A SOCIOLOGY OF POPULAR DRAMA

A SOCIOLOGY OF
POPULAR DRAMA

J. S. R. GOODLAD

822.
09

HEINEMANN
LONDON

Heinemann Educational Books Ltd

LONDON EDINBURGH MELBOURNE TORONTO
AUCKLAND SINGAPORE JOHANNESBURG
HONG KONG NAIROBI IBADAN NEW DELHI

ISBN 0 435 82360 4

© J. S. R. Goodlad 1971

First published 1971

Published by
Heinemann Educational Books Ltd
48 Charles Street, London W1X 8AH

Printed in Great Britain by
Morrison and Gibb Ltd, London and Edinburgh

Contents

Preface

As a child, I found it difficult to believe that the actors of the pantomime really went home to digs by bus from the enchanted castle. But they did. Indeed, they depended for their living on our willing suspension of disbelief. Why did we go there? What gave the theatre its magic? As a schoolboy, I used to sit in the empty school auditorium wondering how those bare boards and hard seats could be transformed into a cockpit of breathless excitement. Later, as a commuter, I have seen from the train window hundreds of ceilings lit by the blue flicker of television sets—flocks of policemen and secret agents hunting their nightly victims, watched often by several millions of my fellow citizens. Here is an astonishing social phenomenon which often escapes notice by its very obviousness. Why do we watch drama at all? Why do so many of us watch such vast quantities of it—particularly when there are so many other things one could see on television. Fact may be stranger than fiction; but fiction seems to be just as interesting. Indeed, some fictions and some imaginary characters command more interest than those who pluck bright honour from the pale-faced moon or dive into the bottom of the sea. Why?

This study is an attempt to answer some of these questions.

I hope that actors, writers, producers, and other students of drama will read this book, and I hope they will not think that the sociological approach devalues their art. My literary mentors, who schooled me in squeezing the last drop of meaning from complex works of individual genius, will no doubt be horrified at the sweeping categorization of whole groups of plays. In trying to identify plays that were outstandingly popular, I am not of course claiming that these plays are necessarily outstanding works of art; nor does it follow that they are not works of art. What is important is that some plays seem to appeal greatly to very large numbers of people. This is an intensely interesting social phenomenon. I hope that my study of it will also shed light on some aspects of dramatic art.

A sociologist has been defined as one who spends £5,000 and then tells you that there is a whore-house on the corner—which, incidentally, you knew already. No doubt theatre people, and indeed audience research people in television, will know already what the mass-popularity plays are all about. They will probably protest that I pay too little attention to the presence or absence of star actors, animals, lavish stage sets, etc. in the plays I survey. But I hope they will follow the argument through the book. The general reader may wish to skip Chapter 6 (which is rather technical) or simply to read the summary sections of it.

Some people may find offensive the parallel I draw between the consumptions of popular drama and certain types of religious activity. But there is a phenomenon which needs a lot of explaining: not why some people commit crimes, but why most people do *not* commit crimes. What sustains their moral convictions? If, as is widely agreed, the influence of churches on the lives of most people is slight, may they not be drawing upon drama as a source of reassurance?

Acknowledgements

This study could not have been carried out at all but for the generous help and facilities provided by the British Broadcasting Corporation. I am particularly grateful to Mr R. J. Silvey, Mr B Emmett, Miss M. Withers and their staff in the BBC Audience Research Department for their help and advice, and to Mr C. H. R. Wade and Mrs M. Muller of the Scripts Unit. I was given access to Audience Research information (from which I selected the group of plays analysed in the book) and I am grateful for permission to quote from the Audience Research special reports cited in the bibliography. It was a singular privilege to have been allowed to read unpublished BBC television plays and to summarize them for this study; the summaries could have been made from viewing the plays, but my task was made much easier by the facilities given me by the Scripts Unit.

It is a pleasure, too, to thank the many people connected with Independent Television Audience Research who gave me help

and advice and who made material available to me—in particular,
Dr I. Haldane and Mr P. Dannheiser of the ITA Audience
Research Department; Miss L. Coles, the ITA librarian (for whom
nothing was too much trouble) and Mr D. Rotheram, lately of
Rediffusion Television. I am grateful to the ITA for permission
to quote *A report on a study of television play viewing* (1965), and to
the Attwood Group of Companies Ltd for permission to quote
A special study on television drama (1965).

For information about factors determining the length-of-run
of plays on the London West End stage, I am indebted to Mr J.
Chapman, author of *Dry Rot, Simple Spymen, The Brides of March,*
etc.; Mr. R Cornish, Assistant Secretary of the Society of West End
Theatre managers; Mr J. Hollingshead, Manager of the Strand
Theatre; Mr J. Peek, Manager of the Haymarket Theatre; and
Mr J. Perry of H. M. Tennent Ltd. I am grateful to the Royal
Shakespeare Theatre Co. for permission to quote from their
audience research study cited in the bibliography.

Many individuals were of help to me in conversations (which
they may well have forgotten by now)—in particular Professor
R. Hoggart, Mr S. Hall, Miss R. Powell, and Mr A. Bear of the
Centre for Contemporary Cultural Studies, University of Bir-
mingham; Dr W. A. Belson, Director of the Survey Research
Centre, London School of Economics; Dr R. L. Brown, Centre
for Mass Communication Research, University of Leicester; Mr
Martin Esslin, Head of BBC Radio Drama; Miss E. Sweeting,
Administrator of the Oxford Playhouse; Professor D. Riesman of
Harvard University; and Professor D. MacRae and Dr D. Martin
of the Department of Sociology, London School of Economics.
My father, Dr J. F. R. Goodlad, a psychiatrist, by his helpful
comments and questions helped me to avoid some nonsenses. In
thanking these people for the insights they afforded me, I exon-
erate them from responsibility for errors and misjudgements that
remain.

Everyone engaged in research experiences the patience and
expertise of librarians. I would like to thank all the librarians who
helped me to locate material. I would also like to thank Mrs J.
Freeman, Mrs K. du Toit, Miss V. M. Taylor, and my sister-in-law
Miss H. Kruse for their help in the mechanics of producing this
study. Finally, I would like to thank my wife, Inge, for all her
patience, help, and support.

Bibliographical Material: a Note

Bibliographical references included in the text of the book give author's name and date of publication. The full reference may be discovered from the primary bibliography (Appendix A) which lists in alphabetical order of authors' names all the publications that have been directly cited and referred to in the book. The secondary bibliography (Appendix B) lists material directly relevant to the subject of this book but which has not been specifically referred to in the text. Additional bibliographical material and a list of useful bibliographical sources may be found in the thesis (Goodlad, 1969) upon which much of this study is based. Table 2 of Appendix C lists the dates and publishers of the plays surveyed that are available in print. Detailed summaries of BBC TV plays not in print may also be found in an appendix of the thesis (Goodlad, 1969).

1

Introduction : A Sociology of Popular Drama

Why do people watch drama?

It is not unusual for 20 per cent of the population of the United Kingdom over the age of five to see a popular television play. In the West End theatre of London, a successful play (such as *Roar Like a Dove*, *Boeing-Boeing*, or *The Mousetrap*) may be seen by over two million people. Huge quantities of drama, especially on television, are available to the public. In July 1965, Raymond Williams (Williams, 1966) counted the number of hours and minutes devoted to fact and to fiction on BBC1, ITV, and BBC2. I myself carried out a similar count in the week August 1–7, 1970. The results of these two counts are presented below. Fact programmes include political, social and economic programmes, religious, magazine, artistic and historical, scientific, farming and nature, sport, music, panel games, and hobbies. Fiction programmes include all plays, crime and espionage series, Westerns, domestic dramas, science fiction, adventure dramas, and comedies.

	BBC1		ITV	
	Hours per week of:			
	Fact	Fiction	Fact	Fiction
July 1965	33	22	28	31
August 1970	51	22	39	36

These figures, which are rounded to the nearest hour, may even under-represent the situation, for the majority of dramatic fiction is screened during peak viewing hours. For the 1970-71 season, the BBC announced that there would be 592 original drama productions and that many of the drama programmes would be longer than before.

A BBC study (BBC, 1959) of listeners and viewers, the time they devote to listening and viewing, the services they patronize, their selectiveness and their tastes, revealed that plays were the most popular single items both for television and for radio.

Authoritative studies have shown that people spend a very great deal of time looking at television (cf. Himmelweit, H. *et al.* 1958; Steiner, G. A., 1963; Belson, W. A., 1967). Belson, for example (pp. 223-225), estimates that since 1960 the average viewer in the United Kingdom has been spending over eighteen hours a week with his television set.

In view of the evident popularity of drama, the quantity of it available especially on television, and the amount of time spent by people viewing it, the time is now ripe for a review of what is known about drama as a social phenomenon and a statement of what should be the next step in research.

Although popular drama has attracted the attention of scholars from a variety of disciplines, no adequate sociological theory has yet been proposed to place drama in cultural perspective. The easy answer to the question of why people watch drama is that they do it to 'be entertained'. But these two words, 'be entertained', beg a very large number of questions. S. D. Forsey (1963) has commented that as long as we continue to accept that people watch television (and other forms of drama) for 'entertainment', with its connotations of lightness and separation from the serious business of life, we cannot hope to reach any realistic understanding of television's effects. The functionalist view of a social phenomenon is that it probably exists to meet a need in the community. In particular, it seeks to relate the phenomenon to other facets of the total social order. As N. S. Timasheff writes (1967): 'Functionalism does not preclude measurement (or other research techniques). But functional analysis directs attention toward meaning; it strives to answer the question: what do specific and diverse phenomena mean from the point of view of the whole social order?'

One of the first modern social scientists to make a systematic study of drama, H. Powdermaker (1947), was an anthropologist who justified her study of motion pictures from a functionalist point of view:

> We define an institution as an organised system of human activities which meets a basic human need. Our frame of reference is both functional and historical. Any study of its functioning will reveal the complex manner in which one institution is intertwined with others, influencing and being influenced by them. In other words, we arrive at an understanding of an institution not by studying it as if it were a separate phenomenon, but in terms of its interrelationships with society as a whole.

Although functionalist theories seeking such understanding may not be amenable to final proof, they are highly desirable if empiricism is not to run riot. Now that computers are readily available to sociologists, there is a temptation to seek correlations of social phenomena almost without reference to any theory that might render the data meaningful. To guard against this danger, and to supply information on which an adequate theory of the function of drama in society can be built and tested, this study seeks to relate the analysis of the social content of popular dramas of a particular period (1955–1965) to ideas and information drawn from several disciplines.

Drama: Mirror or Model for Society?

Culture may be briefly defined sociologically as the reaction to, and handling of, environment by groups of people. In describing the possible function of an activity in the culture of a community, it is convenient to consider the culture as consisting of two elements: an expressive element concerned with the way people reveal their understanding of their environment, their beliefs about it, and their affective reaction to it; and an instrumental element through which people seek to exercise control over their environment. In practice, it is hard to distinguish between these two elements. For example, descriptions in a community of the causes of a particular disease may not only reflect the community's understanding of the causes of disease, but may also determine the way they react to the incidence of the disease. If cancer is regarded as merely a symptom of the displeasure of God, people may take very little action to resist it; alternatively, if the community believes that cancer is a result of identifiable physical causes, there will be considerable activity in the search for a cure.

The interesting question about popular drama in a community is whether it is merely an expressive aspect of culture—reflecting people's beliefs about their community, or whether it is an instrumental aspect of culture—showing people how they should behave, for example. Commentators on drama as a form of mass communication have opted variously for either or both of these descriptions.

R. S. Albert (1957) wonders whether mass media reflect societal dynamics or structure them. In his own study of the role of mass media and the effects of aggressive film content upon children's aggressive responses, Albert assumed the instrumental function of mass media in culture. S. D. Forsey (1963) called for research into the influence of family structures upon the patterns and effects of family television-viewing. He too anticipated an instrumental function for mass media:

> Once we proceed on the basis that people generally are seeking a resolution of conflicts generated in the main in their family of origin, we can start to ask meaningful questions, for example: what are commonly depicted unresolved conflicts presented on television? Does the repeated presentation of these lead to a resolution in the individual or does it merely titillate him, causing him to engage himself again and again in the ever-deferred hope that they will some day be resolved? How does the symbolic working-out of a problem to persons no longer in their families of origin affect them, and how does it affect those still in their families of origin?

Franklin Fearing (1947) anticipated that a study of the influence of the movies on attitudes and behaviour would probably show that movies were a means by which the individual orients himself in a universe of events that appear to occur haphazardly and chaotically. Fearing suggested that every individual needs meaningful experience and order. He suggested that this need has emotional components, since the lack of coherence in experience creates anxiety within the individual, from which he seeks relief. Fearing suggested that the movie-goer seeks an intelligible arrangement of social phenomena. He finds affirmations for his doubts, alternative solutions for his problems, and the

4

opportunity to experience vicariously ways of behaving beyond the horizons of his personal world.

Another suggestion that mass media perform an instrumental function in culture is to be found in David Riesman's study *The Lonely Crowd* (1961) in which he suggests (p. 149):

> The other-directed person has recourse to a large literature that is intended to orient him in the non-economic side of life. This orientation is needed because, with the virtually complete disappearance of tradition-direction, no possibility remains of learning the art of life in the primary group—a possibility that persisted even in the mobile families of the era dependent on inner-direction. The child must look early to his mass-media tutors for instruction in the techniques of getting direction for one's life as well as for specific tricks of the trade.

F. Elkin (1954) represents the view that mass media drama is an *expressive* item of culture. He suggests that Hollywood farces may be replete with significant themes, indirect and hidden though they may be. He suggests that we are less aware that these 'non-message' films have themes and implications partly because the films so directly *reflect* norms and values of our culture and partly because we have so often met the same plot and characters in radio programmes, magazine stories, novels, fairy tales, and other movies. Because we are less consciously aware of their themes, he argues, it does not follow that these films are any the less 'socially significant'. P. H. Ennis (1962), in an elaborate theoretical proposal for the study of the social structure of communication systems, proposes that mass-communications research as a whole might more wisely wed itself to the expressive rather than the instrumental aspects of culture.

Finally, the work of Raymond Williams on *The Social History of Dramatic Forms* (in Williams, 1961) may be taken as a proposal which suggests that drama may be *both* expressive and instrumental:

> Complicated as it is by delay, by the unevenness of change, and by the natural variety of responses to change, only some of which achieve adequate communication, the outline surely exists, in which we can see drama, not only as a social art, but as a major and practical index of change and creator of consciousness. (p. 273)

These varied suggestions as to the possible instrumental or expressive functions of drama in society do not, however, constitute a systematic programme for functional analysis. To discover why people watch drama, it is still necessary to establish at least some of the items necessary for a full functional approach.

The most comprehensive paradigm for functional analysis that has been proposed is that of Robert K. Merton in *Social Theory and Social Structure* (1957, ch. 1, pp. 19–84). Merton's paradigm is a codification of those concepts and problems that have been forced upon the attention of sociologists by critical scrutiny of research and theory in functional analysis. The present study of the function of popular drama in modern Britain does not meet all of Merton's stringent requirements; but, in seeking to isolate suitable topics for further study, it is strongly influenced by Merton's ideas. The following pages indicate how the study is organized.

The Argument of the Book

Throughout this book, it will be assumed that popular drama is a form of mass communication. P. F. Lazarfeld (1947) outlined four main areas of study in the field of mass communications that are still widely followed: (1) The study of output and the control of information in the mass media—how are industries organized economically, who are the people who make decisions, and who create media content? (2) Content-analysis studies—of movies, newspapers, radio programmes, television programmes, drama. (3) Audience research—particularly analysis of the composition of audiences. (4) Study of the long- and short-term effects of media on individuals and on the community as a whole. The present study will concentrate on the last three categories. A major assumption will be made: namely, that the makers of drama for stage and television operate in the same social nexus as that which drama serves functionally. While it may be true that writers and producers may offer to the public highly idiosyncratic dramatic manifestations, it is likely that for drama to achieve the *mass popularity* with which this study is concerned what is offered by the drama industry must be broadly in line with what is wanted by the viewing public.

It should be clear from what has already been said in this chapter that popular drama is an important item of modern British culture. In the following chapters, it will be argued that popular drama is concerned with the survival of the social system. Functions of an item of culture are those observed consequences that make for the adaptation or adjustment of a given system; dysfunctions are those observed consequences that lessen the adaptation or adjustment of the system. For a social system to survive at all, it is necessary that the individual members of the community have a clear understanding of the moral rules that enable the social system to continue in existence. It is possible for moral rules to be rehearsed directly on occasions when a community assembles together. For example, a church service may provide an opportunity for the recitation of Commandments— 'Thou shalt do no murder; thou shalt not commit adultery; thou shalt not bear false witness, etc.' Again, courts of law may provide a community with the opportunity to review its moral code when social deviates are censured for their crimes against the community. Popular drama may serve as the vehicle by which a community expresses its beliefs about what is right and wrong; indeed, it may function instrumentally as the medium through which a community repeatedly instructs its members in correct behaviour. Such an assertion would be very difficult to prove. However, this study offers the prolegomena which may render such a social judgement possible.

The second chapter of this book argues that ritual is concerned with social order. Literature is reviewed which suggests that ritual and myth are interchangeable as items of culture, and that drama as we know it is linearly descended from ritual and myth. It is argued that myth, ritual, and folk-lore perform a cognitive function in informing the members of a community about social structure and about the behaviour expected from individual members of the community if social structure is to be preserved. Myths and rituals are shown to be frequently vehicles for the expression of emotion at matters of tension in social structure. Clearly, not all myths function in this way. It is important to identify which myths are *popular* in a given community. It is suggested that the conflicts forming the themes of popular myths are likely to be those experienced in real life by the members of the community in which the myths are current. As instrumental

7

elements of culture, myth, ritual, and folk tale have the latent (and often manifest) function of exercising social control. As expressive elements of culture, they are likely to be conservative in content, celebrating the *status quo*.

Sociology frequently presents society as unscripted drama. In particular, role-theory uses terminology borrowed from drama. It is therefore interesting to consider the conscious or intuitive use made of roles by members of a community. Literature is reviewed which suggests that members of a community organize their experience of social relationships and structure their participation in these relationships through the manipulation of roles. For this to be possible, it is essential that members of a community become aware of the behaviour appropriate to particular roles. It is suggested that drama offers the individual an opportunity to sharpen his awareness of what is expected from different roles.

Chapter 4 reviews some literary theories about the functions of drama in society. Since the time of Aristotle, literary critics have speculated about the possible social functions of drama. Although their insights have not been subjected to systematic testing, they are nevertheless extremely valuable in suggesting what drama may be about. In particular, literary critics have pointed out forcibly how popular drama provides a monitor of morality, a technique by which the moral order underlying social structure can be identified by contrast with its opposite—immorality, disorder.

Chapter 5 considers drama as mass communication. It is suggested that drama, as a form of mass communication, is likely to exhibit in its particulars the characteristics of mass communication in general. The extensive literature on mass communication suggests that by virtue of its nature as a form of mass communication, popular drama is likely to reinforce prevailing opinion and belief rather than change it and, in its content, to reflect prevailing social norms. The particular case of the supposed damaging effects of violence on television is considered, as is the evidence on the social uses of 'escape' fare in the mass media.

Chapter 6 examines techniques of content analysis and audience research that have been used in the study of drama. If cross-cultural studies are to be made possible, it is essential that a systematic method be devised for describing the content of drama. Similarly, in so far as the *popularity* of drama is an important consideration in this study, it is necessary to specify as clearly as possible how popularity is determined. Chapter 6 is, then, a necessary and important introduction to a survey of a particular group of 114 popular dramas, performed between 1955 and 1965, which is described in Chapter 7—'The Drama of Reassurance'. Although, for practical considerations of convenience, it has been necessary to concentrate on a particular group of dramas performed within the space of ten years, if the theory is correct, it should be possible to apply the same techniques of analysis to *any* group of dramas popular in a particular community.

The eighth chapter, 'Towards a Theory of the Functions of Popular Drama in Society', suggests as a testable sociological proposition: that popular drama deals with the areas of social living in which members of a community find it most difficult to comply with the moral requirements necessary for the survival of the prevailing social structure. The analysis of the content of the popular dramas of the period 1955-1965 suggests that for Britons these areas were: the institution of monogamy; the judgement of the social power which an individual may be permitted to exercise; money; the control of desire for revenge for real or imagined wrongs suffered; the control of the use of violence in pursuing private goals. Although specific social crises may arise from time to time, it is suggested that these areas of social living are the ones in which tensions are regularly felt. For example, people may be outraged by an increase in bus fares. But there are many channels of protest available to them—and it is possible that newspaper discussion and general social gossip will provide sufficient outlet for the individual and the opportunity to test his private reactions against social consensus. However, monogamy goes on being a problem. People probably watch drama to organize and confirm their experience of society, particularly with reference. to socially approved behaviour. If this theory is correct, popular drama will function expressively as a monitor or indicator of prevailing morality in a particular community. Chapter 8 also proposes as a testable sociological proposition that in a given culture popular drama and its functional equivalents are used instrumentally, deliberately or intuitively, directly or through mediating processes of social intercourse, to disseminate and probably determine the moral values upon which prevailing social structure depends. For example, a popular drama—say a farce—may express the belief of a community that the marriage of one man to one woman is a social norm that should not be violated. The drama will only be amusing so long as this belief is held. But the laughter at the expense of the deviant who acts as though this social norm did not exist may serve as a warning to other would-be deviants. To this extent, popular drama may be functioning instrumentally to underpin the morality upon which the community depends.

If this interpretation of the possible instrumental function of popular drama is correct, it is not too fanciful to suppose that popular drama may now be a secular substitute for one aspect of religion. That is to say, where at one time moral guidance was the sole prerogative of a church, it may now have become the prerogative of television, cinema and theatre.

2

The Association of Drama with Ritual

In seeking to define a cultural item and in outlining its possible social function, it is usually valuable to study the primitive original form of that item. Such study does not presuppose that the item to which a function is currently imputed has the same function as its original. Popular drama may have radically changed its social function, may have ceased to have any function at all, or, indeed, may be dysfunctional in modern society. For example, drama may at one time have been functional—instrumentally as a ritual activity controlling awareness of social structure, expressively monitoring the morality of a society. In its present form, it may be severely dysfunctional—distracting the participants in the drama and the audience of it from more important activities necessary for the effective functioning of their society. However, one of the principal values of functional analysis is that it suggests propositions that may be worth testing by experimental technique. The purpose, therefore, of the review in this chapter of the association of drama with ritual is to identify possible items to be studied in the functional analysis of popular drama in modern Britain. Western drama is widely believed to have originated in ritual; it will therefore be valuable to examine the nature of this association and to explore the functions of ritual and also of myth (with which in the opinion of some scholars ritual is interchangeable).

Any review of the possible functions of ritual in society—and of the association of drama with ritual—must record a debt to Emile Durkheim, whose insights into the possible functions of ritual in society have provided inspiration to many subsequent scholars. In *Elementary Forms of the Religious Life* (first published in full in 1912—quotations in this book from Durkheim, 1961),

Durkheim imputes four particular functions to ritual. These have been conveniently summarized by H. Alpert (1961, cf. pp. 198–201) as follows: (a) a disciplinary and preparatory function through which ritual prepares the individual for social living by imposing on him the self-discipline, the 'disdain for suffering', the self-abnegation without which life in society would be impossible; (b) a cohesive function through which ceremony brings people together and thus serves to reaffirm their common bonds and to enhance and reinforce social solidarity; (c) a revitalizing function through which, if society is to be kept alive, its members must be made keenly aware of their social heritage: traditions must be perpetuated, faith must be renewed, values must be transmitted and deeply embedded; (d) a euphoric function through which rituals serve to establish a condition of social euphoria, i.e. a pleasant feeling of social well-being. In counterbalancing the effect of disturbing actions in society, ritual performs its euphoric function by requiring individuals to have and to express certain emotions and sentiments, and by making them express these sentiments and feelings together.

Durkheim starts from the functionalist assumption that all religions satisfy some need and that the needs in different societies are fundamentally the same. This is how he justifies the study of ancient and primitive religion. He notes that religion is something eminently social. Religious representations are, he claims, collective representations that express collective realities; the rites are a manner of acting, which arise in the midst of assembled groups and which are intended to excite, maintain, or recreate certain mental states in these groups. (Durkheim, 1961, p. 22). Durkheim makes a distinction between objects considered in a particular society to be sacred or profane. Religion, he maintains, is a system of beliefs and rites associated with these profane and sacred objects. Religious beliefs are the representations that express the nature of sacred things and the relations they sustain, either with each other or with profane things. Rites are the rules of conduct that prescribe how a man should comport himself in the presence of these sacred objects (pp. 52–56). It is in his treatment of the ritual observances associated with sacred and profane objects that Durkheim's insights are most valuable. Durkheim argues that the only way of renewing the collective representations that relate to sacred beings is to retemper them in the very source of the religious life, that is to say in the assembled groups. By assembling together for acts of ritual representation of the society's beliefs, the members of a society are mutually comforted and come to share a body of belief and opinion. Ritual activity, Durkheim argues, is essential if society is to survive:

> If the idea of society were extinguished in individual minds and the beliefs, traditions, and aspirations of the group were no longer felt and shared by the individuals, society would die (pp. 388–389).
>
> If we are to see in the efficacy attributed to certain rites anything more than the product of a chronic delirium with which humanity has abused itself, we must show that the effect of the cult really is to re-create periodically a moral being upon which we depend as it depends upon us. Now this being does exist: it is society.
>
> Howsoever little importance the religious ceremonies may have, they put the group into action; the groups assemble to celebrate them. So their first effect is to bring individuals together, to multiply the relations between them and to make them more intimate with one another. By this very fact, the content of their consciousness is changed. (p. 389)

Durkheim traces his social interpretation of religion through a wide variety of cults and their associated rites. Representative or commemorative rites are regarded as techniques by which a social group periodically renews the sentiment it has of itself and of its unity; at the same time, individuals are strengthened in their social natures. Piacular rites of mourning have a similar function: mourning is not a natural movement of private feelings wounded by a cruel personal loss; it is a duty imposed by the group. A recent study of *Death, grief and mourning in contemporary Britain* (Gorer, 1966) provides substantial evidence of activity that would seem to support Durkheim's theory.

Finally, it is interesting to note Durkheim's answer to a very difficult question: how do societies full of defects invent idealistic religions? It is worth quoting Durkheim's answer to this question in some detail, because his insight into the importance of ideals in society will become relevant later in the study of the content of popular drama. This is what Durkheim says:

> The formation of the ideal world is therefore not an irreducible fact which escapes science; it depends upon conditions which observation can touch; it is a natural product of social life. For a society to

become conscious of itself and to maintain at the necessary degree of intensity the sentiments which it thus attains, it must assemble and concentrate itself. Now this concentration brings about an exultation of the mental life which takes form in the group of ideal conceptions where is portrayed the new life thus awakened; they correspond to this new set of physical forces which is added to those which we have at our disposition for the daily tasks of existence. A society can neither create itself nor re-create itself without at the same time creating an ideal. This creation is not a sort of work of supererogation for it, by which it would complete itself, being already formed; it is the act by which it is periodically made and re-made. Therefore when some oppose the ideal society to the real society, like two antagonists which would lead us in opposite directions, they materialise and oppose abstractions. The ideal society is not outside of the real society; it is a part of it. Far from being divided between them as between two poles which mutually repel each other, we cannot hold to one without holding to the other. For a society is not made up merely of the mass of individuals who compose it, the ground which they occupy, the things which they use, and the movements which they perform, but above all is the idea which it forms of itself. (Durkheim, 1961, p. 470)

Needless to say, Durkheim's theories have not gone un-challenged. Evans-Pritchard, for example, criticizes Durkheim's theory of elementary religion mainly on ethnographical lines. He points out that most of Durkheim's observations do not permit experimental verification. He does not deny that religion is a social phenomenon, but he insists that it is not profitable to dwell on its origins (Evans-Pritchard, 1965). E. O. James, in his study *Prehistoric Religion* (1957a), argues that religion is more than just collective consciousness. But he agrees that rituals exercise an integrative function in society.

Because of the fascinating implications of Durkheim's theory, it will be valuable to examine the nature and functions of rituals and myths as represented in the writings of other scholars.

The Nature and Functions of Rituals and Myths

Popular drama in contemporary Britain is a form of story-telling —containing, perhaps, elements of folk-lore and myth. In seeking a definition of the possible functions of popular drama, it is therefore profitable to examine the supposed associations between ritual, myth, and folk-lore.

J. Goody (1961) has defined ritual as 'a category of standardised behaviour (custom) in which the relationship between the means and the end is not intrinsic', i.e. is either irrational or non-rational. E. G. Ballard (1957) has defined myth as 'the verbal transformation of the feeling and movement of ritual'. J. L. Fischer (1963), in his major review of 'socio-psychological analysis of folk tales', uses the term 'folk tale' broadly to include any traditional, dramatic, oral narrative. Folk tales include, in his definition, serious myths dealing with the supernatural, as well as tales told primarily for entertainment; purportedly factual accounts of historical events; moralistic fables; and other varieties of narrative. Much academic energy has gone into the discussion of whether myth arises out of ritual or whether ritual out of myth. For example, Jane Harrison, in her study *Themis: A Study of the Social Origins of Greek Religion* (1963), argues that myth is the spoken correlative of the acted rite, the thing done. She argues that myth arises out of rite rather than the reverse, and insists that myth is not anything else nor of any other origin. For the purposes of this book it is not necessary to go into all the arguments for or against either theory. More important is to show from the existing literature the functional similarity between ritual and myth. In an important study, *Myths and Rituals: a general theory*, Kluckhohn (1942) argues that the facts known to anthropologists do not permit any universal generalizations as to ritual being the cause of myth or vice versa.

> Both myth and ritual satisfy the needs of a society and the relative place of one or the other will depend upon the particular needs (conscious and unconscious) of the individuals in a particular society at a particular time. This principle covers the observed data which show that rituals are borrowed without their myths, and myths without any accompanying ritual. A ritual may be reinforced by a myth (or vice versa) in the donor culture but satisfy the carriers of the recipient culture simply as a form of activity (or be rationalized by a quite different myth which better meets their emotional needs). In short, the only uniformity which can be posited is that there is a strong tendency for some sort of inter-relationship between myth and ceremony and that this inter-relationship is dependent upon what appears so far as present information goes, to be an invariant

function of both myth and ritual: the gratification (most often in the negative form of anxiety reduction) of a large proportion of the individuals in a society. (Kluckhohn, 1942, p. 57)

Kluckhohn argues that myth is a system of word symbols, whereas ritual is a system of object and act symbols. Both are symbolic processes for dealing with the same type of situation in the same affective mode.

What then are the supposed functions of myth, ritual and folk tale? Ballard (1957) notes that ritual is usually a spontaneous response to some disturbing aspect of life. An important and authoritative study of a certain category of rites is that of Arnold van Gennep in *The Rites of Passage* (1960). Van Gennep argues that the life of an individual in any society is a series of passages from one age to another and from one occupation to another. Wherever there are fine distinctions among age or occupational groups, progression from one group to the next is accompanied by special acts. Transitions from group to group and from one social situation to the next are looked on as implicit in the very fact of existence, so that a man's life comes to be made up of a succession of stages with similar ends and beginnings: birth, social puberty, marriage, fatherhood, advancement to a higher class, occupational specialization, and death. For every one of these events there are ceremonies whose essential purpose is to enable the individual to pass from one defined position to another, which is equally well defined (van Gennep, 1960, p. 3). The exact details of the rites of passage described by van Gennep are not of primary importance here. What is important, however, is van Gennep's observation that when an individual moves from one stable form of social structure to another, he passes for a time through a limbo state in which he is a member of neither of the two stable groups. It is with this period of passage that rituals are associated. Ceremonies and rituals ease the individual's passage from one sector of society to another. As van Gennep says:

An individual is placed in various sections of society, synchronically and in succession; in order to pass from one category to another and to join individuals in other sections, he must submit, from the day of his birth to that of his death, to ceremonies whose forms often vary but whose function is similar. (p. 189)

This function is to preserve the order of society not only for the individual who must undergo passage from one part of it to another but also for members of the society in their separate sections of it.

Fischer (1963), who argues that myth, folk tale, and ritual are alternative ways of saying the same thing, summarizes the view of social scientists as being that the cognitive function of myth is to inform individuals not about the universe or nature but primarily about social structure, and to help them to understand the workings of their own society (p. 256). The affective functions of folk tale (and thereby of myth and ritual) are to express emotion at elements of social structure that might otherwise give rise to conflict in the mind of the individual and/or in society.

If we regard folk tales as largely a vehicle for the expressing of already existing emotions which have for one or another reason been denied expression, then folk tales have a positive psychological affective function, since once the negative emotions are overtly expressed with regard to a definite object, even if not to the original one, both their intensity and their tendency to provoke an undefined anxiety are reduced. Whether folk tales which evoke negative emotions always successfully fulfil this function of ultimately relieving anxiety is another question. Conceivably, at some times and for some individuals they may provoke more anxiety than they relieve. Presumably, however, the balance is 'profitable' for the individuals who participate regularly as narrators or audience. (p. 257)

Fischer discusses a number of distinguishable but related psychological functions of folk tales. In his view, it is meaningless to ask which of these functions is *the* function of the folk tale, or whether the function of the folk tale is psychological or sociological. All of these functions, and probably some others, can be demonstrated for many folk tales. Fischer argues that it is more useful to ask which kinds of functions are important for which kinds of tales and for what individuals under what circumstances in what societies.

We must not assume that any particular tale has the same function for all members of the society at a given time, or for the typical member at different historical periods. A myth which is liberating for individuals at one period or in certain statuses in a society may be constricting for individuals in other statuses or at other periods. A folk tale which serves as a harmless outlet for the anti-social wishes and emotions of certain individuals may serve to increase the anxiety or promote the overt anti-social behaviour of other more deviant individuals. (p. 258)

Fischer shows that it can be argued that for a folk tale to persist it must be both psychologically and socially adjustive. It is conceivable that myths can be invented which would be psychologically dysfunctional—cause more rather than less anxiety in the narrator and audience—but socially adaptive, i.e. use the anxiety provoked by the myth to motivate the listeners to perform altruistic, self-sacrificial acts for the good of society. Fischer argues that for a tale to persist, some sort of balance must be achieved between two sets of demands: (1) the demands of the individual for personal pleasure and reduction of his anxiety, and (2) the demands of other members of the society that the individual pursue his personal goals only in ways that will also contribute to, or at least not greatly harm, the welfare of the society. This balance can be made in various ways, but Fischer believes that it is always made in folk-tales and other expressive culture, and that analyses dealing with only one of these sets of demands will be less effective than those involving both (p. 259).

Fischer's main contribution, however, to the discussion of the functions of folk-lore (myth and ritual) is his insistence that the most valuable way to determine the functions of a myth in society is to examine the audience's appreciation of the myth and the content of it. He notes that individuals can and do create purely selfish narratives as individual fantasies, but these narratives never gain sufficient acceptance from a stable and persisting audience to become traditional. He raises the question as to whether there is a determinate relationship between folk tales and social reality, and if so, what aspects of social reality are related to folk-tale content, and how they are related. Folk tales, he notes, are obviously not relevant to all of social reality. They are selective in their reference. He argues with considerable force (pp. 261–263) that any theme that is prominent in the folk tales of a group is the subject of considerable conflict in real life. His basic proposition is, then, that folk tales (like rituals) focus attention on elements of strain in a social structure, and that a study of the content of the most popular folk tales—and by inference of the most frequent ritual activity—will provide valuable evidence about social structure, the consciousness of the individuals of that social structure, and their feelings about it.

From the review given of Fischer's analysis of folk tales, it is clear that he regards folk tales as a major division of expressive culture; indeed he expressly states this (p. 236). The Frankforts, in their introduction to *Before Philosophy* (1964), propound a similar view—that myth is a form of poetry that proclaims a truth, a form of reasoning that transcends reasoning in that it wants to bring about the truth it proclaims. There are, however, equally vigorous proponents of the view that myths, rituals, and folk tales are *instrumental* aspects of culture. Maud Bodkin, for example (1934), examines those forms or patterns in which the universal forces of our nature are objectified. She regards the ritual dance, and other such ceremonies, as imaginative achievements, having potential social value through influence over group attitudes towards the unknown forces of reality. In his study *The Andaman Islanders*, A. R. Radcliffe-Brown (1933) states that in the case of both ritual and myth the sentiments expressed are those that are essential to the existence of the society (p. 405). In a monograph on 'The Nature and Function of Myth', E. O. James (1957b) asserts that the function of myth and ritual is to promote social intercourse and stabilize social structure. He notes that literary myths have no connection with ritual, but perform a similar function, i.e. to safeguard custom. In similar vein, Kluckhohn (1942) maintains that rituals constitute a guarantee that in certain societally organized behaviours touching upon certain 'areas of ignorance' which constitute 'tender spots' for all human beings, people can count upon the repetitive nature of the phenomena. Rituals and myths, he maintains, supply the fixed points in a world of bewildering change and disappointment. Myths and rituals deal with those sectors of experience that do not seem amenable to rational control and hence where human beings can least tolerate insecurity.

The body of scholarly opinion, then, seems to point to the principal functions of ritual and of myth as being those of informing the individual about his society and controlling his participation in it. An important recent contribution to the discussion of ritual is contained in Dr Mary Douglas's study *Purity and Danger* (1966), in which she states:

> As a social animal, man is a ritual animal. If ritual is suppressed in one form it crops up in others, more strongly, the more intense the social interaction. Without the letters of condolence, telegrams of

congratulations and even occasional postcards, the friendship of a separated friend is not a social reality. It has no existence without the rites of friendship. Social rituals create a reality which would be nothing without them. It is not too much to say that ritual is more to society than words are to thoughts. For it is very possible to know something and then find words for it. But it is impossible to have social relations without symbolic acts. (p. 62)

The problems of confirmation of these functional interpretations still remain. However, we now have pointers to the possible functions of popular drama in contemporary Britain if this can be considered to be a form of modern folk tale or myth. The connection between myth and ritual and drama now remains to be demonstrated.

The Ritual and Mythic Content of Greek Drama

The literature on the ritual origins of Greek drama is vast and confusing. For the purposes of this study, it is not necessary to demonstrate precisely how Greek drama arose from ritual but simply to give some evidence that there is a strong association between the drama of the Western world and ritual and myth. Several major studies have dealt with the origins of drama: among these may be listed G. Thomson's *Aeschylus and Athens: A study in the social origins of drama* (1941); Gilbert Murray's *Excursus on the Ritual forms preserved in Greek Tragedy*, in Jane Harrison's *Themis* (1963); A. W. Pickard-Cambridge's study *Dithyramb tragedy and comedy* (1927) and his *Dramatic Festivals of Athens* (1953).

The most valuable evidence is the demonstration of surviving patterns of ritual in actual dramas. In *Story Patterns in Greek Tragedy*, Richard Lattimore (1964) shows how the arrangements of religious ceremony are often used by the story-teller to communicate a scene or a story in Greek tragedy.

In our dramatic texts, the lines frequently tell of the placing of persons. In 'The Heracleidae', Euripides has the young sons of Heracles in suppliant posture at the altar through the whole tragedy, though they say nothing.

In 'Œdipus', Sophocles has such a solemn entry and departure of silent suppliants at the opening. Or people do and act and instruct each other. The Suppliant Maidens of Aeschylus are told how and where to advance, the family of Ajax what positions to take as preparations are made to carry the body off. Most elaborate of all are the instructions given to Œdipus by the chorus, the people of Colonus, in the ritual that will help the gods to tolerate his presence in the land. The details are dwelt on with loving deliberate care while the action waits.

These ceremonies are numerous and not surprising in what was after all a contest under religious sanctions on a religious occasion. (p. 69)

W. Schumaker (1960) has traced the basic patterns of initiation ceremonies in Greek tragedy. In a common pattern of initiation ceremony, he claims, the candidates leave their homes with adult guides, undergo trials, suffer a pretended death, are shown sacred objects and taught esoteric lore, and at length return to their homes as adults—quite different persons, whose discontinuity with the uninitiated youth is dramatized in curious ways (cf. van Gennep's *Rites of Passage*). The Greek form of the initiation, Schumaker reports, has been speculatively reconstructed by Thomson as follows. It consisted, in order, of an escorted procession, a contest or trial, a rending, or tearing as in the Dionysian celebrations, an unveiling of the reborn god, a teaching by means of dark sayings or riddles, an examining or catechizing, and finally a festal procession back to the village. All these parts of the total ritual have left an impression, it is claimed, upon mature Greek tragedy. The tragic equivalent of the procession is the entrance of the chorus. The protagonists' trial or contest is initiated by the 'perepeteia', or reversal of fortune, which in turn is followed by a ritual lament, comparable to that which accompanied the rending of the sacrificial victim at the Dionysian ceremonies. The tragic recognition is co-ordinate with the unveiling of the reborn god. Schumaker comments that the correspondences are striking. That both initiation ceremony and tragedy should begin and end in a procession is not in itself very meaningful, since the Greek theatre provided no other means of introducing and dismissing the chorus; and the equating of the tragic recognition with the unveiling of a disguised god is perhaps somewhat forced. Nevertheless, a rather surprising similarity remains. When it is remembered that the tragic competitions were held at the greater or city Dionysia, a festival named from the Dionysian mystery, the hypothesis that there was a direct development of the initiation ceremonies for youths through the mysteries to tragedy becomes very persuasive (cf. Schumaker 1960, p. 166 f.).

Schumaker also equates our judgement of the tragic hero, and our acquiescence in his death, as functionally similar to sacrifice as described in, for example, Hubert and Mauss (1964) and in E. O. James's study *Origins of Sacrifice* (1933). Schumaker observes that in tragedy the impulses given free rein are not harmless; injury results to an imagined social body. Because the spectator's will has assented to the protagonist's rashness, his conscience becomes uneasy. The breach of the moral law demands expiation; hence a scapegoat is offered to the parent-judge-god. When all is finished, the spectator can rise from his seat psychically healthy, 'purged' by the discharge of criminal tendencies, reassured that his habitual observance of moral law is the best policy, and once more resigned to unadventurous living. Schumaker draws the inference from this theory that the low state of modern tragedy can be explained as follows. The modern protagonist dares too little, stays too timidly within the *mores*; he is not so much executed as exterminated. His fate is therefore painful, not satisfying. The usual housewife's objection to tragedy, that she 'has enough trouble without going to sad movies', thus has a certain urgency after all (cf. Schumaker, p. 176). If this theory is in fact correct, the implication would be that to fully enjoy the socially integrative function of a sacrificial ritual, the sacrificer (audience) would need to partially identify with a character of massive proportion, who embodied some deep human lusts, and whose destruction was correspondingly impressive. In terms of popular appeal, the implication would be that the death as a scapegoat of Goldfinger would be more satisfying to an audience than the death of Willy Loman.

Ballard (1957, p. 177) has argued that the central part of tragedy seems to be an analogue of the ritual of aggregation, whereby a primitive man entered into contact with the corporate life of the tribe and drew a sense of power from it. The tragic hero, Ballard explains, enters through his trials into a more rational contact with the intelligible universe around him. Whatever process may be involved in the derivation of Greek drama from ritual origins, it is clear that the ritual is still there even if in latent form. Even

E. Cassirer, having dealt with the proposition that our consciousness of *everything* requires a whole first before parts become intelligible (Cassirer, vol. 1, 1953), finds it necessary to go on in the second volume of his massive work *The Philosophy of Symbolic Forms* (1955) to review the way in which ritual was designed to control nature, to explore how Greek tragedy broke away from a treatment of the symbiotic relation of man and nature to a revelation of man as an independent moral being. Cassirer argues that in contrast to epic, tragedy shifts the centre of events from the outside in, and thus there arises a new form of ethical self-consciousness, through which the gods take on a new nature and form. In similar vein, R. J. Hallman (1961) demonstrates how a feeling of alienation arises when the fate of the hero of tragedy is no longer intimately bound up with his membership of a social group.

To sum up the basic message of the literature on the association of Greek drama with ritual, the following propositions may be made: Greek drama was a social phenomenon similar to church-going in modern Western society; its origins are intimately associated with rituals, which have already been shown to be primarily concerned with order in society; its content, even in its most highly developed form, is concerned with the relationship of the individual to his social group. These observations may provide important pointers to the possible functions of popular drama in modern Britain. However, it may be objected that there was a considerable break in tradition between the flowering of Greek drama and the rebirth of drama in the British Isles. It is therefore necessary to deal briefly with some of the ritual content of early English drama.

The Origin of English Drama: its Ritual Content

As with early Greek drama, a large literature has grown up around the rebirth of drama in England following the barbarian interregnum of the 'Dark Ages'. One of the most interesting items of this literature is J. L. Weston's *From Ritual to Romance* (1920). Chapter 7 discusses the derivation of English mumming plays from ritual concerning the death and rebirth of the year—a counterpart to ceremonies of the driving-out of winter and the bringing-in of spring. Miss Weston notes that the early English survivals of vegetation ceremonies preserve, in a more or less detached form, four symbols—grail, sword, lance, and pentangle or dish. In view of the evidence offered, she claims that it is not a very hazardous or far-fetched hypothesis to suggest that these symbols, the exact value of which as a group cannot be determined (but of which the two most prominent, the cup and lance, are known to be sex symbols), were originally fertility emblems. As such, they would have been employed in a ritual designed to promote or restore the activity of the reproductive energies of nature. Much of Miss Weston's book is speculative.

An authoritative treatment of the origins, background and development of early English drama is that of A. P. Rossiter in *English Drama from early times to the Elizabethans* (1950). Rossiter traces the origins of dramatic elements from the Latin liturgy of the church at great Christian feasts. He notes the hieratic gestures of the celebrant in the dramatic ritual of the Mass. He comments on the pictures in mosaic or enamel, paint or needlework, which were displayed for illiterate people on vestments and on banners. He notes how many rituals touched the edge of mimetic action: among them the Palm Sunday procession with palms or olive branches, etc., which came from fourth-century Jerusalem; the washing of the feet of the poor on Maundy Thursday; the offering of gold, frankincense and myrrh at the Chapel Royal; the Lenten veil which hid the sanctuary at Wells and Sarum, to be split at the appropriate words in the gospel; and an elaborately dismal rite at Durham, known as creeping to the cross. Still nearer to drama, he notes, is the ninth-century dedication ritual in which the Bishops' procession approached the new church to the singing of the twenty-fourth psalm (pp. 42–43).

Rossiter suggests that the simplest explanation of the exit from the church of drama is that the secular world gave more room for developments that were already pressing on inventive 'literary' minds. However, although the drama had broken from the confines of church liturgy, it was still secularized *religious* drama: latterly in the hands of craft guilds; filled with much comedy and farce, especially in England; but forces of ritual still directed it (p. 53).

The early 'dramas' consisted mainly of processions with scenes from scripture represented on drawn vehicles. Even the early dramas, which can be distinctly recognized as plays, contain a very strong element symptomatic of the religious background of the activity. Gradually the personification of moral virtues and vices gave way to an increasing interest in characterization, and the birth of modern drama as we now know it had been achieved.

Before a summary is given of this review of informed opinion on the possible social functions of myth and ritual and their association with drama, one further item merits attention. L. Spence (1947) has argued that certain sports and games also had origins in ritual. Some possible functional equivalents to popular drama will be discussed in Chapter 8. Meanwhile, if a study of the ritual origins of drama as a cultural manifestation can give indications as to its possible present function, it is probable that cultural manifestations coming from similar origins may have similar social functions today.

In discussing the place of blood offerings and human sacrifice in early Mexican culture, Spence describes techniques that were used to secure the many victims essential to the maintenance of the divinities that reigned. Large numbers of captives were necessary for sufficient human sacrifice to ensure the supply of rain, upon which the community relied.

In the early period of Mexican history this [the securing of large numbers of captives for sacrifice] had been a matter of definite treaty and arrangement with a neighbouring state, the 'Republic' of Tlascala. Whether or not Tlascala had been dedicated as a sacrificial reservation by the Azteks of Mexico it would be difficult to say, although the hatred of its people for the Azteks would seem to suggest as much. Indeed, it was the alliance of the Tlascans with the Spaniards under Cortes which helped to bring about the downfall of the Aztek Empire. Be that as it may, the Tlascans agreed to the Aztek proposal that once a year the forces of the two states should meet on a selected battle-ground and should strive to secure, the one from the other, as many sacrificial victims as they could make prisoner. The struggle resolved itself into something resembling a great wrestling match, and must, indeed, have seemed not unlike American collegiate football. Killing was, of course, quite out of order, as the main object was to secure living sacrificial victims, and the sturdy knights of the Aztek 'Eagle' and 'Ocelot' corps—the guards of the Mexican army—usually succeeded in capturing the necessary number of victims. (Spence 1947, pp. 5–6)

In further support of this thesis, Spence demonstrates how many sporting events in the ancient world were connected with various cults. For example, by the middle of the second century of this era, no fewer than 135 days in the Roman calendar were devoted to them. That these sporting events had a very distinct religious significance is revealed by the strictness with which they were observed and organized. Indeed, if they were interrupted or accidentally infringed in any way, it was found necessary to repeat them, lest the wrath of the gods be incurred. They were superintended by the priesthood as well as by the magistracy and subvented by the public funds, frequently at very great cost, and in some cases the sums lavished upon them make the outlays of a modern leading football club appear almost beggarly. Spence describes how the most important among the Roman games were those that celebrated military triumphs, and these were invariably held in honour of the god Jupiter, the head of the Roman Pantheon. Next in popular favour were the games of the Plebs, or people, held in November; those of the goddess Ceres, celebrated in April; those of Apollo, which occurred in July; the games devoted to the great capital Mother early in April, and those dedicated to Flora, the goddess of vegetation, at the beginning of May. The religious character of most Roman games is thus placed beyond doubt. (See pp. 11-12.)

Following on his demonstrations of the ritual associations of many games and sports, Spence shows how a game very similar to football was known in England in the reign of Edward III. Again, prior to the period of the Commonwealth, contests between towns, or parishes, or between two sections of people within the boroughs, were commonly celebrated. For example, Spence recounts how in the town of Derby the inhabitants of the parishes of All Saints and St Peter engaged in a football match annually, the goals being fixed as 'the water-wheel of the nuns' mill', and 'the gallows balk' at the other end of the town. The ball, a massive affair, was thrown into the market place from the Town Hall among the packed crowd of people below, and a furious struggle commenced up and down through the narrow streets of the old town until the ball was 'goaled' by one side or the other. Similar customs were to be found at Dorking in Surrey, at Alnwick in Northumberland, and many other places throughout England. In a revealing passage (p. 91) Spence says:

I find it difficult to dissociate games played with balls from a religious significance of some kind . . . some authorities have believed that these were originally mimetic of the actions of the gods, as they propelled the heavenly bodies throughout space, the powers of good and evil seeking to drive them either to those positions in the 'sky', where they would either act for the good of mankind, or to some point where they would prove of no avail to him. But why men who would naturally benefit from an appropriate position of the sun should seek magically to bring about, by mimicry, his relegation to a sphere of hopeless inutility (as one 'side' at least must have done) I cannot conceive.

The reason may in fact have been that these 'religious' sporting ceremonies had functions similar to those imputed to religious activities by Durkheim—to increase group solidarity. Indeed, the spectacle of a modern football crowd, dressed in fantastic garb in the colours of the home football side, screaming excitedly for the downfall of the representatives of another town, and occasionally involving themselves in physical combat with rival supporters, leaves one in little doubt that one of the principal functions of football nowadays is the maintenance of group solidarity, and the provision for the individual of a sense of communal identity.

Summary of Informed Opinion on the Possible Social Functions of Myth and Ritual: Possible Implications for the Study of Popular Drama

From the foregoing summary of literature, it would seem that five principal functions have been imputed to ritual, myth, and folk tale in society: (a) they perform a cognitive function in informing members of the community about social structure and about the behaviour expected from individual members of the community if that social structure is to be preserved; (b) they are likely to be vehicles for the expression of emotion at matters of tension in social structure; (c) the themes of myths and folk tales (and the elements of social structure controlled by ritual activity) are likely to be those most frequently felt in real life—particularly if audience satisfaction is taken as an indicator of the place of the myth in society; (d) as an instrumental element of culture, myth, ritual, and folk tale has as their manifest or latent functions the task of exercising social control; (e) as an expressive element of culture, myth, ritual, and folk tale represent a force for conservatism.

It must be repeated again, for emphasis, that the task of this study is not to demonstrate the functional necessity of any of these items—myth, ritual, or folk-lore—in society, but merely to derive from the study of their functions some possible questions for the study of popular drama in modern society.

Three principal properties of popular drama are likely to appear if drama does indeed still fulfil similar functions to those of its ritual ancestors: (a) if one of the tasks of drama is to inform members of a community about social structure, emphasis in characterization is likely to be on stereotypes rather than on the individuality of particular persons. It is likely that characters will be required whose social status and anticipated activity can be readily identified, so that their inter-relationships in social structure may be contemplated. (b) If popular drama is indeed functionally similar to ritual, it is likely to deal with subjects where rational control and rules are hardest to maintain (cf. Kluckhohn, 1942). The themes of the most popular dramas (myths) are likely to be concerned with conflicts found in everyday life. (c) If popular drama continues the function of ritual as a method of social control, it is likely to be extremely conservative in outlook.

This review of literature has provided some leads, which can be followed up in later study. Fischer (1963) has commented that in modern literate societies folk tales tend to disappear, and that this is due to their replacement by such functional equivalents as books, motion pictures, television, and comic strips. W. Breed (1958) has indeed suggested that the functional equivalence of religion and mass communication merits investigation:

> The values of religion, as Durkheim said, are linked to *social processes* taking the form of ritual. Durkheim maintained that rituals, with their repeated, rhythmic, tangible form served to concretise and reinforce religious beliefs. While the analogy is far from perfect, it may be that the mass media also, by the repeated, patterned 'ritual' of their dissemination—every month or week, day, hour, etc.—serve a similar function in the conservation of socio-cultural resources. One comes to expect a certain joke from Jack Benny, a 'Tiny Tim' story at Christmas, a boy-gets-girl story in magazine and movie, etc.

People may not so much 'learn' from the media as they become accustomed to a standardised ritual.

Chapter 5 will investigate the social functions imputed to mass communications. But meanwhile it will be profitable to look briefly at the theory of roles, which has many properties common to the theory of ritual, myth, and folk tale, and to examine literary theories about why people should be interested in drama.

3

Roles : Society as unscripted drama

The language of sociology borrows a great deal of terminology from the language of dramatic criticism. However, the emphasis in this chapter will be, not on the ways in which sociologists use concepts of roles to describe society, but on the ways in which members of a society use a conscious or intuitive understanding of role-differentiation to live in society—to organize their understanding of it and control their participation in it. The review, in Chapter 2, of the association of early drama with myths, folk tales, and ritual may have given the impression that an individual's consciousness of the structure of his society is exclusively the product of group interaction and story-telling designed to stimulate group consciousness. This view of society has been severely criticized. It is, therefore, necessary to demonstrate that an individual may be conscious of social structure, with its pattern of role interaction, and yet be intellectually free to move about within that structure.

The beliefs of the majority of existentialist thinkers are directly opposed to what has been called the 'sociologistic' perspective of society; however, existentialists who are fully aware of the 'artificial' nature of ritual activity still participate in it. For example, philosophers still go to church; professors of sociology still take part in academic ceremonials; intellectuals of severely independent cast of mind still take part in 'sit-ins' or demonstrations, fully aware that these ritual activities are an important technique for reinforcing individual beliefs in moral ideas and ideals.

This chapter will review some of the existential criticisms of the sociologistic perspective of society, demonstrating the way in which people may be fully conscious of the roles they play. It will review some of the literature on how role-playing is used, consciously or unconsciously, by members of a society, and how the roles that the members play are differentiated. Finally, it will be argued that even existentialist sociology supports the view that the principal functions of ritual activity—and, therefore, its mythic and dramatic equivalents—are to inform the individual about social structure.

Existentialist Criticisms of the Sociologistic Perspective of Society: the Conscious Control of Roles

The clearest account of the difference in sociological perspective between 'sociologists' and existentialists is that of Edward A. Tiryakian (1962). Tiryakian reviews the way in which Durkheim saw no fundamental conflict between the individual and society. He contrasts this view with the existential perspective, which views society as the seat of objectivity and therefore antagonistic to the subjective existence of the individual. The contrast between these two perspectives of society that Tiryakian explores merits some attention.

Durkheim saw the individual and society as interpenetrating entities, of mutual benefit to one another. The social self, in Durkheim's view, is that which gives us true humanity, because it makes us civilized. Durkheim acknowledged that there would be no society without individuals, but held that what gives society its particular richness is the interaction of individuals. Because of the symbiotic interpenetration of the individual and society, morality is fundamentally a social phenomenon. For Durkheim, the source and the end of moral action is the collectivity. This is not to say that the emphasis on the collectivity denies the value of the individual; the content of morality for Durkheim is focused almost exclusively on the dignity conferred upon the human person by society (cf. Tiryakian, p. 152). In his study of suicide, Durkheim demonstrates how an individual who becomes detached from his social group experiences what is called 'anomie', and thereby becomes a high suicide risk. Indeed, one can trace in a great deal of Durkheim's writing this emphasis on the reliance of the individual upon the group.

As Durkheim's views about the ritual mechanisms of social

interaction and the consequent generation of social consciousness have been used as part of the argument in Chapter 2 for finding functional perspectives in the association of drama with ritual, it will be valuable to explore the ways in which existentialist social criticism emphasizes the independent awareness of the individual and his deliberate choice of the roles he will play. Existentialism is not, however, a coherent or unified system of philosophic or sociological thought. To illustrate the point this chapter is making, examples will be drawn exclusively from the thinking of Jean-Paul Sartre: other examples might show a different emphasis.

In his short essay *Existentialism and Humanism* (1965) Sartre proclaims the fundamental existentialist belief that existence precedes essence. Man first of all exists, encounters himself, surges up in the world—and defines himself afterwards. That is to say, self-conscious awareness—the discovery of self as separate from external reality—precedes the assumption of any role in society. Sartre argues that if man as the existentialist sees him is not definable, it is because to begin with he is nothing. He will not be anything—that is to say he will not assume any social roles—until later, and then he will be what he makes of himself. 'Man is nothing else but that which he makes of himself' (p. 28). Sartre argues that we invent values—that there is no sense in life *a priori*. Life is nothing until it is lived. The individual must make sense of life by choosing what he will do and how he will live. This whole approach to existence, to 'reality', is an approach from inside—an approach from the point of view of the 'actor' as opposed to that of the observer from without.

To acquiesce in roles ascribed to one by society is what Sartre calls 'bad faith'. One can, of course, exhibit this phenomenon of bad faith by the very effort to be sincere in a role one has adopted —or which has been forced upon one. In *Being and Nothingness* (1957) Sartre gives an example of a waiter who attempts to be an object:

> Let us consider this waiter. His movement is quick and forward, a little too precise, a little too rapid, he leans forward a little too earnestly . . . he gives himself the rapidity and pitiless speed of a thing. He is playing . . . at *being* a café waiter . . . What he is trying to realise is the being-in-itself of a waiter, as if it were not precisely in his power to reject the duties and rites of this condition, as if it were not his free choice to get up each morning at five o'clock or to stay

in bed, even though it meant getting fired. As if from the fact that he plays this role it does not follow that he also transcends it, he is something *beyond* it. However, it is undoubtedly true that he *is* in one sense a waiter—otherwise he could just as well call himself a diplomat or journalist. But if he is such, it is not in the sense of the in-itself. He is a waiter in the sense of *being what he is not.* (pp. 98–100)

In his study of Sartre, Anthony Manser (1966) explores in detail the way in which Sartre develops this concept of bad faith in his philosophical writing and in his fiction. Indeed, Sartre was by no means the first person to notice the difference between what people *really* are—in their deepest sense of personal reality—and what they *pretend* to be to meet the requirements of the society they live in. Contrasts between what people want to do and what they are required by society to do are the very stuff of literature. Many novelists have made massive capital of this observation. Comedies of manners depend almost entirely on people's choices of behaviour and their required behaviour.

Semi-sociological observation of considerable wit has probed the ways in which individuals consciously use the role expectations of other persons for personal advantage. One of the most brilliant examples of this technique is that of Stephen Potter in his books *The Theory and Practice of Gamesmanship* (1947); *Some Notes on Lifemanship* (1950); *One-Upmanship* (1952); and *Supermanship* (1958).

Tiryakian suggests that an important task of existential sociology would be to analyse the multiplicity of social worlds to be found within a given society (e.g. the worlds of different social classes, kinship structures, political structures, occupational strata). It would also seek to analyse the worlds of different societies, as well as the inter-relationship of different social worlds (see Tiryakian, p. 165). However, for the purposes of this study, all that will be required is a brief review of sociological commentary on how roles are used (consciously or unconsciously) by members of society, and how these roles are differentiated.

Sociological Commentary of How Roles are Used

The essence of any social situation lies in the mutual expectations of the participants. These expectations rest to a great extent on the norms applicable in the situation. Every culture evolves folkways

33

and mores to cover typical situations, thus furnishing a pattern for the mutual expectations of the interacting parties. In this sense almost every situation is socially defined. Each actor has some conception of what he himself expects of the others, and believes he has some notion of what they expect of him and of what they expect that he expects them to expect. (K. Davis, 1964, p. 83)

This statement by K. Davis in his book *Human Society* is an excellent summary of what roles are used for. Most of the examples summarized below to expand on this brief statement are taken from two studies: that of M. Banton (1965) and that of E. Goffman (1969). Banton shows how society may be pictured as a system of roles; and he demonstrates how this system works for the individual. Goffman starts his study *The Presentation of Self in Everyday Life* with a succinct statement of the practical needs of the individual for knowledge of roles:

When an individual enters the presence of others, they commonly seek to acquire information about him or to bring into play information about him already possessed. They will be interested in his general socio-economic status, his conception of self, his attitude toward them, his competence, his trustworthiness, etc. Although some of this information seems to be sought almost as an end in itself, there are usually quite practical reasons for acquiring it. Information about the individual helps to define the situation, enabling others to know in advance what he will expect of them and what they may expect of him. Informed in these ways, the others will know how best to act in order to call forth a desired response from him.

Banton distinguishes three principal types of role with which expectations of behaviour are associated. First are what he calls basic roles; these are ascribed to people by fixed criteria that are independent of individual merit, such as the criteria of sex and descent, or of seniority of age. These criteria, Banton shows, are 'exhaustive' in that they can be applied to everyone, and their categories are mutually exclusive in that everyone belongs in one or the other: male or female, juvenile or adult. Secondly there are general roles which, while being more differentiated than basic roles, have extensive implications for the other roles open to their incumbents and for inter-personal relationships. He gives as examples from industrial societies: convict, priest, policeman, doctor, lawyer, ambassador, Member of Parliament. Each of these general roles has a much wider significance than most occupational roles in that each of them either restrains the incumbent from engaging in a whole series of activities open to the ordinary person, or confers influence and prestige recognized in many situations. Most of these roles also bring both restrictions and privileges. General roles are usually allocated to individuals in accordance with their qualifications; they are not linked to 'exhaustive' criteria like sex and age. Frequently they are associated with activities important in the moral order of society, such as those of religion and politics. Thirdly, there are independent roles, which have few implications for other roles. Most leisure roles and many occupational roles in industrial societies are examples. Independent roles are usually allocated in accordance with individual merit (see Banton, pp. 39–40).

Summarizing these differences, we may compare the individual role of blacksmith with the basic role of married woman and the general role of policeman in three respects. First, blacksmith is a role which someone assumes for part of the day only; when he has finished work the incumbent is not expected to behave in any way different from people who are not blacksmiths, whereas a married woman and a policeman have obligations they are supposed never to lay aside. Second, both policeman and blacksmith are single occupations among many thousands, unlike the fundamental division of the population into male and female, married and single. Third, anyone who wishes to be a blacksmith and can do the work is in most societies free to take it up; the role can be assumed and laid aside fairly easily and the stress is upon technical competence. Admission to the role of policeman is more restricted: In Britain, age, education, and physique are relevant considerations, but equally a person associating with or related to known criminals would be deemed unsuitable, and a particular religious or racial background is more likely to exclude a man from this role than from that of blacksmith. Being a policeman usually comes to affect a man's whole outlook on life. The role of married woman is open only to females and is obtained by most of them though there is sometimes an element of competition. Assumption of this role (as of the policeman's) is marked by ceremonial, but once taken up it is not easily demitted; a woman cannot be discharged from marital obligations on the grounds of technical incompetence as easily as people are discharged from independent roles. (Banton, pp. 40–41)

Banton uses this classification of roles as a model to separate and identify different spheres of social investigation. Both Banton and Goffman show how the definition of social distance between roles serves important social functions. Banton, for example, shows how much social life is based on the assumption that when one person encounters another he can tell whether he or she is his social superior, equal, or inferior. Goffman draws similar examples from industrial society. However, Goffman's emphasis is on the element of deliberate and calculating management of the impression conveyed by a role for various social purposes. He draws an important distinction between what he calls 'back stage language and behaviour' and 'front stage behaviour language'. When 'off-duty', individuals are technically back-stage—that is to say they adopt a casual manner of language and behaviour, which is in sharp contrast to the behaviour they adopt when they are playing their roles in an organization. The important point in both analyses is that role-playing performs a function in organizing social behaviour. The interest, from the point of view of this study, is particularly in Goffman's evidence that role playing can be a deliberate and calculated activity.

There are of course many functions of role-playing. One important function is that the playing of a particular role increases social awareness. Janis and King (1954) have shown that role-playing, as an artificially constructed exercise, can affect opinion-change. J. L. Moreno has used role-playing as a psycho-therapeutic technique (Moreno, 1946, vol. i).

The weight of evidence is that differentiation of role is not only a useful technique for sociological analysis, but also performs important functions for the individual in helping him to orient himself in society. To show the relevance of this evidence for the present study of popular drama, a short summary of information on how roles are differentiated in society will be appropriate.

How Roles are Differentiated

In arguing that external symbolism upholds the explicit social structure, Dr Mary Douglas (1966) draws on Goffman's evidence that there are no items of clothing, food, or other practical use which are not seized upon as theatrical props to dramatize the way people want to present their roles and the scenes they are playing in. Everything we do, Dr Douglas argues, is significant; nothing is without its conscious symbolic load.

Banton (in his chapter on role signs—chapter 4, 1965) shows for example the importance of clothes in differentiating various types of role. He notes differences in costume between male and female, which are sharper than physiological differences would necessitate, because social organization requires a clear differentiation. More important are the outward signs of general roles. For example, Banton suggests (p. 85) that it is possible to estimate the theological position of a minister of religion from watching the kind of costume he wears in different situations. Again, when a doctor receives patients in his private surgery he will probably not wear a white coat unless considerations of hygiene require it; after all, his patients know who he is. In a large hospital, however, doctors are likely to wear white coats most of the time, not only for technical reasons, but to indicate their role and their claims to privilege (p. 86). The dress of advocates and barristers in Britain, like that of judges, clerks of court, and solicitors, emphasizes that their actions are to be interpreted as stemming not from the likes and dislikes of private individuals but from impersonal rules administered by qualified holders of special office. Wigs, gowns, and other forms of uniform dress conceal individual variations and add an air of authority to their wearers. Like the uniform of a soldier, the costume of the barrister makes people playing this role seem interchangeable (p. 87). Even independent roles have their particular signs. The differences between workers in, say, a department store may not be very important to the person who visits the shop to buy goods, but they may be very important to the social well-being of the staff themselves. Thus, overalls of a particular colour serve as role signs only within a particular organization, compared with the much more general significance of, say, feminine costume.

Banton summarizes his review of role signs as follows:

The more a role is inter-dependent with other roles the more likely it is to be distinguished by some outward sign that acts like a warning light to notify people that the person in question has special rights and obligations either in the immediate situation or in other relations in which the parties might be involved. Role signs are a means of communication indicating the relationship in which someone is prepared to interact with others. Role signs also control behaviour by making any deviant behaviour on the part of the bearer seem more incongruous and by warning other people of the relevant social norms. (p. 91)

Quite apart from the fact that stage drama depends heavily on interaction between fictional roles, there is an important connection between techniques of role differentiation and ceremonial techniques, which were discussed in Chapter 2 as being associated with drama in its origins. Banton has commented on the fact that the division of society into a relatively small number of basic roles creates strains of various kinds, and he suggests that there is an obvious value in customs that permit the discharge of accumulated tension in a harmless fashion. Indeed, he suggests, when any pair of roles—basic, general, or independent—contrast sharply with each other, society may benefit from ceremony that requires the parties to change places for a while. He gives a few examples (pp. 44–45) of rituals involving role reversal. This aspect of ritual behaviour is much more fully treated by L. Spence (1947) in his discussion of the functions of the Lord of Misrule and the Bishop of Fools in early ritual. The importance of ritual when persons are undergoing passage from one role to another had already been noted in Chapter 2—with reference to van Gennep's theories.

Ceremonials containing elements of behaviour practically indistinguishable from stage drama can be found in modern society fulfilling the fundamental function of indicating to persons what their role entails. For example, the Imperial College of Science and Technology in London University is a federation of three colleges—the Royal School of Mines, the Royal College of Science, and the City and Guilds College. The latter comprises the five departments of engineering education. There is no physical difference between the members of each of these constituent, federated colleges, and the buildings of Imperial College are very similar to those of any large office block or factory. So that the students may convince themselves that they are members of a university college, they invent special rituals to demonstrate their collegiate existence. These consist of manifestations in which the union officials dress in strange clothing, in which special chants are sung, in which mascots are paraded around with reverence, and in which 'non-events' are planned—usually involving forays against other sectors of the college. These apparently nonsensical activities seem to perform a valuable function in confirming the students in their consciousness of being students. The content of the dramatic rituals often involves role-reversal activities in which gaily decorated student officials mimic the activities of lecturers, and the students sitting in the seats (in which they normally sit as passive audiences for highly technical lecturing) give vent to wild and eccentric behaviour which, at least in Imperial College, is not usually associated with the role of student as listener-to-lecture.

Dramatic and semi-ritual activity seems then to perform a valuable function in differentiating roles, which in turn function for members of a society as devices for understanding and controlling social structure.

Role Theory: Possible Implications for the Study of Popular Drama

The common concern of sociologism and existentialism is with the predicament of the individual in modern society, who, cut off from his traditional ties, has become deracinated. Where the two sociological perspectives diverge is, of course, in the therapy they propose. For existentialism, the moral reconstruction of the world can only be an individual matter, a matter of inwardness, of choice-making. Its expression does, however, entail the adoption of various types of role, and the use of ceremonial activity and signs to indicate what role is being adopted. For sociologism, the solution to social disintegration is the re-integration of the individual into society by the development of social groupings which will offer the individual meaning for his existence and give him the sense of participating in something greater than his own self. (Tiryakian, 1962, p. 162)

The message of role theory is, then, that the individual perceives the structure of his society through the roles he expects people to play; and that he identifies with his community by his choice of roles to play. Drama is, of course, entirely concerned with the artificial construction of roles. There are clear implications in role theory for the study of popular drama.

First, the function of popular drama may be to sharpen the individual's consciousness of roles, and thus his awareness of the structure of his society. Chapter 2 argued that myth, ritual, and folk tale inform about social structure; role theory suggests that they do so by helping the individual to differentiate between different types of role. If popular drama still has some functions similar to those of myth and ritual, it is likely that it will contain highly dramatic activity that emphasizes the distinctness of roles—such as role-reversal and transvestism.

Secondly, if the individual *needs* popular drama, in the same way that he needs mechanisms by which to distinguish between different social roles, it is likely that he will favour drama in which the emphasis is on social duty and social integration, rather than on existential independence from social obligations.

4

Literary theories about the functions of drama in society

> The overwhelming majority of those concerned with problems related to the social background of art and literature are not sociologists. They are, on the whole, art or literary critics and historians who resort to sociological interpretations for the purpose of increasing their appreciation and knowledge of a work, or a group of works of art or literature. Their enterprise can be illuminating but hardly ever systematic in a sociological sense. (Barbu, 1967, p. 161)

Ever since Aristotle defined tragedy as an imitation of an action of high importance, complete and of some amplitude, in language enhanced by distinct and varying beauties, acted not narrated, by means of pity and fear affecting its purgation of these emotions, generations of literary critics and commentators have waxed eloquent on the social content of drama and on its supposed effects on society. Although, as Professor Barbu points out in his article 'The Sociology of Drama' from which the above quotation is drawn, their activities have hardly ever been systematic, their insights into the quality of drama raise important and valuable suggestions as to the possible functions of drama as a social phenomenon. Some of the systematic attempts to trace the effects of drama will be charted in Chapter 5 of this book; systematic techniques of content analysis will be reviewed in Chapter 6. Meanwhile, as the purpose of the study is to isolate a social phenomenon and to identify the questions that it is meaningful to ask about it, a review of some of the theories of literary critics and observers is appropriate at this juncture. The literature is, of course, enormous; this review will, therefore, be highly selective.

Eric Bentley, in *The Life of the Drama* (1965), raises directly the question: Why do we enjoy looking at drama? Among the answers he gives, six merit note at this point—particularly, because they point to possible functional equivalents, which will be discussed in Chapter 8 of this book. First, Bentley notes our sheer joy in watching impersonation. Reduced to its minimum, the basic theatrical situation is that A impersonates B while C looks on. Impersonation can of course be present in other types of activity—such as acrobatics at a circus. As Bentley points out (p. 154), we know that it is easy for many creatures to fly up and down at great speed: the interest is *only* in seeing men and women do it, because it is not easy for them to do it. To see Olivier as Shallow is to see comparable difficulties overcome, comparable laws of nature defied by human prowess. Hence we are not enjoying the role alone, but also the actor. Another aspect of this phenomenon of impersonation is that we simply enjoy looking at ourselves. We like looking at photographs of ourselves; in a similar way, we are probably attracted to radio and television series like 'The Archers', 'The Dales', and 'Coronation Street', because we see ourselves imitated there.

Secondly, Bentley notes the impossibility of drawing a strict line between drama and gossip, drama and scandal, drama and the front page of tabloid newspapers—which, understandably enough, claim to be dramatic (pp. 156–157). Gossipy newspapers such as the *News of the World, Reveille, The People*, and the *Daily Express*, have a huge sale. People seem to like watching other people's lives—particularly if something smutty or naughty is happening. In the privacy of a darkened auditorium, with one of the four walls of someone's living room taken away, we can be peeping Toms without the danger of being caught at it. Through our television screens we can spy on other people's lives.

Thirdly, Bentley notes the phenomenon of adolescents becoming stage-struck. Puberty, he notes, is a time when the adolescent struggle with parents, with home and the family, often becomes conscious and bitter. The adolescent is not really ready to be independent, to start his own home, to be on his own in the great world, and yet that—or something vaguer or more disruptive—is just what he would like to do. With the perennial human wish to have one's cake and eat it, the adolescent would like to have a rebellion without facing the consequences of a rebellion. One would like to go to another country and yet to stay in this one. On the stage, the wishful thoughts of adolescents become actions. Life is complicated; but the stage solves problems (see Bentley, p. 164 f.). This observation agrees with the theory of roles discussed in Chapter 3. It has been noted that actors are frequently very shy and introverted people, uncertain of their own identity; taking roles on the stage seems to be therapeutic in that it temporarily gives them an identity.

Fourthly, Bentley suggests that theatre provides unembarrassing company for the lonely. Theatre assuages loneliness without imposing the pest of company. Actors provide company—whether on the stage of the live theatre, or on television, or on the cinema screen—without asking anything in return. Indeed, we do not even need to show gratitude; we have paid—either for a licence fee or for a ticket of admission. This is an area of interest that has been extensively explored by mass communications research, as will be shown in Chapter 5.

Fifthly, Bentley suggests that drama invests the trivial with cosmic significance. Details of everyday life seem to matter when displayed in drama. If this is indeed an element of the appeal of drama, it clearly has a wide variety of functional equivalents. The Beatles pictured eating a particular food, the Queen riding on the Victoria Line, a prestige newspaper mentioning the village in which we live—these may all perform similar functions to the ones suggested by Bentley.

Sixthly, Bentley comments on the function of play-acting for children:

> What the three-year-olds mostly do has an element of pretending in it, and so of play-acting: there is a role and there is drama. But it is not acting because there is no audience; it is not there to be looked at, noted, appreciated, enjoyed. Children, notoriously, are audience-conscious; they wish to be noted, appreciated, enjoyed, but what they at first exhibit to their audience is precisely not their make-belief dramas but their conquests of 'reality'. (p. 183)

It has already been noted, in the discussion of the association of drama with ritual, and in the examination of the theory of roles, that drama may function positively in defining social order. In reviewing the comments of literary critics, this chapter will concentrate on the content of drama that has something to say about social structure. The most obvious way in which we recognize the normal is by contrast with abnormality.

Definition of the Normal in Society through Contrast with the Abnormal

Dr Douglas's thesis (1966), that dirt and uncleanness is that which must not be included if pattern is to be maintained, has already been noted. H. D. Duncan's discussion of the comic propounds a similar thesis. For example, in his study *Communication and Social Order* (1962) Duncan demonstrates how a social order *defines* itself through disorder as well as order. Improprieties set limits; they begin the moment of negation where the positive content of a role ends. Without such limits a role cannot take form (p. 281). No social order, Duncan argues, exists without disorder. In tragic communal rites disorder is exorcized through punishment, torture, and death. But comedy can be used to face disorder. Through comedy we can express doubt as to the principles that those in power uphold in the name of social order. In comedy, the ambiguities and complicating contradictions that interfere with the smooth functioning of individuals in social interaction can be uncovered and commented upon. In the permissive atmosphere of comedy, it is possible to discuss openly what cannot be mentioned in normal social intercourse. Comedy, therefore, Duncan argues, offers many clues to the difficulties men find in playing their social roles.

Drama would not be dramatic if there were no consensus of opinion about subjects that should generate social outrage. In an article on 'The Psychology of Farce' (1958), Eric Bentley comments that the marriage joke exists only for a culture that knows itself committed to marriage. In *The Life of the Drama* (1965) he argues that farce offers us the privilege of being totally passive while on stage our most treasured, unmentionable wishes are fulfilled before our eyes by the most violently active human beings that ever sprang from the human imagination. In the bedroom farce, we savour the adventure of adultery, ingeniously exaggerated in the highest degree, without taking the responsibility or suffering the guilt (cf. p. 229). Neither supermen nor babies have a sense of humour. They do not need one. Men and women do because they have inhibited, in the interests of social order, many of their strongest wishes. Underlying Bentley's argument is the insight that farce offers the opportunity to express

44

emotion at elements of social structure that cause conflict, and at the same time, through the resolution of the drama, to contain those elements of conflict.

Duncan has commented that joking is a form of instruction, a kind of social control, directed at those we intend to accept once they learn to behave properly—that is, like us. He notes that a community will laugh at immigrants so long as it is secure in the glory of its principles of social order. Americans may laugh at the thrifty Scot, feeling the glory of their boldness with money, and at the same time make the Scot aware of how he must spend if he is to become a true American. There may be hostility in this laughter, but it is not the hostility of derisive laughter, which ends in alienation and hate. Americans, through such joking, may be trying to prepare the Scot for membership of the American community (cf. Duncan, p. 389). Both Bentley and Duncan have commented that much of the spice of comedy depends upon a knowledge that while some aspect of authority is threatened, the *principles* of authority are not. The individual priest may be a buffoon; the soldier a coward; the scholar pedantic. But exposure of the weak members of a respected sector of the community really argues that the church is still holy, the army still brave, the community of scholars still dedicated to the search for wisdom (Duncan, p. 387).

One of the most comprehensive reviews available of the causes of laughter is that of Arthur Koestler in *The Act of Creation* (1964, part 1). He reviews, with an elaborate account of the physiological mechanisms of laughter, how laughter serves to relieve tension. He demonstrates how the cognitive element of humour depends upon our identifying two self-consistent but habitually incompatible frames of intellectual reference. In the comic situation these two frames of reference intersect. To find the humorous quality of the intersection of these intellectual matrices, it is necessary to find the link—the focal concept, word, or situation that is bisociated with both mental planes. Such analysis can reveal the purely intellectual pleasure we may derive from wit—in which the greatest possible economy is used in showing the incompatibility of the two frames of reference through the use of a single word or an ingenious idea. To analyse the cause of convulsive laughter, where the body shakes with emotion, Koestler recommends the identification of the emotive charge and the location of the unconscious elements that it may contain. Laughter-producing situations permit us to express repressed emotion at abnormalities that offend.

Koestler's whole analysis of humour (which is in fact merely part of a much more ambitious study of creativity) implies that laughter is instrumentally functional. That is to say, laughter functions to preserve our sense of congruity by permitting us occasion to release emotion at incongruity. However, in the study of drama, it remains to be demonstrated whether drama's capacity to deal with aspects of social normality is an instrumental or an expressive aspect of culture.

Farcical comedy is the most extreme example of the contrast of the normal with the abnormal. However, in practically every type of drama some form of contrast between the socially normal and the socially abnormal takes place. The next section of this chapter will demonstrate, by reviewing the work of some literary critics, how this is so.

The Establishment of Social Norms in Drama

In *Anatomy of Criticism*, Northrop Frye (1957) classifies fictions by the power of action of the hero, which may be greater than ours, less than ours, or roughly the same as ours. His analysis is not only a convenient model for classification, but also suggests some interesting implications for the study of popular drama. Within Frye's scheme of analysis, plot structure may, of course, be isomorphic, and themes may be similar. However, Frye's system is worth quoting at some length because of the ease of analysis it permits.

> 1. If superior in *kind* both to other men and to the environment of other men, the hero is a divine being, and the story about him will be a *myth* in the common sense of a story about a god. Such stories have an important place in literature, but are as a rule found outside the normal literary categories.
> 2. If superior in *degree* to other men and to his environment, the hero is the typical hero of *romance*, whose actions are marvellous but who is himself identified as a human being. The hero of romance moves in a world in which the ordinary laws of nature are slightly suspended: qualities of courage and endurance, unnatural to us, are

natural to him, and enchanted weapons, talking animals, terrifying ogres and witches, and talismans of miraculous power violate no rule of probability once the postulates of romance have been established. Here we have moved from myth, properly so called, into legend, folk tale, märchen, and their literary affiliates and derivatives.

3. If superior in degree to other men but not to his natural environment, the hero is a leader. He has authority, passions, and powers of expression far greater than ours, but what he does is subject both to social criticism and to the order of nature. This is the hero of the *high mimetic* mode, of most epic and tragedy, and is primarily the kind of hero that Aristotle had in mind.

4. If superior neither to other men nor to his environment, the hero is one of us: we respond to a sense of his common humanity, and demand from the poet the same canons of probability that we find in our own experience. This gives us the hero of the *low mimetic* mode, of most comedy and of realistic fiction. 'High' and 'low' have no correlations of comparative value, but are purely diagrammatic, as they are when they refer to Biblical critics or Anglicans. On this level the difficulty in retaining the word 'hero', which has a more limited meaning among the preceding modes, occasionally strikes an author. Thackeray thus feels obliged to call *Vanity Fair* a novel without a hero.

5. If inferior in power or intelligence to ourselves, so that we have the sense of looking down on a scene of bondage, frustration, or absurdity, the hero belongs to the *ironic* mode. This is still true when the reader feels that he is or might be in the same situation, as the situation is being judged by the norms of a greater freedom.

Looking over this table, we can see that European fiction, during the last fifteen centuries, has steadily moved its centre of gravity down the list. (Frye, 1957, pp. 33-34)

Myth, in the sense used by Frye, is almost totally absent from modern fiction. However, there is a large amount of romance. Frye divides his category 'romance' into two main forms: a secular form dealing with chivalry and knight-errantry, and a religious form devoted to legends of saints. There is a great deal of romance fiction in popular drama in the form of Westerns, detective stories, and stories of secret agents.

In the high mimetic mode of drama, particularly in tragedy, the relationship of the hero to his community is usually that of leader. The position of leadership makes the character exceptional and isolated. The nature of the hero's isolation is frequently in terms of some ideal he holds that does not fit in with the norms of his society. In *The Hyacinth Room* Cyrus Hoy (1964) has argued that the protagonists of tragedy and comedy alike are deficient in their knowledge of human limitations, of what they can hope to achieve and what it is the better part of wisdom not to attempt. They lack self-knowledge. The tragic protagonist's lack of self-knowledge typically leads to destruction. The comic protagonist's lack of self-knowledge leads ideally to enlightenment from which he cannot but benefit.

In comedy, the hero may have some misconception of what society is all about; he adjusts himself to society and, frequently, the society to whose membership he aspires often adjusts itself towards his point of view. In tragedy, because of the high-minded nature of the hero's ideals, it is not possible for the prevailing society to move towards his ideal. Typically, in tragedy, a chorus represents the society from which the hero is gradually isolated. However sympathetic the chorus may be, it usually expresses a social norm against which the hero's ideal may be measured. In Greek tragedy, the chorus may be a group of citizens who recite the ideals of the normal society from which the hero is deviating. In Shakespearian tragedy, the 'chorus' may be an individual. For example, Enobarbus in *Antony and Cleopatra* fulfils this function from the very first lines of the play: 'Nay but this dotage of our generals o'erflows the measure . . .' In modern tragedy the idealist hero usually has a foil whose views represent those of the ordinary community, against whose views those of the hero are contrasted. For example, a heroic army officer may have a heightened sense of duty—a form of idealism—which is set in contrast to the instincts of his subordinates for mere self-preservation. Frequently the audience recognizes that the ideals for which the tragic hero stands are the correct ones. He represents a moral norm that the society might wish to achieve, but which it is in normal circumstances incapable of achieving. The destruction of the hero produces a feeling of awe.

It is interesting to note at this point that the further the ideal of the hero deviates from what is considered normal by a specific society the more difficult the drama is to play. For example, it is notoriously difficult for amateurs—for instance in a school—to act a Greek or Shakespearian tragedy really convincingly. The tragic hero is somehow excluded from the group by virtue of his ideals; but the audience knows the actor to be 'one of them', a member of the upper fifth form, and unless the amateur actor is unusually competent, it is extremely difficult to believe his protestations of idealism to be true.

In the low mimetic mode of drama, the equivalent to tragedy is the exclusion of an individual on our own level from a social group to which he is trying to belong. The central tradition of sophisticated pathos (the low mimetic version of tragic pity and fear) is the study of the isolated mind, the story of someone recognizably like ourselves broken by a conflict between the inner and outer world, between imaginative reality and the sort of reality that is established by a social consensus (cf. Frye, p. 39). The conflict can be between animal passion and reason—informed by social consensus. In tragedy, the isolation of the individual by virtue of his different conception of the way things should be typically results in disaster. However, the important point is that on the way to the disaster the hero achieves self-knowledge. He begins to comprehend the difference between his view of life and the social norm from which he is deviating.

The root conflict of comedy may be similar: a conflict between the personal wishes of the hero and the social expectations of the group to which he seeks to belong. Unlike that of tragedy, where the hero is typically alienated, isolated, expelled, or destroyed, the theme of comedy is usually that of social integration. The common factor in both traditions is the establishment of *reason* in terms of social consensus.

> The reason of comedy is social reason. Like tragedy, it is based on convictions about what is necessary to social order. But comic reason holds that reason must keep convictions about social means and ends *open* to reason. Tragedy seeks belief, even though such belief may not be subject to reason. Comedy seeks belief, but never at the price of banishing doubt and question. Tragedy treats disrelations and incongruities as heresy and sin, comedy as misunderstanding and ignorance of proper social ends. (Duncan, 1962, p. 406)

Typically, the theme of comedy is the integration of society, which usually takes the form of incorporating the central character into it. Frye shows how in New Comedy what is normally presented is an erotic intrigue between a young man and a young woman, which is blocked by some kind of opposition, usually paternal, and resolved by a twist in the plot, which is the comic form of Aristotle's 'Discovery'. At the beginning of the play, the forces thwarting the hero are in control of the play's society, but after a 'discovery' in which the hero becomes wealthy or the heroine respectable, a new society crystallizes on the stage around the hero and his bride. The action of the comedy moves towards the incorporation of the hero into the society that he naturally fits. Frye notes that, in conformity with low mimetic decorum, the hero is seldom a very interesting person; he is ordinary in his virtues, but socially attractive (Frye, p. 44). The movement of the play is, typically, a movement from one kind of society to another. The final society reached by comedy—the society that incorporates the hero—is the one that the audience has recognized all along to be the proper and desirable state of affairs. The tendency of comedy, Frye notes (p. 165), is to include as many people as possible in its final society: the blocking characters are more often reconciled or converted than simply repudiated. Comedy often includes a scapegoat ritual of expulsion, which gets rid of some irreconcilable character. But exposure and disgrace make for pathos, or even tragedy. More common is the conversion of the obstructive character, so that he may be fitted in to the new and desirable society that has emerged.

The blocking character in this sort of comedy is usually someone with a good deal of social prestige and power, who is able to force much of the play's society into line with his own will. When the blocking character becomes the butt of the play's humour, the process of social control through humour is coming into play: that is to say, the individual whose power and prestige is holding a society in a state of undesirable moral organization is laughingly made to see the unreasonableness of his views.

If it is true, as has been suggested in Chapters 2 and 3, that drama is historically derived from ritual—and is concerned mainly with social integration—and that the organization of roles within society is also concerned with social integration, it might be expected that dramas concerned with social integration would have a greater mass popularity than those concerned with social alienation. That is to say, dramas of social inclusion would be more popular than those of exclusion. Where we are expected to identify with the central character, comic integration would be more likely to satisfy a need for social integration than would drama in which the hero is excluded. However, a society can be defined by those not permitted to be members just as much as by those who are permitted. It is, therefore, necessary to examine briefly the mechanism of the ironic mode of drama.

In Frye's ironic mode, the audience has the sense of looking down on a scene of bondage, frustration, or absurdity. The audience may still feel that they could be in the same situation as the central character; but the character's situation is judged by the norms of a greater moral independence. Frye argues (p. 45 f.) that ironic comedy brings us to the figure of the scapegoat ritual and the nightmare dream, the human symbol that concentrates our fears and hates. Outside the boundaries of art, the scapegoat may be the black man of a lynching, the Jew of a pogrom, the old woman of a witch-hunt, or anyone picked on at random by a mob. But the element of *play* is the barrier that separates art from savagery, and playing at human sacrifice seems to be an important theme of the ironic mode of drama.

> The fact that we are now in an ironic phase of literature largely accounts for the popularity of the detective story, the formula of how a man-hunter locates a 'pharmakos' and gets rid of him. The detective story begins in the Sherlock Holmes period as an intensification of low mimetic, in the sharpening of attention to details that makes the dullest and most neglected trivia of daily living leap into mysterious and fateful significance. But as we move further away from this we move toward a ritual drama around a corpse in which a wavering finger of social condemnation passes over a group of 'suspects' and finally settles on one. The sense of a victim chosen by lot is very strong, for the case against him is only plausibly manipulated. If it were really inevitable, we should have tragic irony as in *Crime and Punishment*, where Raskolnikoff's crime is so interwoven with his character that there can be no question of any 'who-dun-it' mystery. In the growing brutality of the crime story (a brutality protected by the convention of the form, as it is conventionally impossible that the man-hunter can be mistaken in believing that one of his suspects is a murderer), detection begins to merge with the thriller as one of the forms of melodrama. In melodrama, two themes are important: the triumph of moral virtue over villainy, and the consequent idealising of the moral views assumed to be held by the audience. In the melodrama of the brutal thriller we come as close as is normally possible for art to come to the pure self-righteousness of the lynching mob. (Frye, 1957, pp. 46–47)

This brief review of the high mimetic, low mimetic, and ironic modes of fiction has shown how in each of the three modes drama may in some way be concerned with the interplay of the central character's ideals and activity with the norms of the society in which he finds himself.

In much popular drama there seems to be a marriage of the romance mode of fiction (with its connotations of wish-fulfilment) with the ironic mode of fiction, involving drama of sufficient realism, even if remote in time or place, to convince. Much critical commentary on this popular drama has been concerned with its social content.

Critical Commentary on Some Types of Popular Drama

At bottom, the gangster is doomed because he is under the obligation to succeed, not because the means he employs are unlawful. In the deeper layers of the modern consciousness, all means are unlawful, every attempt to succeed is an act of aggression leaving one alone and guilty and defenceless among enemies: one is *punished* for success. This is our intolerable dilemma: but failure is a kind of death and success is evil and dangerous, is—ultimately—impossible. The effect of the gangster film is to embody this dilemma in the person of the gangster and resolve it by his death. The dilemma is resolved because it is *his* death, not ours. We are safe; for the moment, we can acquiesce in our failure, we can choose to fail. (Warshow, 1948, p. 244)

This comment by Robert Warshow on 'The Gangster as Tragic Hero' is typical of the increasingly vast critical literature dealing with popular drama. This literature is an uneasy mixture of psychoanalytical, sociological, philosophical, and literary criticism. Its common feature is that it is eclectic and unsystematic in its use of material for analysis. However, a common theme running through most of the literature is that the drama expresses emotion about items normally repressed in the individual's experience of his culture, and contains the action expressing this emotion within some sort of moral framework, however crude. With the poorest of the material reviewed, the containment of emotion is imposed probably only by the censor, and by the backing of laws of obscenity. It is, however, useful to review some of the critical literature because it suggests insights into the sociological functions of drama in society. Although the main subject of this book is drama as contained in single plays, this critical literature (which deals principally with series, serials, and fiction with repeated appearances of heroes of known cultural dimensions) points to questions which it will probably be valuable for the functional analyst to raise when trying to come to an overall picture of the place of popular drama in society.

In dealing with the hero of the Western, Robert Warshow (1954) asks the question: why does the Western movie especially have such a hold on our imagination? He thinks it is because the Western offers a serious orientation to the problem of violence such as can be found almost nowhere else in our culture. One of the well-known peculiarities of modern civilized opinion, Warshow argues, is refusal to acknowledge the importance of violence. This refusal is a virtue, but like many virtues it involves a certain wilful blindness and it encourages hypocrisy. Violence is, therefore, a subject of conflict between the individual and his culture. The Western 'myth' deals with violence in a stylized fashion and thus permits it to be contemplated. Other writers, for example W. J. Barker (1955) and F. Elkin (1950), have argued in similar vein to Warshow. The growth of literature on Westerns has in fact now become luxuriant. A review of a brief selection of some of it will reveal the principal preoccupations.

N. A. Scotch (1960) noted a change in the image of Indians shown in Westerns from lying and violent savages to strong, silent, and virtuous persons of singular civilization. He even notes the presence in one Western of a Harvard-educated Indian who becomes a marshal. Why, Scotch wonders, has this sentimentalization taken place? Among the reasons he gives is an admiration among Americans for a fantasy group with strong morals. 'There is a wistfulness in our time for great moral strength.'

M. Nussbaum (1960), exploring the sociological symbolism of the adult Western, explains that the adult Western has evolved in American culture as a new art-form, delineating our motivations and psychoses and permitting their catharsis. He notes some of the more obvious attractions of the Western: the Western as foreign adventure involving wide open spaces, majestic scenery and a new frontier; the Western hero, serious, quiet, relaxed, achieving law and order like the heroes of ancient mythology— Joshua, Ulysses, Sir Lancelot; the independence of the hero who, unlike the commuter returning by tube to his canned food, rides off into the sunset; the individualism of the hero and his direct contact with nature. But Nussbaum's particular contribution is his interest in the shades of grey given in the adult Western in its treatment of the conflict between good and evil. Adult Westerns, as opposed to the stereotyped Western, seek to explain why Blackie was bad, and that he was not completely bad. Similarly they show that the hero was not all good and that he was capable of making costly mistakes. What adult Westerns accomplish, Nussbaum argues, is to graft onto Western characters the emotions, fears, inadequacies, and psychoses of modern man. But the hero is still seen as one who takes it upon himself to judge between good and evil. Today when all our problems are so complicated that there is really no right and wrong but rather many shades of grey, it is gratifying to see complex problems reduced to an either-or proposition, adjudicated and resolved by a single action (p. 27). This single adjudicating action is the use of the gun. The gun, Nussbaum argues, coupled with the fast draw, symbolizes maleness, individualism, and the equivalent of the Greek *deus ex machina*. He goes on to draw analogies between the gun which solves all problems and the phallus.

One of the most intriguing treatments of the Western is that by Peter Homans in 'Puritanism Revisited' (1961). He noted that in 1961 more than thirty Western stories were told each week on American television, with an estimated budget of $60,000,000. Four of the five top night-time shows were Westerns, and of the top twenty shows, eleven were Westerns. His method of choosing Westerns for content analysis was extremely unsystematic—as was his content analysis itself. However, he notices a variety of characteristics of the typical Western hero. The hero emerges from the desert and returns to it. His life is one of austerity and simplicity; if he is not one who rides in from the desert, but is a town marshal, his office is a place of singular austerity. This is contrasted sharply with the rich carpeting, impressive desk, curtains, pictures, and liquor supply of the saloon owner or evil gambler. The asceticism of the Western hero is not, apparently, due to the hero's lack of funds or low salary; the point is rather that because of his living habits there is no need of anything else. Indeed, we are led to suspect that such austerity is in some way related to the hero's virtue. The traditional resources of society—doctors, teachers, ministers, lawyers—have failed to cope with the presence in a community of 'an evil one'. The action of the typical Western, Homans explains, consists of three basic parts: before fight; fight; after fight. In the opening phase, the audience is prepared for the action by learning the moral characteristics of the hero. The hero is, first of all, a transcendent figure, originating beyond the town. Classically, he rides into town from nowhere; even if he is the marshal, his identity is in some way disassociated from the people he must save. He apparently has no friends, relatives, family, mistresses—only a horse. He is shown as detached and self-controlled. Although he has opportunities for self-indulgence, he does not yield to them. He never seems passionately attracted to women; he gulps his drink, rarely enjoying it; he gambles, but he appears uninterested in winning. He seems indifferent to money, regardless of its quantity or source. The hero is in the sharpest possible contrast to the evil one, who unhesitatingly involves himself in most of the following activities: gambling, drink, the accumulation of money, lust, and violence. Evil is the failure to resist temptation—and this is precisely what the evil one represents. The key to the Western, Homans argues, is that temptation is indulged while providing the appearance of having been resisted. Each of the minor temptation episodes contrasting the hero with the evil one takes its unique shape from this need—the scenes setting forth the characteristics of hero and evil one as each encounters drink, cards, money, and sex. Each temptation episode is a climax-less Western in itself, a play within a play in which temptation is faced and defeated, not by violent destruction as in the climax scene, but by inner-willed control. The temptation scenes are, of course, interchangeable; that is why they do not all need to occur in one Western.

The evil one who is contrasted with the hero has disturbed the life of a community. He must be destroyed by the hero, before the town can return to normal. But the restoration to normalcy of the community is merely the vehicle by which the Western myth may be shown. This is a myth in which evil appears as a series of temptations to be resisted by the hero—most of which he succeeds in avoiding through inner control. When faced with the embodiment of these temptations, his mode of control changes, and he destroys the threat. But the story is so structured that the responsibility for the final act—the killing of the evil one—falls upon the evil one himself, permitting the hero to destroy while appearing to save (see p. 82). Homans presents the Western as a Puritan morality tale:

> Whenever vitality becomes too pressing and the dominion of the will becomes threatened, the self must find some other mode of control. In such a situation the Puritan will seek, usually unknowingly, any situation which will permit him to express vitality while at the same time appearing to control and resist it. The Western provides just this opportunity for . . . the entire myth is shaped by the inner dynamic of apparent control and veiled expression. Indeed, in the gun fight (and to a lesser extent in the minor temptation episodes) the hero's heightened gravity and dedicated exclusion of all other loyalties presents a study in Puritan virtue, while the evil one presents nothing more or less than the old New England Protestant devil—strangely costumed, to be sure—the traditional tempter whose horrid lures never allow the good Puritan a moment's peace. In the gun fight there is deliverance and redemption. Here is the real meaning of the Western: a Puritan morality tale in which the saviour-hero redeems the community from the temptations of the devil.
>
> The Western is also related to Puritanism through its strong self-critical element, i.e. it attacks, usually through parody, many aspects of traditional civilised life . . . the story is well-removed from (his own) locale, both geographically and psychically. Because it is always a story taking place 'out there' and 'a long time ago', self-criticism can appear without being directly recognised as such. (p. 83 f.)

Like Westerns, detective stories have also been subjected to psychoanalytical treatment. George Orwell's essay on 'Raffles and Miss Blandish' (Rosenberg and White, 1957, pp. 154–163) was one of the earliest. G. Pederson-Krag's treatment of detective stories (1949) equals in psychoanalytic boldness K. J. Munden's study of the cowboy myth (1958). But the main emphasis in this brief review will be on sociological interpretations. Once again, the main emphasis is on a saviour redeeming society from moral evil. The hunt for and sacrifice of the scapegoat victim is lavishly treated. C. J. Rolo's treatment of 'Simenon and Spillane' (Rosenberg and White, 1957, pp. 165–185) describes the hero of Spillane's novels, Mike Hammer, as Jehovah's messenger, the avenging hand of the Jehovah of *Proverbs* who ordains that 'destruction shall be to the workers of iniquity'. Hammer is the superman who fights evil for us in a compensatory day-dream. C. La Farge discussing 'Mickey Spillane and his bloody Hammer' (1954) describes Mike Hammer as the logical conclusion, almost a sort of brutal apotheosis, of McCarthyism: when things seem wrong, let one man cure the wrong by whatever means he, as privileged saviour, chooses. Hall and Whannel (1964) devote a whole chapter to what they call 'the avenging angels' (pp. 142–163) in which Mike Hammer's fearful redemption of capitalist society from Communist evil features largely.

Rolo describes the detective story, with whichever type of hero seems to appear, as modern man's Passion Play.

In the beginning is the murder, and the world is sorely out of joint. There appears the detective-hero and his foil, the latter representing the blindness of ordinary mortals—Dr. Watson, or the police, or, if the hero is a policeman, his bumbling associates. The detective is a man like the rest of us, with his share of human failings—Nero Wolfe swills beer; Maigret is helpless without his pipe; Hammer goes in for venery. But this mortal has The Call—he is Saviour. In him is grace, and we know that he will bring the light.

The hero suspects everyone, for the murderer is everyman; the murder is the symbol of guilt, the imperfection that is in all of us. In his search for the hidden truth, the hero is exposed to danger, thrashes about in darkness, sometimes suffers in the flesh, for it is by his travail that the saviour looses the world of its sins. In the detective's hour of triumph, the world is, for a moment, redeemed. Unconsciously we die a little when the murderer meets his fate, and thus we are purged of guilt. We rejoice in the reassurance that beyond the chaos of life there is order and meaning (the writer who leaves bits of chaos lying around condemns the reader to purgatory). We exult that the Truth has been made known and that Justice has prevailed. All this the lowly who-dun-it offers. And still that is not all.

By his personality, his deeds, his methods, the hero bears witness to a system of belief, a secular credo for a religious doctrine. He is the apostle of Science like Holmes, or of pure Reason like Hercule Poirot. He may, like Maigret, believe that Understanding is the highest good and that its fruit is Compassion. He may, like Hammer, be the vessel of wrath which executes Jehovah's vengeance on those who ploughed iniquity. There are other kinds of hero detectives, and they are true prophets all. For in the detective story Paradise is always Regained. (Rolo, Rosenberg and White, 1957, pp. 174–175)

A similar sort of analysis is that of H. Dienstfrey in his study of 'Doctors, Lawyers, and other T.V. heroes' (1963) in which he shows police and other professionals as saviours of society's morals. Dienstfrey attributes the remarkable success of the story of professionals to the image of society which they present. Again, his criticism is worth quoting at some length:

> In the midst of the urban jungle—and usually in one of its bureau-cracies—the professional dramas are matter-of-factly able to uncover all the signs of a healthy, serene and on-going community. Where others mainly have seen the ravages of anomie, they find a plenitude of well-being.
>
> There is, first of all, the work of their main characters . . . on these programmes one finds men in the very bosom of the city, pursuing occupations that provide them with nothing but the deepest satisfaction. . . . It is in their work that all alike find their identity . . . their jobs, are the best of all possible jobs: they offer both inner-meaning and public worth. Television's city-dwelling professionals thus serve as living proof that work in the modern world can be beautiful . . .
>
> The goal of the professionals is to render aid, their vision is social, and their richest reward is obviously the knowledge that they have done their job well. When the public has such men to serve (or defend), the fundamental decency of the surrounding society follows as a matter of course.
>
> It follows also from the way the main characters analyse the social problems with which they are always coping. In deciding the right or wrong of an issue, their only criterion is the effect a given action will have on the common good. (Dienstfrey, 1963, pp. 523–524)

Over and over again, moral disintegration in society is cured even when the manifest tasks of the heroes, like Dr Finlay and Dr Cameron, are medical. If low-budget TV productions showing dedicated professionals at work are not sufficiently satisfying to the imagination, there are always the vast spectacle films of the James Bond novels. In his study *The James Bond Dossier* (1965), Kingsley Amis presents the James Bond magic as a type of political catharsis. As usual, an orthodox moral system pervades the Bond stories. Some things are regarded as good: loyalty, fortitude, a sense of responsibility, a readiness to regard one's safety, even one's life, as less important than the major interests of one's organization and one's country. Other things are regarded as bad: tyranny, readiness to inflict pain on the weak or helpless, the unscrupulous pursuit of money or power (see Amis, pp. 84–85). The situation that the hero saves is one of greater magnificence than that which the hero of the Western saves. Not only is the local social and moral order in danger: the entire structure of Western civilization has to be saved by Bond. Throughout Bond's adventures, Amis notes, no Englishman does anything bad. Even Bond's superiority to his American counterpart Leiter is part of the overall picture. As Amis says: 'those who hold that violent films, TV shows, and the like are useful in safety-valving off our private aggressions should hail Mr Fleming as a comparable therapist working in the field of politics' (p. 93).

A complicating factor in Bond films, as in Westerns, is the sheer spectacle. The sub-title to Siegfried Kracauer's *Theory of Film* is 'The Redemption of Physical Reality' (1960). Film can emphasize physical as opposed to social reality. But this review of critical commentary on popular drama suggests insights that may be useful when we come to consider single plays in Chapter 7, and the tentative conclusions of this study in Chapter 8.

Summary of Non-Sociological Commentary on Drama: Possible Implications for the Study of Popular Drama

There is a sense in which the whole effort of civilisation is an effort at imposing form on unruly matter—matter in this case being the fleshly desires and lusts of human kind. The formalising process is variously implemented: by a legal code, a moral code, a code of manners, to name the three that most regularly operate to curb the lust for one's neighbour's blood, or one's neighbour's property, or one's neighbour's wife, or which serve merely to brand as offensive acts which violate society's standard of good sense and good taste (Hoy, C. 1964, p. 147)

Four principal points seem to emerge from this review of non-sociological (that is to say literary, and other) commentary on drama: first, an important function imputed to drama is that of containing unruly instinct by stylized dramatic technique. Bentley (1965) has drawn attention to the abstract quality of farce —in which human beings move around with maniacal speed, violating convention with machine-like detachment. Farce is funny because we really believe in the social institutions its characters appear to be attacking. Similarly, the stylized treatment of violence in the Western helps us to be rational about an element of experience that might be socially disruptive.

Secondly, critics have commented on the way in which order is most clearly defined by its opposite—disorder. Morality is understood by immorality. Identification of criminality, and discussion of it, seems to serve a function in increasing social coherence. This is a phenomenon that was commented upon by Durkheim in *The Division of Labour in Society* (1893). The treatment of crime in drama may be functionally instrumental, or functionally expressive, with regard to people's deepest and most sinister instincts. It is obvious, though still worth stating, that crime dramas would cease to be dramatic if we did not believe that the crimes portrayed were disruptive of social harmony.

Thirdly, if the function of drama, like that of ritual and myth, is primarily to express or control the moral cohesion of society, the implication is that the most popular form of drama will be that in which social integration takes place. From the comments of critics recorded in this chapter, the expectation would be that comedy would be one of the most popular forms of drama.

Fourthly, critics have commented on how the hero of the high mimetic mode has ideals that are unattainable. The hero of the low mimetic mode has ideals that are attainable—indeed, they are the ideal standards by which society sustains itself. If these ideals are to be expressed, it is probable that they will be most frequently expressed when social disorder is at its highest. That is to say, it is likely that idealists in low mimetic, realistic drama, will be found in dramas that deal with the total or almost complete disruption of society.

The principal implication of the literature reviewed in this chapter, as of the literature reviewed in Chapters 2 and 3, is that popular drama, as opposed to drama favoured by social revolutionaries, innovators, and intellectuals, is likely to be conservative in orientation. If it is concerned with crime, it is likely to show who is to be excluded from the conventional society and why. If it is comic drama, it is likely to give expression to those strained points in social structure that cause most conflict to the individual, to show how these can be accommodated, and to deal with social integration. It remains to be seen whether these theoretical predictions from critics who have not sought to adopt a systematic sociological approach are borne out by sociological evidence.

5

Drama as Mass Communication

> Mass Communication is directed toward relatively large and hetero-
> geneous audiences that are anonymous to the communicator.
> Messages are transmitted publicly; are timed to reach most of the
> audience quickly, often simultaneously; and usually are meant to be
> transient rather than permanent records. Finally, the communicator
> tends to be, or to operate within, a complex formal organisation that
> may involve great expense. (C. R. Wright, 1960, p. 606)

The form of drama being dealt with in this study, particularly
television drama, is a form of mass communication within the
definition proposed by Wright in the above quotation. Before
embarking on the detailed study of popular drama in the theatre
and on television, it is necessary to examine the nature and some
of the effects imputed to mass communications in general. In
seeking a clear definition of the possible satisfactions to be found
in drama, it is necessary to compare drama with other types of
mass communication; such a comparison should suggest another
range of questions pertinent to the study of popular drama.

Communication basically involves the transfer of information
from one system to another. In studying the communication of
information through electronic media, engineers constantly battle
with the problem of 'noise'. That is to say, the information—in
the technical sense of the word—is usually entangled with un-
desired properties resulting from the nature of the electronic
medium. Communication between individual human beings is
even more subject to interference—a social version of 'noise'.
Mass communication, by implication, is a subject of bewildering
and daunting complexity. In his article 'Toward a General Model
of Communication', George Gerbner (1956) outlines ten basic
aspects of communication. In drawing up his model, he compares

a verbal model of communication with areas of study necessary in the field of mass communication.

Verbal Model	*Areas of Study*
1. Someone	Communicator and Audience Research
2. Perceives an event	Perception Research and Theory
3. And reacts	Effectiveness measurement
4. In a situation	Study of physical, social setting
5. Through some means	Investigation of channels, media, controls over facilities
6. To make available materials	Administration; distribution; freedom of access to materials
7. In some form	Structure, organisation, style, pattern
8. And context	Study of communicative setting, sequence
9. Conveying content	Content analysis; study of meaning
10. Of some consequence	Study of over-all changes.

(p. 173)

Gerbner comments that this model represents shifts of emphasis in study rather than tight compartments. In fact, nearly every aspect of the model he proposes can be viewed in terms of any of the others. His model is noted simply to illustrate the staggering complexity of mass communications research. It is clearly impossible, in this brief review, to do justice to all the items proposed by Gerbner.

L. Lowenthal, in his essay 'Popular Culture' (1960), suggests that study should concentrate on patterns of influence, content, and evolution and transmission of particular standards. Chapter 6 of this book will deal with the techniques of content analysis relevant to the study of drama. It will also comment briefly on some of the patterns of influence that control the material available to the consumer of drama. This chapter will concentrate on what is known, from mass media research, of the function of mass communication in reinforcing existing opinions; of the effects of crime and violence in the media; of some of the proposed functions of 'escape' fare in the media; of the effects of media on behaviour—a problem of cause and effect; and of the way in which media in general tend to reflect social values. It will conclude with a brief summary of the implications of mass media research for the study of popular drama.

C. R. Wright's (1960) inventory of possible mass-communication functions requires a clear contrast between the supposed manifest and latent functions and dysfunctions of mass-communicated surveillance material (news), correlation material (editorial activity), cultural transmission, and entertainment, for society, sub-groups in society, the individual, and the cultural system. In dealing with entertainment, of which drama forms a part, his model suggests that for society the functions (manifest and latent) are respite for the masses and the dysfunctions (manifest and latent) are diversion of the public from necessary social action. For the individual, the functions are respite—which may be therapeutic—and the dysfunctions an increase in passivity, a lowering of tastes, and escapism. For specific subgroups (e.g. a political élite) entertainment would function to extend control over one more area of life. He sees no dysfunctions in this category. For culture in general, he sees no positive functions; but he suggests that entertainment might be dysfunctional in weakening aesthetic perception at the expense of 'popular culture'. Although his model of analysis is based on Merton's functional paradigm, Wright does not seem to do justice to the possibility that items of surveillance, of correlation, and of cultural transmission may be functional equivalents (positively, or dysfunctionally), for the items of entertainment for society, for sub-groups, for the individual, or for the cultural system at large. In seeking the appropriate questions to ask about drama as a form of mass communication, it will be more satisfactory to follow the set of questions outlined, and in part answered, by J. T. Klapper in his authoritative survey *The Effects of Mass Communication* (1960). As this study is seeking to delineate the possible functions of drama in society, it is probably too early to use the fine distinctions of Wright's model.

Klapper's book is basically a collation of findings of published research on mass communication as an agent of persuasion and of the effects of specific kinds of media content. The basic argument of his book is for a shift away from the tendency to regard mass communication as a necessary and sufficient cause of audience effects, towards a view of media as influences, working amid other influences, in a total situation. Two generalizations are central to Klapper's organization of the research findings he reports: (a) mass communication by itself does not act as a necessary and sufficient cause of audience effects; (b) mass communications typically reinforce existing conditions rather than change them. His classification of research findings is itself a valuable source of questions to be asked about drama as a cultural phenomenon. However, a good deal of important work has been done since Klapper's book was published (and there is some work that is not reported by Klapper); so, although this chapter will basically follow in outline Klapper's reporting of research, it will also seek to recount other research findings that are likely to prove important in the study of drama.

The Effects of Mass Communication in Reinforcing Existing Opinion

In Chapter 2 of his book (pp. 15–52), Klapper reports that communications research strongly indicates that persuasive mass communication is in general more likely to reinforce the existing opinions of its audience than it is to change such opinions. He outlines five principal reasons why this is so. It has already been argued in the first four chapters of this book that popular drama is more likely than otherwise to reinforce existing beliefs; so what Klapper reports about the effects of mass communications in this respect, and what can be learned from other research, is of extreme interest and importance.

First, mass communications operate in conditions of selective exposure, selective perception, and selective retention. It has been found that people tend to expose themselves selectively to communications in accordance with their existing beliefs, in order to avoid exposure to unsympathetic opinions. If, by accident, they expose themselves to unsympathetic material, they not infrequently distort, or selectively perceive, its meaning in order to bring the received message into accord with their existing views. People have also been found to retain sympathetic material more effectively than unsympathetic material. Although these phenomena are extremely common, Klapper notes that they are rarely if ever experienced by all persons in any communication situation. A large body of evidence is being built up in the field of social psychology to support the sociological research reported by Klapper on the processes of selectivity. By selective perception and selective retention, individuals tend to minimize the gap between what they believe already and what they are being invited to believe. The writings of L. Festinger, i.e. *A Theory of Cognitive Dissonance* (1957) and *Conflict, Decision, and Dissonance* (1964) examine the variations of this phenomenon, as does the book *Explorations in Cognitive Dissonance* (1962) by J. W. Brehm and A. R. Cohen.

A typical experiment demonstrating the effect of cognitive dissonance is that reported by L. Berkowitz in 'Cognitive Dissonance and Communication Preferences' (1965). Berkowitz had fifty-three male and female college students listen to a tape-recorded speech on the topic of mercy-killing, supposedly given by an authority on the subject. The students were classified within each sex into three groups, depending upon their response to an attitude questionnaire administered before and after hearing the recording: consonant subjects, moderately dissonant subjects, and strongly dissonant subjects. It was found that: (a) the strongly dissonant people, particularly the men, tended to prefer to communicate with others holding views close to their own shaken beliefs; (b) the somewhat more confident men in the moderately dissonant and consonant groups were more inclined to seek out people holding different opinions; (c) the moderately dissonant men, although they indicated a preference for writing to fellow group members moderately far from them on the attitude continuum, tended to write the longest messages in the communications experiment, and seemed most likely to ask the others for their opinions—possibly seeking people with opinions near to their own. It is a commonplace of social observation that 'birds of a feather flock together'. It is hardly surprising, therefore, that in exposing themselves to mass communications, and in paying attention to what they see and hear there, individuals are highly selective, and tend to reinforce with the material presented to them the beliefs they hold already.

A second extra-communication factor that mediates the reception of mass-communication content is the social group to which the audience member belongs. Research has shown that predispositions that reflect norms of groups to which an audience member belongs are particularly resistant to change. Social groups may increase the reinforcement characteristic of mass communication in various ways. For example, they often increase selective exposure. The hand on the control knob of the television set is a notorious phenomenon in television research. Again, social groups provide arenas for discussion of the sympathetic content of communications, for the exercise of opinion leadership, and consequently for discussion that minimizes the effect of unsympathetic communication content. In an article on 'Communication Research and the Concept of the Mass', Eliot Freidson (1953) argues from awareness of group behaviour against the loose use of the word 'mass' with reference to communications research. Freidson acquiesces in the conception of the mass audience as having four distinctive features. First, it is heterogeneous in composition, its members coming from all groups of a society. Second, it is composed of individuals who do not know each other. Third, the members of the mass are spatially separated from one another and in that sense, at least, cannot interact with one another or exchange experience. Fourth, the mass has no definite leadership and has a very loose organization, if any at all. These features, Freidson notes, are all implied by the commonsense notion of a mass and are logically compatible with each other (see p. 314). However, Freidson argues that it is wrong to regard an audience as merely an aggregation of discrete individuals, whose social experience is equalized and cancelled out by allowing only the attributes of age, sex, socio-economic status, and the like, to represent them, except by subscribing to the assertion that the audience is a mass. While one can *describe* such an aggregate without reference to the organized groups that compose it, one cannot *explain* the behaviour of its members except by reference to the local audiences to which they belong. The importance of these comments by Freidson will be appreciated when techniques of television audience research are considered in Chapter 6.

Since Klapper's summary of research, more experimental evidence has been published stressing the importance of group norms in the audience's receptivity to mass-communicated material. E. Levonian (1963) has shown how a film tailored to audience interests was more effective in changing the opinion of the group whose interests had been taken into consideration than in changing the opinions of a control group. In a doctoral dissertation on 'A Social Psychological Study of Motion Picture Audience Behaviour', S. W. Bloom (see Dissertation Abstracts, 1956) has illustrated how individual reaction and perception is subordinated to group norms. However, in common experience, it does not need a doctoral dissertation to remind one of the singular force of group norms in mediating reaction to communicated material. The 'Well, really!' of a fierce maiden aunt can severely temper a timorous individual's enjoyment of particular material on the television screen.

Thirdly, Klapper has reported the importance of inter-personal dissemination of communication content among people who share pertinent opinions on the topic being discussed. Discussion of mass communication among people of similar opinion is likely to increase the potential of the communication for reinforcement without increasing its potential for conversion. It is by no means clear how opinion 'gets around' about the excellence of a West End theatre play; but it is highly likely that the channels of inter-personal dissemination of opinion about the content of a stage play will have a great deal to do with its likelihood of achieving a long run. In this way, conservatism is likely to be perpetuated in plays of mass appeal in that the mass of the population will be conservative in its tastes.

Fourthly, Klapper has shown that people are more crucially influenced in many matters by 'opinion leaders' than they are by mass communications. Such opinion leaders are typically 'super-normative' members of the same group as their followers, but are more exposed to mass communications and serve as transmission agents or interpreters. Klapper notes (p. 51) that although most studies of opinion leadership have to date focused on the leaders' role in producing change, there is good reason to postulate that they frequently exercise their influence in favour of constancy and reinforcement. In an article on 'Communication Research and the Image of Society: convergence of two traditions', E. Katz (1960) has shown parallel findings from rural sociology and mass-communication sociology that support the evidence cited by Klapper. In both urban and rural settings, personal influence appears to be more effective in gaining acceptance for change than are mass media and other types of influence. Rural sociologists have found that mass media and other sources help in providing information; however, personal influence is crucial in determining the decisions that are made.

With reference to the study of popular drama, it is not difficult to see that plays which break new ground in terms of either artistic format or thematic content must gain favour with opinion leaders in order to gain mass appeal. In so far as opinion leaders represent to a heightened degree the values of the groups they lead, the 'dice are loaded' against innovation in popular drama, as in other types of media communication.

Fifthly, Klapper has cited the nature of commercial mass media in a free-enterprise society as yet another force of conservatism. It has been held that in order to avoid offending any significant portion of their necessarily vast and varied audience, the media have been forced to show only such attitudes as were already virtually universally acceptable. Content analyses of entertainment fare prevalent in the 1940s and early 1950s bear out these allegations. Impresarios with a sharp eye on the box office or the audience ratings for television are very unlikely to be innovators. M. L. De Fleur, in an article 'Mass Media as Social Systems' (see Larsen (ed), 1968) has provided a model showing how the mass-media social system is based on money and votes. The ultimate dependence of the providers of media content on the money of consumers and of the controllers of media content on the votes of consumers is some guarantee that one of the major assumptions underlying the present study is correct: namely, that the providers of popular drama operate within the same social nexus as the consumers of it and that drama that is not in line with the tastes of the consumers will not in fact be popular.

These research findings on the effects of mass communications in reinforcing existing opinion heighten the probability that popular drama, as a form of mass communication, will be conservative in orientation.

The Effects of Crime and Violence in Mass Media

Chapter 4 of this study argued, among other things, that contemplation of disorder—particularly in the form of crime—is likely to function positively in increasing group cohesiveness in a community. Durkheim's views (as given in *The Division of*

Labour in Society) support this hypothesis. The point was made that crime drama would not be dramatic if violence were an everyday and accepted form of social behaviour. A considerable amount of mass-media research has concentrated on answering the question as to whether violence in mass-media content increases or decreases aggressive behaviour in the beholders of it. For example, a major report to the National Commission on the Causes and Prevention of Violence (USA, 1969) is mainly concerned with this vexing question. If it is to be posited as a testable functional hypothesis that popular drama functions positively either as an expressive aspect of culture or as an instrumental aspect of culture—in expressing the individual's understanding of social norms and controlling his participation in his society—it is important to review the evidence from mass-communication research that argues that violent content in mass media tends to increase the likelihood of viewers behaving violently. J. D. Halloran (1964), for example, reports in his study on *The Effects of Mass Communication* that research results from controlled experiments

> . . . leave little doubt that violent programmes on television do not serve to reduce aggression vicariously as some people have attempted to show, but if anything increase it and encourage its later expression. We know that children with high levels of aggression are especially attracted to violent programmes on television. If television now feeds rather than reduces children's aggressive tendencies, and if it gives them hints as to how to take out aggression with fists, knives, or guns, then an opportunity may come to use those weapons at a moment when they are angry. (p. 24)

Several major studies on television and children have demonstrated the massive quantity of violence available on television—for example, Himmelweit, Oppenheim, and Vince (1958); Schramm, Lyle, and Parker (1961); USA (1969). Two principal topics have been the subject of mass-communications research: first, what factors determine a person's preference for violent television fare? secondly, does exposure to violent fare increase aggressive behaviour in the beholder, or the opposite? It is the latter question that has been the cause of considerable public concern.

In view of this widespread public concern, it is surprising how

little research appears to have been done about whether individuals actively *want* aggressive material as such in their mass-
media fare. The social psychologist is, naturally, interested in the
reactions of the individual to what he is confronted with. The
psychiatrist is especially interested in pathological cases. Violence
may have unfortunate effects on those who see it; the arguments
as to whether or not this is the case will be reviewed below. But
in determining the possible social functions of *popular* drama in
society, it is important to note that violence is *not* popular with
television viewers. Evidence about the tastes of British viewers
will be given in Chapter 6. The American Report to the National
Commission on the Causes and Prevention of Violence (USA,
1969) gives some evidence of American tastes. Two items bearing
directly on this question were included in the Violence Commission National Survey. The first enquired: 'How do you feel
about the amount of violence portrayed in television programmes
today, not including news programmes—do you think that there
is too much, a reasonable amount, or very little violence?' A
representative sample of adult Americans gave the following
responses to this question: (1) 59 per cent said that there was
too much violence, (2) 32 per cent said that there was a reasonable
amount, (3) 4 per cent said there was very little and (4) 4 per cent
were not sure. Thus a majority of adult Americans think there is
too much violence on television. A second item was asked of the
same sample: 'Apart from the *amount* of violence, do you generally approve or disapprove of the *kind* of violence that is portrayed on TV?' In reply, 25 per cent said that they approved,
63 per cent *disapproved*, 12 per cent had no views. The report
suggests (p. 333) that Americans may not be getting what they
want in television programming when the issue is the kind of
violence portrayed.

Setting aside the question of whether or not television violence
is approved of by the majority of viewers, it is still a serious
question as to whether the violence portrayed incites viewers to
behave violently. But first the question must be answered: who
is it who wants violent television? Various types of study have
been designed to discover what makes people want violent
amusement. It is significant that the principal evidence about the
desire for aggressive media content of various sorts is based upon
experiments for which subjects were deliberately provoked into

aggressive frames of mind, exposed to media, and then tested for their immediate response.

For example, J. F. Strickland (1959) studied 'The Effect of Motivation Arousal on Humour Preferences'. Thirty-three cartoons, from a selection of 150, were categorized by fifteen independent judges. Seventy-five students were taken as experimental subjects. Some subjects were made angry by being left alone in a bare room and by being treated rudely by the experimenter. Some had their sexual interests aroused by being shown photographs of nudes. The experiment was designed to test the hypothesis that the arousal of different types of motivation would produce differences in humour preferences. It was predicted that in the hostility-arousing situation, subjects would prefer humorous material of a hostile and aggressive nature, while subjects placed in a sexually arousing situation would prefer humorous material with a sexual theme. This prediction was confirmed by the experiment, in Strickland's view. An explanation of the results was offered in terms of suppression. A similar experiment had been performed by D. Byrne (1956) with similar results. Earlier (1955), E. E. Karp, in a study on 'Crime Comic Book Role Preferences', had found *no* difference in preference between normal, aggressive, and over-socialized groups of children.

This apparent conflict of results is echoed in the research on the *effects* of drama. Himmelweit, Oppenheim, and Vince in their study (1958), and Schramm, Lyle, and Parker in theirs (1961), found the evidence about aggressive content and subsequent aggressive tendencies inconclusive with reference to television. A doctoral dissertation (1956) by A. E. Siegel argued that the case for violent television content increasing aggressiveness was 'not proven', but that violence tended to increase anxiety. F. E. Emery (1959), studying the psychological effects of the Western film on Australian boys, concluded that although certain temporary changes may be brought about in the way in which an individual sees himself in relation to his social environment, these changes do not appear to involve systematic changes in aggressive drives. Similarly, S. Feshbach (see Arons and May, 1963, p. 83 f.) noted that the results of research were inconclusive.

Indeed, Feshbach has gone further to suggest that the evidence is positive; he has suggested that television violence in fact has a cathartic effect. Excerpts from his paper 'Effects of Exposure to

Aggressive Content in Television upon Aggression in Boys' are included in Appendix IIIe of the Report to the National Commission on the Causes and Prevention of Violence, *Mass Media and Violence* (USA, 1969). The experiment upon which this report is based sought to measure the effects of television as viewed in the normal viewing conditions. Feshbach concludes (p. 468) that

> within the restrictions of sample characteristics, range of stimuli utilised and the duration of the experimental period, there are two major conclusions indicated by the experimental findings:
>
> 1. Exposure to aggressive content in television does not lead to a noticeable increase in aggressive behaviour; and
> 2. Exposure to aggressive content in television seems to reduce or control the expression of aggression.

The major evidence suggesting that the effect of violent and aggressive content on television *increases* aggressive behaviour and drives is based upon research carried out in controlled laboratory conditions. For example, P. Mussen and E. Rutherford (1961) tested the hypothesis that exposure to aggressive fantasy in an animated cartoon might intensify children's impulses to aggression. Their conclusions are based on experiments with thirty-six children. The intensity of a child's aggressive impulses was inferred from his responses to questions concerning desire to 'play with' or 'pop' a large yellow balloon held by a tester. The experimental findings were held to support the conviction that exposure to aggressive fantasy in an animated cartoon would stimulate children's aggressive behaviour in play. Two possible explanations for the results were discussed: that intensification of aggressiveness may have resulted from the child's identification with the aggressive cartoon characters; that the relaxed 'fun' context of animated cartoons may lead to a reduction of inhibitions against aggressive expression in a permissive play situation. It is to be noted that the children in the experiment showed their aggressive behaviour in the very room in which they had been shown the cartoon.

O. I. Lovass (1961) conducted similar experiments with pre-schoolchildren who were exposed to five-minute films and then allowed to play with a lever-pressing toy that could cause one doll to beat another on the hand. Exposure to a film that portrayed aggressive behaviour increased the child's indulgence in this symbolic kind of aggression; exposure to a film of non-aggressive behaviour did not.

Two studies by A. Bandura, D. Ross, and S. A. Ross (1961 and 1963) produced similar results in similar conditions with test groups of similar size.

L. Berkowitz, R. Corwin, and M. Heironimus (1963) carried out experiments with groups of Yale students, angering one group by messing them about with tiresome psychological tests, and comparing them with a control group. The students were then shown seven-minute clips of a Kirk Douglas film in which a man was beaten up. The results of this experiment were not very conclusive. However, in a later experiment, L. Berkowitz and E. Rawlings (1963) tested the possibility that recently-angered people can 'purge' their anger through viewing film sequences of aggression. A hundred and sixty college men and women were shown a seven-minute prize fight scene after having been either deliberately insulted or treated in a neutral fashion by a male graduate student. Just before the subject saw the film, E, a female graduate student, provided them with one of two synopses of the film plot. In half of the cases E told the subjects that the film protagonist (who took the bad beating in the fight) was a downright scoundrel. The fantasy aggression witnessed by this group was presumably regarded as justified. The remaining subjects were told that the protagonist was not really bad, and they presumably came to regard the filmed aggression as less justified. All subjects rated the male graduate student (the one who had insulted half of the group) after seeing the film. In opposition to the thesis of vicarious hostility reduction, Berkowitz and Rawlings predicted that the justified fantasy aggression would produce heightened overt hostility towards the insulting male graduate student by lowering inhibitions against aggression. Questionnaire ratings supported their prediction.

In the previous section of this chapter it was suggested that mass media tend to reinforce existing behavioural norms. Young children, however, who have few socially induced norms, are learning behaviour from scratch. The possibility that they are learning to achieve their social goals through violent behaviour is one that merits serious concern. A further study by Bandura (1965) confirms his earlier findings that children learn from

aggressive dramatic representations to imitate aggressive behaviour. However, this study shows that children acquire from
watching television a capability of performing imitatively many
more acts of aggression than they spontaneously exhibit. The
sixty-six children who participated in this study were of nursery-
school age, averaging just over four years. They were assigned at
random to three categories—'Model Rewarded', 'Model Punished', and 'No Consequences'. The child in the first category
began his participation in the experiment by watching a five-
minute television show in which an adult exhibited physical and
verbal aggression toward a doll. In the closing scene of the
'Model Rewarded' film, a second adult appeared, bearing a large
supply of sweets and soft drinks, informed the model that he was
a 'strong champion', and that his superb performance of aggression clearly deserved a treat. He then gave the model various
foods, and while the model ate these he continued to describe and
praise the model's feats.

A child in the 'Model Punished' category saw a performance
that was identical to the above in its initial sequences, but concluded with a second adult reproving rather than praising the
model.

Finally, a child in the 'No Consequences' category saw a
performance involving only the initial section of the film, the part
showing the adult's aggression toward the doll.

Each child was then observed in a ten-minute play session
while alone in a room containing a variety of toys, among which
were some similar to those used by the adult model on the film.
Judges observed through a one-way screen and recorded the
occurrence of imitative aggressive responses. Then the experimenter returned to the play-room, bringing an assortment of fruit
juices and booklets of pictures to be presented to the child as
rewards. She then asked, 'Show me what Rocky did in the TV
programme,' and 'Tell me what he said,' promising to reward the
child for each imitation performed. The object of this experiment
was to see how much imitative aggression each child performed
spontaneously in the ten-minute session as compared with how
much imitative aggression he showed himself capable of performing when offered an incentive.

As in earlier studies, the children in the 'Model Rewarded' and
the 'No Consequences' categories mimicked the adult model in

their own free play, doing so more frequently than those in the 'Model Punished' category. This was supposed to suggest that children imitate aggression they observe on television and that punishment of the adult in the television show serves to inhibit the children's tendency to imitate spontaneously. The new finding, however, was that when requested to imitate the adult's behaviour and offered an incentive, each group of children performed more imitative acts of aggression than had been performed spontaneously in free play. This demonstrated that the children were capable of more imitative aggression than they had initially shown. Further, those in the 'Model Punished' category could imitate aggressive acts just as efficiently as those in the 'Model Rewarded' and 'No Consequences' categories. This study suggests very strongly that children learn some of the behaviour they observe on television; that some sequences of their learning are exhibited spontaneously in their play; and that others can be elicited if the setting is right.

A related study (1966) by Bandura, Grusec, and Menlove produced supporting evidence and, in addition, showed that children who verbalize what they are seeing show an even greater capacity to remember what they have seen.

Other experiments offer further evidence of the possible dangerous effects of viewing violence in television drama. A study by Hicks (1968) dealt with the long-term retention of aggressive behaviours learned through observation. Children saw a filmed model perform a number of novel acts, some of which were clearly aggressive. After an interval of two months, the acts were shown again and subjects were given an opportunity to perform the responses. The tests for immediate retention given at this point showed that more than 60 per cent of the aggressive responses were recalled. A final test for retention was conducted after an interval of eight months. By this time, about 40 per cent of the acts were still recalled.

An experiment by Meyerson (1966) was carried out to examine the possibility that the similarity of a real situation to a situation once viewed on television might act as a cue to aggressive behaviour. Children in this study were exposed to the filmed aggressive performance of a model and were then observed in a test situation having either high, medium, or low similarity to the observed setting. The results showed that the level of imitative aggression increased with increasing similarity between the film and the post-film settings.

Greenwald and Albert (1968) have shown that similarity of setting between film and real life affects adults as well as children. The speed with which adults learned complex motor responses was found to vary directly with the proportion of stimulus elements common to both the performance they observed and the later situation in which they were tested.

It may be objected that filmed acts of aggression isolated from any social context may be totally unlike the acts of aggression that viewers can see in television drama. The context in which violent or aggressive behaviour takes place is, surely, of crucial importance. However, Berkowitz and Geen (1967) demonstrated that the inhibitions of male undergraduates at Wisconsin against aggressive behaviour could be reduced by showing a filmed episode of 'justified aggression'. The *Mass Media and Violence* report (USA, 1969) comments (p. 292) that it is somewhat ironic that the self-regulatory media codes of good practice insist that violence should not be shown *unless germane to the dramatic development of the story*. One test of relevance is that it produces a desired outcome; another is to have the violence directed toward a character who is defined as 'deserving it'. In either case, the studies seem to have shown that the conditions for effective observational learning through vicarious reinforcement have been ensured. It would seem that, in the very process of seeming to preach that 'crime does not pay', the media may actually undermine the moral restraints against violent and anti-social behaviour. Tannenbaum and Greenberg (1968) comment that screen plays based on the precept of 'an eye for an eye and a tooth for a tooth' can lead to 'socially harmful consequences'. If the criminal or 'bad guy' is punished aggressively, so that others do to him what he has done to them, the violence appears justified.

Yet another danger of the massive and repeated presentation of violence in television drama is that the emotional responses of viewers to violence become blunted. Psychologists and physiologists have long accepted that the repeated stimulation of an emotional response results in the progressive decrease in the strength of this response. The phenomenon has been variously called habituation, satiation, accommodation, and adaptation. It is possible that this process of habituation takes place with the emotional responses repeatedly evoked by the observation of violence in television drama. The danger is that the viewers' reaction to violence—as an unusual, anti-social, and unnatural form of behaviour—will be progressively removed, just as a phobia can be removed through psychological treatment.

In a study of 'Vicarious Extinction of Avoidance Behaviour' (1967), Bandura, Grusec, and Menlove showed how children's fear of dogs could be removed. In this study, children were selected because they showed consistent fearful avoidance behaviour towards dogs. In the course of a number of brief sessions, the children saw another child engaged in a variety of interactions with a brown cocker spaniel. Control groups were either shown the dog alone or were given no special treatment at all. When subsequently tested, the subjects in the experimental groups showed a sharp reduction in avoidance behaviour. Many were now able to engage in intimate and potentially fearful interactions not only with the dog they had seen before, but also with an unfamiliar dog. The differences between the children in the experimental group and the control group were maintained in a follow-up test a month later.

A second study by Bandura and Menlove (1968) is even more significant. In this study, films were used. Over a period of time, groups of children who were initially fearful of dogs were shown a number of different films showing another child playing with a single dog, or alternatively, 'numerous dogs varying in size and fearsomeness'. A control group of dog-fearing children were shown a parallel series of non-threatening films containing no dogs at all. Again, there was a striking reduction of fearful avoidance behaviour in the experimental groups. The untreated children in the control group, however, continued to be fearful and maintained their avoidance of dogs at a high level.

These experiments suggest that films can be very effective in reducing the emotional responses of children to subjects that would otherwise frighten them.

R. E. Goranson has produced an admirable 'Review of Recent Literature on Psychological Effects of Media Portrayals of Violence' as Appendix IIIa of the report *Mass Media and Violence* (1969). He summarizes the research findings as follows (pp. 409–410):

Learning effects: novel, aggressive behavior sequences are learned by children through exposure to realistic portrayals of aggression on television or in films. A large proportion of these behaviors are retained over long periods of time if they are practised at least once. The likelihood that such aggressive behaviors will be performed is determined, in part, by the similarity of the setting of the observed violence and the cues presented in later situations. The actual performance of aggressive behaviors learned from the media is largely contingent on the child's belief in the effectiveness of aggression in attaining his goals while avoiding punishment. The mass media typically present aggression as a highly effective form of behavior.

Emotional effects: frequent exposure produces an emotional habituation to media violence. There is suggestive evidence that this results in an increased likelihood of actually engaging in aggression.

Impulsive aggression: aggressive impulses may be held in check if the viewer has been made especially aware of the 'wrongness' of aggression or of the suffering that may result from violence. The target person's prior association with media violence serves to heighten the intensity of aggressive attacks on him.

The weight of evidence from the laboratory experiments seems to be against the catharsis hypothesis. Bandura (1965) has pointed out that we would scarcely recommend that adolescents be shown libidinous films as a means of reducing sexual behaviour, nor would we advise that a starving man watched the eating of a delicious meal in order to diminish his hunger pangs. Similarly, we should not expect that the outpourings of violence in the mass media will have the effect of reducing aggressive behaviour.

However, this view slightly over-simplifies the situation and there is clearly room for considerably more research—as Bandura and his colleagues are the first to admit. For example, W. P. Davison (1960) has drawn attention to some of the intrinsic difficulties of these laboratory situations—particularly those involving student participants. Most of the laboratory experiments offer difficulties of interpretation since they make use of communication habits that do not play a role in other situations. When confronted with a communication in a classroom or laboratory, the subject may make conscious or subconscious assumptions about the instructor or experimenter. He may, for example, try to produce the effects that he thinks the experimenter wants to find. Again, television is usually viewed in the comfort and permissive atmosphere of home. This factor may increase or decrease the nefarious effects of television violence. Feshbach's research was designed to simulate as nearly as possible the traditional and usual viewing situation; it is noteworthy that his conclusions support the catharsis hypothesis. Again, the experimental work of Bandura and his colleagues has been criticized on other points. For example, Dr Ruth E. Hartley (see Larsen (ed), 1968) has raised various objections to the experimental techniques upon which the evidence is based. For example (p. 135), the physical 'aggression' shown by the children in Bandura's studies consisted of hitting, kicking, and otherwise attacking a Bobo doll, which is a toy rather than a person. It is also a toy that is specifically designed for this purpose, and virtually invites attack. Again, the stimulus material for the experimental group consisted largely of exhibitions of such attack by adults, outside any context at all, and untempered by exhibitions of other activities, or by the presence of other adults in the exhibition. Or again, she suggests that play behaviour cannot serve as an accurate predictor of non-play behaviour since because of its permissiveness children act in ways in which they would not act in non-play behaviour.

One might also suggest that the permissive play context of the acted-out aggression has parallels in other social activities. For example, normally gentle and law-abiding citizens can behave with extreme violence and aggressiveness in the 'play' situation of field sports—such as rugger, football, hockey, etc. Their aggressiveness can be artificially stimulated by 'hate-songs' rehearsing the evils of the opposing side and celebrating the virtues of the home side. In amateur manifestations of this sort, it is not uncommon for the participants who have been attacking each other violently on the field to drink beer in peace and amity afterwards.

However, the real solution to the vexed problem of violence in television drama has still to be found. It is possible that aggression —with notable and measurable after-effects—is an inevitable incidental feature of the achievement of socially desirable goals by characters in drama. It may, indeed, be an unwelcome excrescence on an otherwise laudable activity that functions positively for a community. That is to say, the violence exhibited in the pursuit of socially desirable goals may be dysfunctional in the same way that obsession with the care of buildings or with the minutiae of ritual may be dysfunctional for churchgoers. Buildings and detail of ritual may be important in the activities that express the deep-felt beliefs and social solidarity of a church group; but they can be dysfunctional in diverting the attention of church members from religious activities that more effectively express what they really believe. In like manner, violence shown in television drama in the pursuit of goals that are otherwise wholly laudable may work *against* the overall effectiveness of a particular television drama in producing the deepest form of satisfaction for the audience.

It is possible that concentration on the violent way in which goals are achieved is distracting attention from the actual *goals* that drama characters are seeking. If the themes of drama are indicators of stress-points in the moral and social structure of a community, may it not be possible that viewers accept violent solutions to problems because they are passionately interested in seeing the *problems solved*? People frequently resort to physical violence when the processes of rational argument have broken down. War is an extension of foreign policy. In so far as television drama is social argument, it is to be expected that when problems seem incapable of solution by rational means, the characters in the dramas will resort to violence. The violence itself may be irrelevant. The goals of the characters for which violence is employed are the items to which attention should be paid.

It is worth repeating that research has shown that television viewers *dislike* violence. The presence of violent and aggressive behaviour in television dramas may be an expression of the views of producers and writers. It may, indeed, be more a symptom of the medium than of the message—that is to say, physical violence is more spectacular than verbal or other types of violence. While drama containing excessive amounts of violence may satisfy the felt needs of small sectors of the community, it is probable that *popular* drama satisfies the needs of the larger section of the community. The presence or absence of violence may in fact be a distraction. But, in view of the possible damaging effects of drama violence on those who see it, the subject is one that needs to be kept open.

In conclusion, a comment of W. M. Gerson is worth quoting. In an essay 'Violence as an American Value Theme' (see Larsen (ed), 1968, pp. 151–162), Gerson writes (p. 158):

The mere frequency of an activity . . . does not necessarily mean that the behavior constitutes highly valued behavior socially. For example, American men tie their shoe-laces every single day, year in and year out—a consistent, frequent activity. It does not follow, though, that shoe-lace-tying is an American value. We can, however, say that the habitual shoe-securing ritual is often an indirect pre-requisite to several cultural goals—social mobility, occupational success, marrying the 'right' person, being liked by others, etc.—and these goals do represent cultural values. Much violent behavior, then, may not appear to be a value theme, but indirectly it might be part of an overall value complex.

Mass Media and 'Escape'

In dealing with the mass media as a whole, it is necessary to con-sider the question as to whether television-viewing, in particular, is functional or dysfunctional. The general effects of television (and therefore drama included as an aspect of television) will be considered in more detail in the next section. Meanwhile, it is important to deal with the criticism that mass-media fiction—of which drama forms the major part—offers the viewer a form of 'escape', and that this escape from his normal activity is dysfunc-tional. Furious critics, of whom the seventeenth-century Puritans were typical examples, have always accused dramatic fictions of diverting the public from serious concerns. In a sense, any activity can be considered as escape. In commenting upon this point, Klapper quotes Mott (1957) as follows:

What is this crime of escapism? Escape from what? Apparently it is escape from work and worry. Escape to what? Apparently to play and fun. Now the difference between work and play is that the one consists of activities performed under the compulsion of duty after the freshness and novelty have worn off, while the other is activity which is not compulsory but is engaged in because its novelty is not exhausted to the point of boredom. Thus big game hunting is still play despite its fatigue and hardship, but professional base-ball is work for the 'player' because the sport has, for him, passed from the status of an activity enjoyed for its own rewards to that of a job required by duties under a contract. And so reading, if required and onerous (as professional study may often be), becomes work; but if done for pleasure, as most of our reading is, it is play—whether it is the light literature of romance and adventure or in the heaviest dissertations in science and philosophy. In other words, all general reading is escapism.

But critics usually concentrate their attention on dramatic fiction as being the sinister type of escape. To clarify the possible functions, or dysfunctions, of drama as a form of mass-media 'escape', it will be valuable to examine the effects that escape material has been found to have.

First is the obvious effect of providing relaxation. The mild hypnotic trance induced by the 50-cycle flicker of British television sets may be, in itself, a form of relaxation and thus for the individual positively functional. However, as R. J. Silvey (1962) has shown, the particular way in which television is used by Britons produces an uncritical frame of mind.

> Because viewing is play, at home, and for nothing, one of the pleasures it offers is that of not having to make decisions. Hence some viewers will always, and most viewers will sometimes, not so much choose as drift, taking the line of least resistance. This may result in the set being 'left on' to whichever channel it happens to be tuned or to the effective abdication of the right to choose in favour of a set of invariable habits.
>
> The important point is that the frame of reference serves to release the viewer from any obligation to 'better himself' or to consider his immortal soul. If you are only out to enjoy yourself why do it the hard way? This loads the dice against any programme which stretches the mind or the imagination, which calls for thinking rather than feeling. Not only because such programmes call for effort, but because notoriously all new ideas are potentially disturbing, for they may threaten the comfortable assumptions with which we cushion ourselves. By contrast, programmes which make few demands upon viewers, and above all those which are built into a cosy framework of familiarity, minister positively to the needs for reassurance and emotional security which are in some measure universal.

Silvey's point, basically, is that television functions positively; and that material that is conservative in nature will be the most acceptable.

Secondly, escapist fare in the media may stimulate imagination and fantasy. This use of escapist fare, particularly by children, has been noted several times. Himmelweit, Oppenheim, and Vince (1958) note that escape fare stimulates the imagination of the child with lightheartedness, glamour, and romance, and permits the child to identify himself with different romantic heroes. Similarly, Schramm, Lyle, and Parker (1961) define the chief needs for which children go to television as the needs for both fantasy and reality experiences. By comparing pre-television with television behaviour, they were able to show that it is overwhelmingly the *fantasy* needs of children that television is meeting. E. B. Parker (1960) in a doctoral dissertation on 'The Functions of Television for Children' comes to similar conclusions; he notes that comic books, pulp magazines, movies, and radio are all significantly displaced by television for children. Both this finding and the finding that there are significant correlations among them (and between comic-reading and television-viewing) indicate that they are similar in function for children. Parker claims that this function is the facilitation of fantasy.

Again, E. E. Maccoby, in asking 'Why do children watch television?' (1954), studied the extent of a child's interest in television as a symptom of a need for vicarious satisfaction through fantasy when the child is frustrated in his efforts to obtain satisfaction in real life. In a later study, with W. C. Wilson (Maccoby and Wilson, 1957), films were shown to twenty-five classrooms of seventh-grade children, and the children were tested a week later on their knowledge of the films' content. Using an indirect measure of identification, Maccoby and Wilson found that viewers did indeed identify themselves with the like-sexed leading character, in viewing a film that included both strong male and strong female leads.

M. W. and J. W. Riley (1951) noted a difference in behaviour between different groups of children with reference to animal cartoons in which the animal heroes successfully evaded adult standards. Children who belonged in family groups but not in peer groups expressed a greater preference for comic books dealing with these types of animals.

> One key to such a difference lies, we believe, in the social structure itself. The children who belong in family groups but not in peer groups are offered a set of adult values by their parents. This usually means that they are expected to help at home, to do well in school, to learn to strive in order to achieve, and in general to prepare for a future life as adults. For many 10–12 year old children these goals may often seem difficult, or even completely unattainable. Small

wonder, then, that they love to read about little animals like Bugs Bunny, whom they perceive as the complete negation of the goals and conventions established by adults. . . . On the other hand, the peer group members, though still tickled by his humour, are less engrossed by Bugs Bunny (75% as compared with 92%). This is perhaps because they have less need to defy parent values, since they, as members of two groups, have a choice between two sets of values—those of their parents and those of their peers. Peer values are usually far less discouraging, having to do with being just like the group (not too poor but also not too good at anything) and involving certain routines of keeping up with base-ball and with the latest tunes, hanging around with the gang, and seeing the funny side of things.

In so far as fantasy can be regarded as positively functional in helping the individual to orient himself to the community, television escapist fare, in providing fantasy material, is performing a positive function.

Thirdly, escapist television fare has operated to provide vicarious interaction particularly for people in social isolation. M. E. Olsen (1960) sought to demonstrate that migrants to a community tended to go to films more frequently than existing members of the community. L. Pearlin (1959) studied 736 television owners in Southern City and measured their felt stress. He compared groups who felt stress or did not feel stress with reference to the indicated importance of a lack of opportunity or advancement in one's occupation; fearfulness of intimate social relationships on the one hand and blind faith in people on the other hand; and personal feelings of depression, despair, and futility regarding the world. He found that significantly more 'escape' television viewers were fearful of establishing relationships, not selective in forming them, or felt that the world was in a muddle.

H. Mendelsohn (Dexter and White, 1964, pp. 240–248) found that among other things radio was used by people as a sort of companion. W. McPhee and R. Meyersohn (1955) studied the use made of radio by residents in cities where television was available. They found that radio programmes involving social interaction were more commonly enjoyed by people who were lonely. These radio programmes provided them both with a vicarious sense of participation and a feeling of kinship and concern. The Schramm,

Lyle, and Parker study announced as a basic rule that when a child has unsatisfactory relationships with his family or his playgroup, he tends to retreat to television where he can for a time leave the field of real-life problems and possibly reduce his tension. More conflict, more television (p. 172). Evidence from the Himmelweit, Oppenheim, and Vince study bears out this assertion.

One final item of evidence may be cited: the study of 'The Radio Daytime Serial' by W. L. Warner and W. E. Henry (1948). Women listeners to the 'Big Sister' radio serial experienced vicarious social interaction with the characters of the programme. All these findings bear out the assertion of Eric Bentley (1965) referred to in Chapter 4, that drama may provide unembarrassing company for the lonely. In doing this, it acts, like participation in ritual, to make the individual feel more a member of the society to which he in fact belongs.

Fourthly, escapist fare in the media has been shown to operate as a common ground for social intercourse. J. T. Klapper (pp. 176–177) reports the findings of L. Bogart (1955) that adults talk about newspaper comics, just as Britons are reputed to talk about the weather, to permit sociability without personal commitment or discussion of controversial matters. Mendelsohn (1964) noted that one of the reasons why radio was enjoyed was that it provided a social lubricant—providing things to talk about. As yet another mass media phenomenon, drama may function similarly. That is to say, by providing neutral ground for social intercourse, it serves to increase social coherence.

These relatively straightforward uses of escapist media all seem to function positively with reference to social structure. Indeed, Warner and Henry (1948), on the rather slender evidence of a study of sixty-two women who regularly listened to 'Big Sister' and a 'control group' of five who did not, argued that listening to the serial provided an important social function for the women by reaffirming the basic security of the marriage ties; accentuating the basic security of the position of the husband; demonstrating that those who behave properly and stay away from wrong-doing exercise moral control over those who do not; showing that wrong behaviour is punished; dramatizing the significance of the wife's role in basic human affairs, and thereby increasing the woman's feeling of importance by showing that the family is of the highest importance and that she has control over the vicissitudes of family life; decreasing the feelings of futility among some women by making them feel wanted; and condemning unregulated impulses in life by always connecting them with characters who are condemned and never relating them to those who are approved (see p. 63).

This experimental evidence is fruitful in suggestions of the likely functions of drama in society.

Effects of Media on Behaviour: Problems of Cause and Effect

The reading of detective stories is simply a kind of vice that, for silliness and minor harmfulness, ranks somewhere between smoking and crossword puzzles. This conclusion seems borne out by the violence of the letters I have been receiving. Detective-story readers feel guilty, they are habitually on the defensive, and all their talk about 'well-written' mysteries is simply an excuse for their vice, like the reasons that the alcoholic can always produce for a drink.

This assertion by Edmund Wilson in 'Who Cares who Killed Roger Ackroyd' (Rosenberg and White, 1957, pp. 149–154) points to the commonly imputed dysfunction of media consumption. The criticism is not that the media content corrupts morals, although theatres have been closed on these supposed grounds in the past. But, in Merton's phrase, mass communication is feared to have a 'narcotizing dysfunction'. In their article 'Mass Communication, Popular Taste and Organised Social Action', P. F. Lazarfeld and R. K. Merton (see Rosenberg and White, 1957, pp. 457–473) state the fear very clearly:

Exposure to this flood of information may serve to narcotize rather than energise the average reader or listener. As an increasing amount of time is devoted to reading and listening, a decreasing share is available for organised action. The individual reads accounts of issues and problems and may even discuss alternative lines of action. But this rather intellectualized, rather remote connection with organised social action is not activated. The interested and informed citizen can congratulate himself on his lofty state of interest and information, and neglect to see that he has abstained from decision and action. In short, he takes his secondary contact with the world of political reality, his reading and listening and thinking, as a vicarious performance. He comes to mistake *knowing* about problems of the day for *doing* something about them. His social conscience remains spotlessly clean. He *is* concerned. He *is* informed. And he has all sorts of ideas as to what should be done. But, after he has gotten through his dinner and after he has listened to his favourite radio programmes and after he has read his second newspaper of the day, it is really time for bed.

In this peculiar respect, Mass Communications may be included among the most respectable and most efficient of social narcotics. They may be so fully effective as to keep the addict from recognising his own malady. (p. 464)

In view of the positive functions of 'escape' fare in the media, E. Katz and D. Foulkes (1962) question whether in fact there is a severe narcotizing *dysfunction*. They note that, by virtue of the number of hours invested in mass-media exposure, the performance of the individual's social roles must be affected. But, they insist, the more subtle problem is to specify exactly the way in which particular patterns of exposure feed back to particular social roles, whether the feedback is functional or not, and whether it is a consequence of exposure 'per se' or exposure to particular content. Indeed, the problem for functional analysis is even more serious. The findings of the Himmelweit, Oppenheim, and Vince study and the Schramm, Lyle, and Parker study that heavy use of media is correlated with insecurity, maladjustment, and inadequate contact with friends, is merely a correlation. It is not altogether clear whether heavy use of the media causes feelings of insecurity, maladjustment, and lack of contact, or vice versa. Most of the evidence is that in fact those who are already maladjusted and socially isolated are the heavy users, and that the relationship is not causal in the other direction. Maccoby's research (1954), for example, would bear out the implication that alienation causes heavy media-use rather than the other way round.

There is some evidence worth mentioning at this stage, that suggests that the use of television for the average viewer does not deter him from taking part in other activity. Himmelweit, Oppenheim, and Vince found that television-viewing did not make children listless, nor did it lead to poor concentration at school and reduced interest in school. Children's love of activity and exploration is very strong; they noted that when there was a choice between sports or hobbies and viewing, television was often the loser. Indeed, if reading is evidence of positive involvement with life, and with intellectual matters, television's power for children was found to be positive in stimulating interest.

For adults, the most important evidence is from the researches of W. A. Belson. In two articles (1958 and 1959) he describes the method by which he measured the effects of television on the interests and initiative of adult viewers in Greater London (in the 1958 article), and reports his findings (in the 1959 article). Belson based his work on the measurement of the effects of television on a representative cross-section of the interests of viewers in the one case, and of their acts of initiative in the other. His final survey was based upon about 800 cases, and the construction of measuring devices upon about 3,000. He found that the effect of television had been to reduce both interests and initiative. The reduction of interest was not only in terms of activity level, but in viewers' *feelings* of interest as well. Even when interests are featured in television programmes themselves, the loss to television is made up to only a very small degree. Television's effects do, however, vary markedly from one group of interests to another. The loss in initiative and in interest extends over a period of five to six years. Generally speaking, the loss is greatest in the first few years, after which there is a gradual recovery. For the purposes of this present study, the particular interests are important. For all television viewers, Belson found that cinema-going was reduced by 33 per cent. Cinema-going, as a method of consuming drama, may be regarded as functionally similar to theatre-going. In this respect, the finding is neutral. Gardening, as a typical British activity, tended to return to its pre-television level. With sporting events, increased attendance and increased interest was noted. The reading of books and magazines was reduced, but some subjects started to read about material that they had not read about before. After five or so years of television ownership, membership of clubs and associations—an indicator of social involvement—returned to pre-television levels. Basically, the weight of evidence is that television reduces activity in areas that are functionally similar, but, after a period of television-set ownership, does not reduce other activities that may be deemed indicators of participation in the life of a community.

It has already been noted that drama constitutes a large part of the content of television fare. It is hardly surprising, therefore, that acts of initiative in seeking out drama elsewhere, for example in the cinema, fall off when drama is offered in the home.

Do the Mass Media of Communication Reflect or Control Social Values?

Although this study is primarily concerned with the content, and possible functions, of popular theatre and television drama, it is important to note the views of mass-media researchers about the instrumental and expressive functions imputed to mass communications. None of the studies cited so far, and none of the studies to be cited in this section, has tried to deal with the media content that is 'the most popular' with the particular social groups being studied. However, some of the information is relevant to the present study.

In asking the question 'Does literature reflect common values ?', M. C. Albrecht (1956) sampled 153 magazine stories—62 from 'lower' cultural levels, 59 from 'middle', and 32 from 'upper' levels. The main hypothesis of his study he suggested was largely upheld: that short stories in wide-circulation magazines, though representing different reading levels, in general reflect the cultural norms and values of the 'average' American family. Lazarfeld and Merton (Rosenberg and White, 1956, pp. 457–473) report that the media in general enforce social norms principally by exposing deviants. The implication of this finding, of course, is that in so far as drama serves this function, there are likely to be functional equivalents in other types of media. Again, M. Janowitz (1959) reports as a substantive generalization that the vast majority of mass communications appear to have little content directed toward challenging existing normative patterns, encouraging critical thought, or stimulating individual or collective actions disruptive of the more or less orderly flow of existent social processes (p. 142).

A contribution to the instrumental view of mass media in controlling social values is contained in the article 'Mass Media Socialization Behaviour: negro white differences' by W. M. Gerson (1966). Gerson sought to test the implications of previous research that media can function as an agency of socialization in at least two ways: (1) by reinforcing existing values and attitudes, and (2) by serving as a source of norms and values that offer solutions to personal problems. Gerson administered a questionnaire to 638 adolescent boys and girls in four communities in the

San Francisco Bay region. Data were obtained in two kinds of settings: in schools and in the adolescents' homes. When unreliable responses were excluded, 623 respondents remained in the population studied. The final study population included 272 whites (43·6 per cent of the sample), and 351 negroes (56·2 per cent). To determine respondents' perceived use of the mass media as a reinforcing agent, they were asked the following questions: 'Do you ever *try out* ideas you already have about dating and things like that by watching to see if that really happens in T.V., movies, books, or magazines? (1) I do this all the time. (2) Very often. (3) I do this sometimes. (4) Once in a while. (5) I never do this.' Similar questions were included about getting ideas from the media. Gerson defined a media 'socializee' as one who is high in either media-reinforcement or in media-norm-acquiring, or who is high in both types of behaviour. Defined in this way, 60·4 per cent of the study population of 623 adolescents used the media as an agency of socialization in cross-sex behaviour. Again, Gerson found definite differences between negro and white respondents. Among the negroes, 66 per cent were media socializees, compared to 53·3 per cent of the white teenagers (p. 44). Gerson noted that regardless of how the data were grouped, the findings were consistently in the same direction: more negroes than whites used the media in their cross-sex socialization behaviour. Gerson queried *why* whites and negroes apparently used the media in different ways. He noted that the data of his study suggest that many negro adolescents were using the mass media to learn how to behave like whites (i.e. behave in a socially acceptable way). Gerson suggests (p. 50) that if the interpretation of negro media-socialization could be generalized to other population groups in somewhat similar social structural situations, the findings might have more impact on the mainstream of sociology. For example, it might be expected that vertical-mobility-oriented people, immigrants into metropolitan areas, and white adolescents who are not socially integrated, might also use the media as a significant agency of socialization.

Gerson's study not only represents a determined attempt to study the use of mass media as an *instrumentally*, positively functional aspect of culture; it also suggests possibilities for the future study of drama.

Finally, the report to the National Commission on the Causes and Prevention of Violence, *Mass Media and Violence* (USA, 1969), contains two papers arguing that mass media, and therefore television drama as part of mass-media content, teach social values to children. In his article on 'The Effects of Media Violence on Social Learning' (pp. 261–283), A. E. Siegel notes that American children spend many hours each week watching television. They begin watching at a very young age, and are faithful to the television set on week-days and week-ends, throughout the summer, and during the school year, with the result that at the age of sixteen the average American child has spent as many hours watching television as he has spent in school. Siegel asks: is it a fair bet that the two sources of information have affected his social learning equally? Again, W. R. Catton, in his paper on 'Value Modification by Mass Media' (pp. 285–299), examines the effects of mass media in modifying social values. His chapter includes a review of some of the short-term effects of mass media, including the possible effects of violent television content reviewed earlier in this chapter, and also comments on the possible long-term effects of the media. When exposure to mass communication can be shown to produce little or no immediate effect on attitudes, but an appreciable delayed effect shows up, this is called the 'sleeper effect'. Catton observes (p. 297) that whatever the explanation for sleeper effects, it is clear from the fact that such phenomena do occur that mass media produce long-range changes in values that would escape notice in short-range studies. He notes that it should be clear, too, that previous exposure to the mass media may be among the factors that shape the perceptual selections, which in turn shape the effects of subsequent exposures to mass media. Thus the fact that perceptions are selective is no warrant for complacent assumptions that the impact of mass communication upon values is either negligible or necessarily benign.

Summary of Opinion on the Effects of Mass Media: Implications for the Study of Popular Drama as Mass Communication

The unique function of the mass media is to provide both to the individual and to society a coherence, a synthesis of experience, an awareness of the whole which does not undermine the specialisation which reality requires. The supreme test of the mass media, then, is not whether it meets the criteria of art or the criteria of knowledge, but how well it provides an integration of experience. Neither art nor knowledge is excluded as a standard, but they are secondary. (T. McCormack, 1961, p. 488)

In brief, this review of literature on the effects of mass communications suggests the following points relevant to the study of popular drama.

First, most forms of mass communication have been found to reinforce rather than change opinion. It has already been suggested, in the first four chapters of this study, that by virtue of its association in origin with ritual and by virtue of its dealing with roles, popular drama is potentially conservative and thus potentially conservative in its likely effects. Evidence cited in the present chapter suggests that drama may act to reinforce views about social structure rather than change them simply by virtue of its character as mass communication.

Secondly, the work on aggressive content in media and the instrumentality of the media in increasing or decreasing aggressive behaviour is, at present, inconclusive. The behaviour of children in the laboratories of American colleges, or of students of psychology assisting their instructor, are likely to differ significantly from the long-term behaviour of audiences enjoying drama in their homes or visiting theatres in conditions of middle-class respectability. It has not yet been demonstrated that the impact of aggressive content in media on the emotions of the viewer significantly alters his long-term behaviour in his social group. The main point, which bears repetition, is that if violence were a normal and socially sanctioned phenomenon it would cease to be of any dramatic value. It is possible that drama, particularly those types of drama that stylize aggressiveness in the form of farce or in the form of stereotyped crime drama, expresses social concern at aspects of the moral order that cause stress in the community. Appreciation of violence in drama may indicate the depth of the audience's feeling about the elements of stress. But, again, the available evidence is that British and American television audiences dislike violence in drama.

Thirdly, the evidence on the uses of 'escape' fare in the media suggests the necessity of seeking functional alternatives to popular drama. After all, drink and drugs provide a form of escape.

However, the apparent need for fantasy/vicarious interaction supports the idea that drama, particularly that which contains elements of social inclusiveness, is likely to perform positive functions—either as expressive or as instrumental culture. If drama, like the weather, acts as a social lubricant by supplying material for day-to-day social intercourse, it must necessarily, to be popular, avoid highly contentious and controversial issues.

Fourthly, there does not appear to be evidence of television in general having a 'narcotizing dysfunction'. At least, television does not appear to be dysfunctional in deterring people from participating in other types of social activity. However, if people catch opinions from popular drama on television (even if they do so through mediating processes of social intercourse) it is possible that popular drama, by virtue of its conservative content, could be dysfunctional by impeding necessary social change.

Fifthly, the weight of evidence is that most types of mass media reflect prevailing social norms. It is possible that popular drama may be a monitor or indicator of morality more by virtue of its transmission via a mass medium of communication than by virtue of its particular characteristics as drama. Again, it becomes clear that other forms of mass communication (for example, news broadcasts) may be functionally equivalent to popular drama.

In all discussions of drama as mass communication, it is important to distinguish between what is *available* and what is *popular*. Because money underlies the social system of mass communication, it is unlikely that those providers of television and stage drama who have to make a profit will deviate far from what they believe people to like. However, it is *possible* that they may do so—through artistic laziness, by misjudging the popular temper, by indulging in idiosyncratic fantasies of sex and violence, or even by missionary fervour. It must be emphasized that this study is concerned only with *popular* drama. It is, therefore, necessary to specify in some considerable detail how the popularity of the group of plays reviewed in this study was determined, and what techniques have been used to classify the contents of plays.

6

Content Analysis and Audience Research in the Study of Drama

Content Analysis Techniques used in the Study of Drama

Chapter 4 described the insights of literary critics and observers of popular drama, and what they deemed to be the content of the drama they have observed. In that chapter it was pointed out that these studies have the merit of insight, but the limitation of being unsystematic. Even studies of dramatic material that seek to draw conclusions from the content of that material have been notoriously unsystematic until recent years. For example, J. G. McManus and L. Kronenberger in their study (1946) of motion pictures, the theatre, and race relations give little indication of how the particular pictures were chosen for analysis, and do not specify any categories for the systematic analysis of the treatment of race relations. Their views on the effects of motion pictures and the theatre on race relations are eclectic in the extreme. The important study by M. Wolfenstein and N. Leites 'An Analysis of Themes and Plots' (1947) gives a penetrating analysis of a particular social type to be found in American films, the 'good-bad girl'; but their analysis is unsystematic in its selection of films to be discussed, and no indication is given of how the subject-matter of the films was classified. Again, a PhD thesis by C. G. Wiley, *A Study of the American Woman as she is presented in the American Drama of the 1920s* (1957), considers only plays included in Burns-Mantle 'Best Plays of the Year' series 1919–20 to 1930–31. This can hardly be called a systematic choice of popular material for analysis, because 'best' refers only to the choice of the editors of the series.

Systematic analysis of content received its main impulse from the necessity to analyse war propaganda. A typical example, *Propaganda Analysis* by A. E. George (1959), shows how inferences were made from Nazi propaganda on the Second World War. But although the necessity to analyse the content of propaganda accurately provided the impetus, systematic content analysis has a very mixed parentage. Bernard Berelson, in an article on 'The State of Communication Research' (printed in Dexter and White, 1964, pp. 501–520), gives a clear account of this mixed parentage. An authoritative study on *Trends in Content Analysis* by I. de Sola Pool (1959) contains a collection of articles demonstrating the widespread use of varying techniques of content analysis in differing fields of activity from political science to the study of folk-lore and language. The most massive review of the varying techniques of content analysis is contained in a PhD dissertation by F. E. Barcus (1959) with the title *Communications Content: Analysis of the Research, 1900–1958 (A content analysis of the content analysis)*. Barcus's thesis contains a bibliography, which may be considered definitive up to the year 1958.

G. Gerbner, in an article 'On Content Analysis and Critical Research in Mass Communication' (reprinted in Dexter and White, 1964) notes some of the possible materials for content analysis, and points to the necessity for relating communication content to other aspects of communication:

> In what way does the material reflect physical and social qualities of communicating agencies (publishers), and their relationships to other systems such as markets, advertisers, audiences, and their world of events? What points of view about life and the world as M sees them are implied and facilitated? What social arrangements of ownership and control of communicative means and facilities are revealed by the prevalence of this material? What patterns of selection, context, and availability are inferable from this body of content? How valid, adequate, and coherent is the correspondence of these representations to any actual system of events (truth quality)? What might be the consequences (aside from sales, likes and dislikes, conventional meanings, or 'effectiveness' in terms of conscious objectives) of social relationships and points of view mediated through this content as a social event system? (Dexter and White, p. 488)

The need to be objective in analysis of content and yet realistic about the context of content is the principal problem vitiating all content analysis. R. E. Carter (1960) mentions the problem of selectivity of perception on the part of the person who devises content-analysis categories. The problem of validity versus reliability, which occurs in most social-science research, appears in the field of content analysis as a conflict between the needs for quantitative precision and qualitative sensitivity. Barcus, for example, notes that one of the most common faults discovered in his examination of previous content studies was the lack of adequate definition of categories. It is necessary for the content analyst to state as precisely and thoroughly as possible what is and is not to be included, both to ensure his own consistency and to guide the coders who may be applying the categories. Clear definition of categories is also essential for the reader and for future analysts who may wish to make use of the study results (see Barcus, p. 47). However, even if the categories are clearly defined and meaningful in the context of the analysis, they are of very little use unless the quantitative aspect of the analysis is adequate. The problem is that of maintaining perspective and at the same time being analytical in a detailed way. An analogy would be that of describing a rose. One could take the rose to pieces, count the number of petals, measure the dimension of the stamen and sepals; one could classify the colour with some spectrographically-sound colour-code; one could analyse the chemical composition of the stem—but in the process of this methodical work, all the qualities that make a rose a rose would have been destroyed.

A few examples from different schools of analysis may illustrate the dilemma faced by the content analyst. The qualitative approach to content analysis is well represented by S. Kracauer. In an article on 'National Types as Hollywood presents them' (1949), Kracauer describes the appearance of English and Russian characters in American fiction films since 1933. He gives no indication that the content was approached systematically. In a later article, 'The Challenge of Qualitative Content Analysis' (1952–1953), Kracauer argues that qualitative analysis is, in fact, usually more reliable than quantitative analysis in textual criticism. Qualitative analysis is resolutely impressionistic and is not fearful of straying from the safe haven of statistics when this is necessary.

One may legitimately ask whether communication research, as such, should really try to match exact science. Documents which are not simply agglomerations of facts participate in the process of living, and every word in them vibrates with the intentions in which they originate and simultaneously foreshadows the indefinite effects they may produce. (p. 640)

Robert Warshow's work has already been commented on in Chapter 4. Another analyst of mass-media drama, H. A. Grace, studied 'Charlie Chaplin's Films and American Cultural Patterns' (1952). In this he examined seventy-six Charlie Chaplin films—1914–1947, that is to say the complete range of Chaplin's artistic production up to that date. Grace's study of Chaplin's films is systematic to the extent that it surveys the entire output of Charlie Chaplin. However, Grace makes no attempt to show whether the films were typical or exceptional among films of the time or whether they were popular with their audiences. He announces no systematic categories for analysis, but nevertheless succeeds in making some penetrating observations. However, his conclusion that 'film theme analysis may be used as a method for the study of the real and ideal patterns of culture' (p. 361) claims more for the analysis than is really justified. Similarly, Grace's 'Taxonomy of American Crime Film Themes' (1955) discusses how emphasis in US crime films shifts from the 1920s onwards, changing from emphasis on good and evil, through attitudes, personal or impersonal, of the characters in the films, to involvement. Again, his choice of films is highly selective—but none the less perceptive. Although he asks three questions about each of the films he studies: (a) Does the theme emphasize good or evil? (b) Do the central characters reflect a personal or an impersonal attitude toward crime? (c) Are the characters agents or creators of incidents in which they are involved?—he gives no systematic description of how he reaches answers to these questions. To this extent, although his analysis is interesting as aesthetic commentary, it has little value for the content analyst.

The opposite extreme is represented in content-analysis studies which emphasize *quantitative* aspects but which are insufficiently precise about qualitative matters. J. Harvey, in an analysis of 'The Content Characteristics of Best-selling Novels' (1953–1954), attempts a fantastically complex analysis of his selection of novels. He monitors readability; recency of events in the novel; sentimentality of theme; centrality of male characters' affectionate attitude toward other characters; centrality of male characters' total of level 1 emotion (anger, love, etc.); prior date of the same author's publications; and wordage of novel. His technique was to sample thirty pages of each of the novels chosen and apply no less than 510 variables to these. Having pressed his material beyond the conceivable limits, he concludes a little despairingly:

> The causal factors behind the sale of best-sellers are sufficiently complex and are embedded so deeply in the psychological and sociological aspects of modern culture that their description cannot be attempted, although the correlative factors found important in the two studies obviously suggests avenues of approach to the problem.

Two other studies, those by M. C. Albrecht (1956) and by L. W. Shannon (1954–1955), show evidence of massive industry in the study of magazine stories and comic strips respectively. However, the value of their studies to future content-analysts is vitiated by a lack of definition of qualitative categories of analysis.

The combination of qualitative and quantitative techniques in the hands of sensitive analysts has produced some remarkably interesting results. Before moving on to the combined quantitative and qualitative analysis of dramas, it is worth noting some of the dimensions of analysis used in the study of other types of dramatic and semi-dramatic fiction. Some of these dimensions of analysis are used in the study of drama; but in the present study they are by-and-large rejected. It is, however, important to record *why* they are rejected, and it is therefore necessary to mention them briefly.

A pioneering study in the realm of quantitative analysis was that of D. B. Jones (1950) in her analysis of motion-picture content. She studied 1,200 films of the period 1917–1947. Although the commercial interests of the industry prevent her publishing the results of her analysis, she did adopt a technique of qualitative analysis which, by virtue of its simplicity, merits note. Each film story was analysed with a view to listing the principal items of subject-matter contained in the film. To be listed as a picture topic, Jones required that the subject-matter meet one or more of the following tests: (a) the topic was essential to the structure of the story; (b) the topic was one present throughout the film; (c) the topic provided the subject-matter of an entire sequence. She eliminated from her study minor or incidental topics. This elementary system made it possible to describe what a particular film was *about*, without pretending to extract from the material more than it could yield.

M. L. de Fleur, in 'Occupational Roles as Portrayed on Television' (1964), studied 250 half-hour time periods selected randomly from four channels of area television. Commercials, news broadcasts, and Westerns were excluded. From this selection of material, a total of 456 occupational portrayals were analysed. Twenty were subsequently discarded—impostors in crime and comedy dramas—leaving an analysis of 436 roles. Because the qualitative content categories by which the roles were described were chosen with great care, the results are of some value. They are reported on pp. 108–109.

Himmelweit, Oppenheim, and Vince (1958) adopted content-analysis techniques to describe adult plays, Westerns, crime and detective programmes, to help answer the following questions:

1. Does television drama teach good or bad morals? For example, how are honesty and dishonesty treated?

2. Is the criminal sometimes a sympathetic character? Is he ever allowed to 'get away with it'? Do people advance themselves by being virtuous or is virtue considered to be its own reward?

3. What values do television plays put over? Do they depict success in terms of money, independence, domination? What does it teach about appearance and manners? Does it invite the questioning of socially desirable values? How far do values cancel each other out within any one programme or as between one programme and another?

4. What are the heroes and heroines like? Since children often identify themselves with the principal characters, what types of models are offered? What characteristics are presented as sympathetic and unsympathetic? How far are they 'black' or 'white' in character, or how far 'grey'—containing elements of both good and bad?

5. Does adults' television drama present themes and relationships involving children? How are children's relationships portrayed—with one another and with adults, especially parents? Are families shown as contented or rebellious?

6. How are violence and aggression depicted? When is violence considered justified? Who is allowed to be aggressive and why, whose aggression is condemned and why? Does the end justify the means?

7. How far are the characters victims of a capricious fate? How far do television plays use 'deus ex machina' solutions?

8. How are lighting, music, close-ups, and camera work used to stress situations and produce effects? What situations are given special treatment? (pp. 432–433)

Their analysis of characterization (see pages 181 and 187) is particularly thorough. For Westerns they range the personality-characteristics of hero, henchman, and villain, and for detective stories the characteristics of heroes and criminals, along five-point scales dealing with such factors as whether the characters were just–unjust, kind–unkind, assured–insecure, polite–impolite, satis-fied–dissatisfied, honest–dishonest, happy–unhappy, courageous-cowardly, enterprising–unenterprising, intelligent–stupid, etc. Again, they classified violence in Westerns in terms of verbal threats or abuse, seizure by arms, fisticuffs, shooting matches, wounding, and killing. They also deal with setting, themes, and values portrayed. With an analysis so commendably thorough, the amount of time involved would have been prohibitive but for the fact that in their analysis they chose at random (by methods described on p. 433) six short and two long ITV plays, and five BBC plays, which together occupied the same amount of time as the (shorter) ITV plays. Their analysis of Westerns, crime, and detective programmes was limited to ten Westerns selected at random, from both BBC and ITV, four episodes of 'Dragnet' and three episodes each of 'Fabian of Scotland Yard' and 'Inner Sanctum'. If the sample had been very much larger, and selected on grounds other than that of simple availability, such com-prehensive analysis would have been prohibitively expensive in time and money. This choice, which every analyst has to make, between a limited number of dimensions of analysis for a large number of productions, and a large number of dimensions of analysis for a limited number of productions, is a serious one: it will be referred to again later.

A further dimension of analysis that has been used is that of the goals or motives of the characters involved. In two studies (1952 and 1953), M. Spiegelman, C. Terwilliger, and F. Fearing examined the goals and means to goals of characters in comic strips. Some of their results are reported later in this chapter. In another study, H. Goodrich (1964) categorized goals in terms of love; happy marriage; domination–power; benefit–rescue–pro-tection; excitement; success; comfort–emotional security; and idealist objective.

A major content-analysis study of 'The Television World of Violence' was carried out for the National Commission on the Causes and Prevention of Violence by G. Gerbner; it is reported in *Mass Media and Violence* (USA, 1969, pp. 311–339.) For this study, all network television programmes transmitted during prime evening time and on Saturday mornings during the weeks of October 1–7, 1967 and 1968, were monitored. Regular television dramas, cartoon programmes, and feature films presenting one or more plays were analysed. The analysts were, of course, primarily interested in the incidence of violence. They recorded observations about the prevalence and 'seriousness' of violence in each play; rates and types of violent episodes; the role of major characters inflicting or absorbing violence; the role different times, places, people, and 'the law' play in the world of dramatic violence; the significance of violence to the plots; and, when violence was an integral part of the plot, the rates and characteristics of encounters between parties inflicting and suffering violence.

The Gerbner study must have been one of the most massive and thorough investigations ever carried out. Appendix III-J of the report *Mass Media and Violence* (USA, 1969, pp. 519–591) describes in detail the content-analysis procedures used and the results obtained with them. The content-analysis recording instrument is likely to be of great value for future research workers in the field.

Other analysts have evolved techniques likely to be of value to the student of drama. In *An Experimental Study of Comedy*, E. G. Gabbard (1954) defined seven comic devices and five elements through which these devices function. The devices he studied were overstatement—the expression of an element with more force than the truth, situation, or convention warrants; the reversal—an about-face of plan or expectancy of an element; impropriety—the expression of an element that is indecorous; substitution—the deliberate or accidental expression of an element for the purpose contrary to or different from customary usage; double meaning—the expression of an element that is capable of having two or more meanings; understatement—the expression of an element with less force than the truth, situation, or convention warrants; and repetition—the obvious pattern of recurrence of an element. The elements through which these devices function, he records, are idea—thought, verbalized concept, or notion; characteristic—a trait or disposition of an individual; emotion—the state of feeling of an individual; sound—that which affects the sense of hearing; sight—that which affects the sense of sight.

In *A Study of the Image of the American Character as Presented in Selected Network Television Dramas*, R. H. Bell (1961) studied 192 programmes from March 25 to August 23, 1960, representing 3·8 per cent of all network television drama presented over the three networks in Phoenix, Arizona, in one year. To evaluate these dramas, he developed a ten-point form:

A. Tendency of work as a whole.
   1. What is the manifest theme of the drama? Generalised theme?

B. Subjects of crisis catalogued.
   2. What problem creates the conflict in drama?
   3. How is the conflict resolved? Who is responsible for its resolution?

C. Description of individual characters and their motivations.
   4. What is the (a) sex (b) age (c) race (d) occupation of the protagonist?
   5. What motivates the protagonist? The antagonist?
   6. What relationship exists between the leading characters?

D. Actions recommended and disapproved.
   7. What behaviour is rewarded, what punished?
   8. What is valued highly?

E. Symbols and referents.
   9. What symbols are used? Of what are they symbolic?
   10. What beliefs are assumed in the story? (Bell, 1961, p. 35)

Some of Bell's principal findings are noted on p. 109.

Another major study of television drama was that by S. W. Head, *Television and Social Norms: an analysis of the social content of a sample of television dramas* (1953). Among the dimensions included in Head's study were the following: an interaction dimension—including play types, conflicts, motives, goals, themes, outcomes, group relations; a temporal physical dimension—including locales and periods; a character dimension—including the following details about characters: function, importance, age, sex, occupation, socio-economic class, nationality–race, beliefs, attitudes, motives–goals, affective status, ethical status, physical deviation, marital status; a behaviour dimension—including crime–delinquency, consumption, aggression. Head noted the difficulty of establishing a satisfactory method for classifying plays as to type. The principles generally employed in classifying plays are: outcome (e.g. tragedy); style or format (e.g. situation comedy, Western); and subject-matter or theme (e.g. romance). But inevitably principles of classification become confused with one another; often the outcome of a play is ambiguous or completely misleading as to the type of play. For his study Head adopts seven categories: crime, situation comedy, love, political and social problems, history, biographical, general drama, and children's drama. He claims no systematic virtue for these. They are based on a combination of categories previously used for motion pictures and for television. Much more important than classification of type of play is classification of theme.

Head takes over bodily the classification of themes used by McGranahan and Wayne (1947), which are, briefly: love; morality; idealism; power; outcast; career; and 'unclassifiable'. Classification by theme is, of course, the most important single aspect of drama—for the theme of a drama is what the drama is fundamentally *about*. The present study (see Chapter 7) will also make use of extensive McGranahan and Wayne's classification by theme; so it will be dealt with at some length in the following paragraphs.

McGranahan and Wayne, in a study described in 'German and American Traits reflected in Popular Drama' (1947), attempted to compare German and American traits reflected in the forty-five most popular plays in each country in 1927. They took it as an uncriticized assumption that popular drama can be regarded as a case of 'social fantasy'—that the psychological constellations in a dramatic work indicate sensitive areas in the personalities of those for whom the work has appeal; their needs, assumptions and values are expressed ('projected') in the drama. The successful play, to be successful, must be attuned to the audience. Their study is nearest in spirit to the present study of all studies of popular drama that have been done. Their method of selecting 'popular' plays is open to some criticism; the present study uses what is hoped to be a more reliable method.

McGranahan and Wayne attempted to select the forty-five most popular plays in each country as follows. In the United States, popularity was judged on the basis of firstly, success on Broadway as measured by the recorded number of performances. (They did not, however, take into account the size of theatre in which the performances took place.) Secondly, they noted the success in the rest of America as indicated by the frequency and content of reviews in theatre journals and local newspapers (there is evidence, as will be shown in Chapter 7, that the success of plays is independent of reviewing). Thirdly, overall success was noted by various 'end-of-the-season' discussions, tabulations, and over-all reviews from a variety of publications such as *The Theatre*, *The Theatre Arts Monthly*, *Variety*, *Commonweal*, *American Mercury*, etc. In the case of the German plays, popularity was judged on the basis of, first, the success of the play in spreading through the theatres in the various German towns, as indicated by the speed with which reviews of the play followed each other in special theatre periodicals, the over-all frequency of such reviews, and the estimate of popular reaction contained in them. Secondly, it was judged by over-all success as indicated by retrospective summaries, etc. It is clear that not only do these measures of success leave much to be desired in themselves; but they also provide a rather unsatisfactory system of international comparison. However, these considerations apart, the classification of themes used by McGranahan and Wayne is the best that has been used to date.

To classify the plays, seven independent judges were provided with the ninety summaries (each summary averaging a third of a single-spaced typewritten page in length), the detailed definitions of basic themes, and directions to classify a play under a given thematic category 'only if the theme is central to the plot'; that is, if the theme could not be eliminated without significantly changing the essential nature of the plot and leaving it logically or psychologically incomplete. If a love theme, for example, was merely thrown in for incidental interest, this was not to be counted. Subjects were told that a play might contain only one, or it might contain several, of the basic themes (p. 432). Not surprisingly, agreement among judges was high on the matter of the thematic content of the plays. The themes, then, can be listed as follows (this quotation is given at great length because it has been used for the classification of plays in Chapter 7).

Definitions of the Basic Themes

The following are the detailed definitions of the basic themes as given to the judges who analysed the plays. THE LOVE THEME: This category includes only heterosexual love of the boy-girl, husband-wife, master-mistress variety. It does not include family love—unless incest is clearly indicated—or love of any non-sexual object. However, plays dwelling on the problems married people have in getting along with each other are ordinarily included, even if romantic love is not high-lighted. In plays falling under the love theme, dramatic interest usually centres about the question whether two lovers, or potential or would-be lovers, will be united in the end. Opposed to the love relationship may be any number of factors: parents, personal misunderstandings and grievances between the lovers, career ambitions, character defects, higher ideals of one form or another. These forces must be overcome or reconciled before the happy union can ensue. Love may, of course, lose to any of the forces conflicting with it.

THE MORALITY THEME: Plays built around a morality theme deal with the problems that arise from the moral standards of society and human weakness or sinfulness in falling below these standards. Morality is used here only in the sense of *conventional personal* morals such as are treated in the Bible and in Western criminal law. We are not here concerned with good and bad philosophies of life, political faiths or social systems, but with specific individual behaviour. Typical immoralities or sins are: personal crimes of any sort, individual dishonesty, sexual looseness, intentional injury to other persons. Opposed are such virtues as, law-abidingness, honesty, 'true love', kindness, and consideration of others. The good and evil forces may be represented externally by good and evil men (e.g. honest folk and criminals) or internally by good and evil impulses. In plays with a basic morality theme (as here defined) the moral is assumed to be the conventional, the expected, the normal behaviour of the social majority; the immoral is the deviant, the behaviour of the man who falls below the social norm. Indeed, the moral is often treated as having the force of society and perhaps even of 'nature' behind it, while the immoral is unsocial, unwholesome, and unnatural. Ordinarily, in plays with a basic morality theme, the guilty person who falls below the social norm must *either reform* (i.e. readjust to society and nature) or *suffer punishment* (or both). The play clearly implies the superiority of virtue, both as desirable and as necessary. Finally, it is assumed in these plays that the choice between good and evil paths of actions is a matter of free choice between possible alternatives, that the individual is therefore responsible for his morality or immorality. Plays of the morality type may be said to provide the spectator with a certain excitement by dramatising immoral impulses but at the same time they provide him with a moral lesson to the effect that 'crime does not pay'. Because nearly all plays involve crimes or immoralities of one sort or another, it is desirable to define the morality type negatively and indicate the kinds of play that do not fall under this category: (1) plays that present illicit love-making as charming or amusing, and involve no moral judgment, no character reform or punishment, fall only under the love theme; (2) plays that justify an ordinarily immoral or criminal act in the name of a higher ideal or value (patriotism, 'liberalism', art, etc.), or treat ordinary morality as petty and narrow, in comparison with the hero's higher vision, or present a hero who stands far above a corrupt and evil world, fall under the category of 'idealism'; (3) plays that present merely a primitive conflict in which moral forces play no role fall only under the power themes; (4) if the central character is a criminal or other deviant type and the play presents him sympathetically, or makes it clear that he is not responsible for his sins, but society or fate is responsible, then the play belongs under the outcast theme.

THE IDEALISM THEME: Plays featuring the idealism theme have a central character who is consciously attempting to pursue a set of high principles. He may be a revolutionary idealist, a humanitarian idealist, or a devoted supporter of the old regimes; a nationalistic patriot or an internationalist; a free-thinking liberal, a priest or an art-lover. The important point is that his motives and his character set him apart from, and above, the masses of the people. He is not merely seeking to live an average, conventional private life, and he does not behave in a manner that can be expected of the average citizen. In the pursuit of his principles, he may have to sacrifice some conventional personal value—his reputation, his life, love, social acceptance, personal happiness, normal creature comforts. He may very well commit some act against conventional morals, as in the case of the patriot who kills his friend for the sake of his country. The idealist theme is thus concerned with the conflicts engendered by those who stand above the ordinary; the morality theme with conflicts engendered by those who fall below the ordinary. Unlike the moral individual, the idealist has convention and normality usually arraigned against him. Idealism plays often imply the desirability of reforming society as a whole or redefining values, or of preventing a social change that is under way. The idealist typically has to fight against materialism, conventional moral scruples, self-interest, prejudice, pettiness, stupidity, weakness of character, personal desires, lesser loyalties, conflicting systems of ideals. These forces may be external or within himself. Included under idealism are plots that stress an extraordinary sense of duty, loyalty or patriotism, or a single-minded devotion to a 'cause'.

THE POWER THEME: The power theme deals with the problems that arise from the conflict between two individuals or groups for the same object, territory, position of authority, or controlling influence over the situation. It includes personal conflicts for power, class conflicts, ideological conflicts, revolutions, war, etc. Also included are plays in which the central character seeks power against such obstacles as his own inferiority or his more tender impulses. Frequently the struggle involves the use of violence, ruthlessness, trickery or cold-bloodedness on the part of one or both adversaries. In power conflicts, the more powerful side usually comes to dominate the situation; but it is not necessarily the better side that wins— in fact, the reverse is true if the worse side is stronger. Plays that are principally structured and resolved in terms of who is right and who is wrong, or who is good and who is bad, do not, of course, fall under the power category. Power may be represented by a number of different factors: physical or material means, strength of character, ruthlessness of purpose in pursuit of a goal, lack of 'soft' emotions, courage, cunning, trickery.

THE CAREER THEME: In career themes the central character is attempting to win personal success in his occupation, to make money, create a work of art, or advance his professional status. The goal is personal achievement, not the success of an ideal, system, way of life, nation or other super-individual institutions. Various obstacles block the path to success.

THE OUTCAST THEME: In a number of plays we find as a central character a person who is placed outside normality or normal society by some handicap, abnormality, inferiority or stigma. This may be a physical handicap—deformity or extreme ugliness or illness; a mental handicap—some form of mental disease; a political handicap—a condition of being an exile; or any one of a number of social handicaps, such as being a criminal, prisoner, outlaw, vagabond, pauper, negro, bastard, prostitute. The play dwells upon the relationship of this person to normal society, his reactions to society or society's reactions to him. It may show, for example, how he seeks normal love and acceptance, how he reacts with cunning or brutality to his outcast status, how he is not himself responsible for his status, how society misunderstands and abuses him. Sometimes the outcast has a superior perspective and is also an idealist. *If a criminal or other outcast is the central character of a play, the play ordinarily falls into the outcast theme.* But if the central character is clearly a normal individual and the criminal is his adversary, representing evil forces, then the play is to be classified under the morality theme, since the interest here is not in portraying the problems of the outcast, but the conflict between good and evil. Not included in this category are plays in which suspicion or accusation of say, murder, is falsely attributed to innocent persons, and the action of the plot is centred about revelation of the true situation. The outcast's status must be real, recognised as such by both society and the individual. Plays are not included in which a person, normally a deviant, enjoys popularity because of his deviance. (McGranahan and Wayne, 1947, pp. 433–436)

It is to be noted that none of these studies of drama, with the exception of that of McGranahan and Wayne, attempts to isolate popular drama from drama which is simply available. It has also been noted that the indicators of popularity chosen by McGranahan and Wayne are open to some objections. Before examining techniques of Audience Research, it is worth noting the results of some of the content analyses referred to above.

SOME RESULTS OF CONTENT ANALYSIS IN MASS-MEDIA RESEARCH
Following his massive study of content analysis, F. E. Barcus (1959) reports that dramatic and fictional material offers primary source data for the study of cultural values and attitudes. These values and attitudes are reflected in many disguised forms such as in the personal, social, and demographic relationships of the characters in the media world. All of the popular media show consistent configurations with respect to these relationships. He does, however, note considerable variation in the configurations in the specialized media. He recommends that more study should be made of materials designed for various groups—upper, middle, lower social classes, male, female, and child audiences, and other audiences such as housewives, hobbyists, etc. His main point, however, is that the importance of the results of content analyses depends upon the validity of the theoretical framework in which content is viewed. A 'good' content analysis depends ultimately upon the theory on which the analysis is based—its problems, hypothesis, and basic assumptions.

De Fleur, in his study of 'Occupational Roles as portrayed on

Television' (1964), records that the most frequent occupations portrayed were associated with the enforcement or administration of law, with nearly a third of the televised labour force involved. He remarks (p. 62), *'the consistent fascination of the viewing public with criminals, cops, and courtrooms remains to be explained'*. De Fleur also notes that occupations as portrayed in the media have a bias towards professional work.

> Among both males and females, professional workers were sub-stantially over-represented. Nearly a third of the labour force on television was engaged in professional occupations of relatively high social prestige. A similar concentration was noted in the category of managers, officials, and proprietors. The bias in the direction of the higher socio-economic strata is especially sharp for males. Well over half the men shown at work in the televised roles held jobs that would be rated high in occupational prestige. (p. 64)

R. H. Bell (1961), in his study of the image of the American character as presented in selected network television dramas, notes a similar over-representation of middle- and upper-middle-class persons. Fifty-three per cent of the major characters lived in American cities, were middle-class, and were upwardly mobile.

In the realm of conflict, Bell notes that the major themes dealt with life and death (30·7 per cent) and right and wrong (26·6 per cent). Crime was an element in 62 per cent of the dramas. Pro-tagonists resolved the conflict in 70 per cent of the cases, changing character in the process 27 per cent of the time. By the end of the dramas, Bell notes, 95 per cent of the protagonists and 54·5 per cent of the adversaries were sympathetic. Crimes were solved by the protagonist on 87·4 per cent of the programmes, in one third of which he was a law-enforcement officer. In 57·7 per cent of the programmes the crime was punished by legal means.

S. W. Head's findings support much of Bell's work. In his thesis *Television and Social Norms* (1953), Head records the follow-ing:

> Some of the typical empirical findings are the following: 59% of the plays are either situation comedies or crime plays; 44% have a morality theme and 20% a love theme. In 75% of the plays the protagonist is successful. 90% of the major characters are white Americans of native stock. Over half the major characters are classified as 'independent adults', and 83% (exclusive of professional

criminals) are upper or middle class. The most common occupations are police-protective (17%) and professional criminals (17%). Ethnic deviants more frequently have either socially inferior occupations or no specified occupations than non-deviants. In over three-quarters of the plays acts of violence, crime, or aggression occur. The most common acts are battery and homicide. . . .

Comparison of demographic norms of the dramas with those of actual society shows that the dramas do not reflect the literal, objective facts of social environment. (Head, 1953, pp. 2–3)

McGranahan and Wayne (1947) record that German plays are more ideological, philosophical, historical and social-minded than US plays. US plays dwell on private problems and the difficulty of achieving love and virtue in daily life. The German hero tends to be an individual with distinct aspirations; the US hero is usually an ordinary person. US love plots concentrate on the solution to difficulties from hazards from external objects. German love plots concentrate on conflicts between love and higher ideals. The German orientation in the dramas studied was essentially idealistic; the US orientation essentially moralistic. In the US plays, the good side usually won; reform was typically by persuasion. The German plays showed the individual as inflexible and uncompromising; conflicts were typically resolved through power.

One observation may be added to the observation in Head's study of the frequency of situation comedies. E. G. Gabbard, in his experimental study of comedy (1954), makes the following overall observations about the presence of various comic devices that produced satisfaction in the audiences studied. Overstatement was involved in two-thirds of the total number of responses. In these responses one or more of the following appeared: strong conflict of idea and character, strong emotion, loud noise, and broad movement. Sight, characteristic, and idea were the elements through which comic devices functioned two-thirds of the time. The comedies in Gabbard's study that elicited the most response contained the widest variety of combinations of device and element. The implication of this, in so far as the experimental results are to be trusted, is that farce is more likely to be popular as a form of comic expression than other types of expression.

However, the principal overall observation that emerges from all these different types of studies is that the content of the media reinforces social norms.

The study of the content of comic strips by Spiegelman, Terwilliger, and Fearing (1952) noted that comics reflect the cultural patterns of acceptance and rejection of ethnic groups in American society. This, however, is only a detail. From his analysis of 209 individual dramas from television, S. W. Head (1953) concludes that: 'In so far as this sample of content may be indicative, it is concluded that commercial television reinforces the social status quo and is likely to increase cultural inertia' (p. 3).

The most impressive evidence of all, however, is that contained in the doctoral dissertation *Man and Society in Mass Media Fiction: the pattern of life in the mass media as revealed by content-analysis studies* (1964), by H. Goodrich. Unfortunately, Goodrich specifically excluded stage drama from his study: 'It has traditionally been written for, played for, and published for sale to a relatively small, educated, and sophisticated set chiefly concentrated in the larger urban areas' (p. 4). However, his study does cover content analyses of television; and it has already been noted that media other than drama are likely to be functionally equivalent in some respects. So Goodrich's observations are worthy of note. He describes the pattern of content selection in the fictional representations of life found in television drama, feature motion films, magazine short stories, radio day-time serials and crime shows, and comic strips during the period from 1900–1960. He concludes that the status quo in society has been affirmed by the media's avoidance of hints of social or institutional weaknesses and by the denial or minimization of the existence of social wrong or injustice. He too, notes concentration in the media on the portrayal of crime and romance.

It is because the mass media seem, by and large, to reflect cultural norms that concern is currently being expressed over the quantities and type of violence on television. The debate as to whether the violence in television drama does or does not induce violent behaviour in its beholders has been reviewed in Chapter 5. However, a few of the findings of G. Gerbner (USA, 1969) should be noted. Gerbner's analysts found that some violence occurred in eight out of every ten television plays. The average rate of violent episodes was five per play and seven per programme hour. Most violence was an integral part of the play in which it occurred.

Violent acts were usually performed at close range. They were inflicted primarily through use of a weapon, half the time upon strangers, and, in the majority of encounters, upon opponents who could not or did not resist. Those who committed acts of violence generally perceived them to be in their own interest rather than for some other reason (p. 315).

Pain was difficult to detect except when severe or fatal. Some injury was evident in half of all violent episodes. The casualty count of injured and dead was at least 790 for the two weeks reviewed, and one in every ten acts of violence resulted in a fatality. Most violence took place between the forces of good and evil. The 'good guys' inflicted as much violence as the 'bad guys', suffered a little more, but triumphed in the end.

The two weeks of dramatic programming featured 455 leading characters. Of this number, 241 committed some violence, 54 killed an opponent, and 24 died violent deaths. The dramatic lead thus inflicted violence 50 per cent of the time, became a killer 20 per cent of the time, and was killed 10 per cent of the time.

The past, the future, and the far-away loom large in the world of violence in American television. The settings of plays without violence tended to be contemporary, domestic, and civilized. By comparison, the settings of violent plays were more global, more distant in time as well as in place, more mobile, and more exotic. Violence rarely appeared to violate legal codes, and when it did, the law itself was likely to be violent (p. 316).

It is interesting to note that the forces of law and of lawlessness together made up a quarter of the total lead population of television drama, a third of all violent characters, and a half of all killers (p. 324). Gerbner notes that the level of violence employed by agents of law appeared to be no more than that necessary to accomplish their objectives on eight out of every ten occasions. Their actions were portrayed as justifiable on seven of every ten occasions (p. 326).

Space does not permit a more detailed review of this study. However, before this brief review of content analysis is completed, one further point is worthy of note. From his survey of content-analysis studies, H. Goodrich observes that there is an almost total neglect in the media of religion (p. 362 f.). From the theoretical suggestions of the present study, Goodrich's finding is hardly surprising. Of all forms of social interaction, religion is the most widely provided-for in Western society in terms of ritual and mythic expression. If there is functional similarity between ritual and drama, one would expect to find drama dealing with subjects that do not normally find expression elsewhere in the ritual/mythic life of the society.

SUMMARY OF CONTENT ANALYSIS: TECHNIQUES ADOPTED FOR THE PRESENT STUDY OF POPULAR DRAMA

This review of techniques of content analysis as applied to mass media fiction, and drama in particular, has drawn attention to the fundamental dilemma of content analysis: that the analyst can either apply very detailed analysis to a limited amount of material, or apply relatively simple analysis to a relatively large amount of material. Unless considerable resources can be deployed—as in the American study (USA, 1969)—a choice has to be made. The present study adopts the following principles.

First, assuming that drama is dramatic because of its fundamental subject-matter—its theme—the content analysis used in Chapter 7 will focus on the analysis of themes. The classification of themes used by McGranahan and Wayne (1947) is taken over in its entirety. It has the important merit of being less liable to subjective misrepresentation than other dimensions of possible content analysis.

Secondly, themes will be dealt with on D. B. Jones's principles (1950) that the theme must be essential to the structure of the play and that it must be a theme present throughout the play. Additional dimensions of content analysis relevant to the present study will be noted in Chapter 7.

Thirdly, all the content analyses referred to in this section of the chapter have concentrated on mass-media material that is simply *available*; no analyses have taken into account the *popularity* with audiences of particular media material. In Chapter 2, Fischer's (1963) insistence on the need to study *popular* myth and ritual was noted. So that the element of popularity can be given adequate treatment, this study concentrates on justifying a particular definition of popularity and on treatment of a relatively large amount of material. This in itself will limit the number of content dimensions capable of being studied.

Television Audience Research: Measures of the Popularity of Drama

The purpose of this section of the chapter is to review what is known from television audience research about the popularity of different types of drama, and to determine which, if any, of the techniques of audience research in day-to-day use are valuable for identifying popular drama. A comprehensive review of techniques of television audience research, with recommendations for new techniques, is contained in Chapter 25 of *The Impact of Television* by W. A. Belson (1967). The present chapter, however, concentrates on audience research as applied to drama. It reviews six special studies of television drama that have been carried out; it summarizes the information derived from these studies about audiences and their tastes for drama; it reviews the value of normal audience research techniques in determining audience satisfaction with drama; and it summarizes the information on the usefulness of existing audience research techniques in defining *popular* drama for the purposes of the present study.

Special Studies of Television Audiences: Information about Preferences in Drama

In this section, six major studies are reviewed. The first, a BBC Audience Research Report *The Public and the Programmes: A Study of Listeners and Viewers, the Time they devote to Listening and Viewing, the Services they patronise, their selectiveness and their tastes* (1959), reports a study in which lengthy interviews were carried out with over 1,800 persons, some 1,200 of whom had television receivers, in a stratified random sample of the United Kingdom population. In assessing the tastes of listeners and viewers, people were confronted with categories of programme output and invited to say how much they 'liked' or 'disliked' them. The results were presented in the form of a scale (p. 59), the maximum of which was +100 points (which could only be scored if *every* informant had 'particularly liked 'it') and a minimum of −100 points (which could only be scored if every informant had said he 'particularly disliked' it). The report records that for television-viewers, plays came top of the list in order of preference—scoring +57, followed by news (+44), variety and sport (+35), documentaries (+29), light music ($+24$), religious services ($+19$), serious music (-6). opera (-15). With radio listeners, too, plays came top of the list —with a score of $+51$. Information about categories of programme content were classified by the informants' sex, age, and educational level. With plays, it was found that they were slightly less popular with men than with women; that they were much the same in popularity with all age-groups; and that they were much the same in popularity with all educational levels.

The second major study is by D. McQuail. It is reported briefly in *Media Sociology* edited by J. Tunstall (1970, pp. 335–350). This report is, however, based upon a doctoral dissertation. The evidence in the study is so important to the argument of the present study that references in this chapter will be taken from the more detailed information available in the thesis, *Factors Affecting Public Interest in Television Plays* (1967). McQuail chose single plays on television for his study, first because television drama represents material that can be considered either 'high culture' or 'mass culture'; secondly, because many variations of form and content are likely to be contained in any sizeable group of television plays; thirdly, because television plays are popular at all social levels, and the audiences attracted to them are large and relatively undifferentiated in terms of occupation—thus size of audience as a proportion of the total population makes an approach by means of survey feasible; fourthly, because of the representativeness of the drama audience and the wide range of content, a situation presents itself where very different kinds of dramatic material presented over a mass medium can be compared in terms of the reactions of different social groups. McQuail's study was designed to exploit these possibilities (see p. 31).

To obtain his results, McQuail recruited a panel of viewers in the Leeds area who could be contacted at intervals, and asked to keep records of their viewing and their opinions about television plays broadcast during a specific period. (McQuail describes his procedure in detail on p. 49 of his thesis.) In selecting material to be studied, McQuail considered only full-length drama productions, of an hour or more in length, and distinct from serials, series or films. Three exceptions were made to this rule—three BBC productions were included which were in fact episodes in series— 'Maigret', 'Z Cars', and 'Jack and Knaves'. A period of two or three weeks was chosen, and informants were questioned about all drama productions shown within that period.

The first of McQuail's findings of particular interest in the present study is that there was apparently no sign of any progressive variation in response to drama as one moved along the occupational scale. The rank ordering of plays in terms of popularity for each occupational group was also very similar. Only four plays showed any difference in appreciation between members of different occupational groups. Secondly, McQuail found a general absence of correspondence between audience size and the eventual judgement that the plays received from the viewers. There was, however, a difference between BBC and ITV plays in that the BBC plays had smaller audiences and did on the whole show a greater degree of correspondence between audience size and the plays' rating (see p. 175). Thirdly, McQuail noted that people's choice of television plays was largely governed by their habits of viewing at certain times and habitual attachment to one or other of the main television channels. There was some evidence of differences of expectation from each of the two main television channels (BBC1 and ITV), and these expectations were to some extent related to differences of education, occupation, and age. However, and this is the important point, the process of selection did not appear to be efficient if the degree of accord between the level of eventual satisfaction and the size of the audience is taken as a measure of efficiency (pp. 200–201). Having noted that variations in the extent to which plays were liked, and variations in the extent to which people choose to watch plays, could not for the most part be explained in terms of differences of social characteristics, McQuail suggested that variations in response must be attributable to differences between the plays themselves.

From a brief classification of play types, and measure of audience response, McQuail concluded (p. 208) that the plays most unanimously liked could be classified under two headings: either they were detection or suspense stories, or they were comedies—usually with a semi-romantic basis. These plays, he noted, as a whole tend to have in common a familiar or undisturbing quality. Plays that were deemed unpopular were apparently unpopular because of their specific themes—usually because they raised inherently tragic issues or dealt with political or social conflicts that could not be shown to be resolved—for example the colour bar, nuclear disarmament, Irish nationalism (p. 210). McQuail subjected the plays, their audiences, and the responses of the audiences to a wide range of cross-tabulations. From this he concluded that if one wants to classify plays according to the response they receive, differences of subject-matter are more relevant than social differences between the individuals making up the audience (p. 228).

A total of 499 respondents gave some answer to a general question included in McQuail's questionnaire, 'What is the main thing you would look for in a good television play?'. Among the words used most frequently in respondents' answer to the question about the qualities they looked for in general in television plays, and the types of plays most liked, were the following: realistic, credible, true to life, about ordinary people, homely, domestic, modern, gripping, holding interest and attention, mystery, murder, thriller, good drama, good story, humour, comedy, comics. (McQuail tabulates the responses on p. 236 of his thesis.) Although informants were not specifically asked to state their dislikes, a number did so, and these dislikes were also categorized by McQuail under some major headings. The most frequently used words in describing dislikes for television-play material were: sex in plays, romance, love, sloppy material, violence, murder, brutality, thrillers, plays with beatniks, Teds, teenagers (see p. 237).

McQuail notes that an account of audience 'needs' derived primarily from evidence of a *post facto* kind about satisfactions derived from plays is open to objection, and must rely heavily on inference and assumptions. With this proviso, however, he separated the categories of expectation that emerged from his data, suggesting audience needs that may eventually be served by drama. These were as follows:

Television plays are expected to
  (i) Hold attention, keep in suspense, be gripping.
  (ii) Have an intrinsically interesting subject matter or (less often) setting, satisfy curiosity, possibly to be about something of topical interest.
  (iii) Amuse, cause laughter.
  (iv) Be relaxing, pleasant, light-hearted (not always distinguishable from (iii)).

(v) Be true to life—i.e. show events or situations which within the viewers' own experience are authentic and credible.

(vi) Be down to earth, about 'ordinary' people and problems, in everyday surroundings. (This is close to (v), but narrower in scope.)

(vii) Be out of the ordinary, unusual, strange in settings, motivations or meanings.

(viii) Have a good moral or meaning—i.e. to have a meaning which is approved of because it is thought to be true and worth pointing out, and not in conflict with the viewers' own values.

(ix) Be exciting, fast-moving, with a good deal of 'action' and not too much talking. (This is linked with (i), but the two are not identical in meaning.)

(x) Be thought-provoking. (This may be categorised with either (ii) or (viii) above.) (p. 245)

Having noted these expectations, as recorded by response to the initial questionnaire, McQuail raised the question as to whether some people look predominantly for one kind of satisfaction, or whether the same people tend to have different expectations at different times. He attempted to answer this question by sending an additional questionnaire to his respondents. The purpose of the questionnaire was to confront people with a list of characteristics that television plays could have, and to ask them to say how important they regarded each one to be. The composition of the group of 257 people actually returning a satisfactorily completed questionnaire was inevitably biassed. Compared to his initial sample, the group replying to this additional questionnaire over-represented those in the more skilled occupational groups and those with longer education. However, the additional questionnaire provided more systematic evidence about tastes than the unstructured replies to the general question in the original questionnaire. Following this additional questionnaire, the qualities to which most importance was attached emerged as follows: a good moral or meaning, credible and realistic, tense and exciting, fast-moving action, suitable for the family, true to everyday life. The qualities that emerged as least looked-for by the sample population were: a modern setting, about ordinary people, a happy ending, light and amusing.

McQuail then went on to test whether there was any relationship between the factors noted as being appealing and actual reaction to plays. Did those people, for example, who thought excitement important in television plays actually *like* plays that were exciting more than other plays? From his analysis McQuail concluded that these 'factors' did not provide any better prediction or indicators of appreciation than the social factors previously studied. Concluding his overall review of preferences, McQuail notes that the evidence tends to confirm the view that occupational differences do not provide a very useful predictor of tastes and interests in television drama any more than they provide a predictor of reaction to drama.

McQuail acknowledges that his sample was quite small in size, and in some respects unrepresentative—first because it was specifically chosen to include those with some interest in viewing plays on television, and secondly because of losses from the original sample during the survey itself (see p. 285). However, in view of the evidence cited from the BBC study, interest in television plays seems to be a very widespread characteristic of the British population. Having hedged his conclusions with wise provisos, McQuail notes that the implications of his study are that television content is providing something universally acceptable, and meeting widely distributed needs, and that the classlessness in the use of television is to be attributed to this as much as to anything else. People do not primarily orient themselves to the cultural fare available to them in terms of value judgements. They consider it, not as being of a 'high' or 'low' quality, but as serving, or failing to serve, some immediate or simple purpose. On the evidence available, McQuail notes that the needs involved and the expectations present among the audience do not seem to vary greatly along the lines suggested by social class or educational differences (p. 296). McQuail quotes J. T. Klapper's view (1960) that audience members select from the vast supply of television fare the sort of material that serves their immediate needs, and reacts to the material in accordance with those needs. McQuail indicates that his study reinforces this view, and suggests that it is only in these terms, and in terms of a resulting pattern of tastes and preferences, that some coherence can be given to variations in use of and response to mass-media material (p. 299). The main needs that McQuail's evidence points to are summarized by him as follows, listed in descending order of importance:

(a) a need for amusement.
(b) a need to satisfy curiosity, to follow an intrinsically interesting story.
(c) a wish to see a portrayal of everyday life.
(d) a need to have a moral or 'meaning' presented.
(e) a need for excitement and vicarious involvement in action.
(f) a need for something which is unusual, outside normal experience. (p. 300)

When plays were grouped according to the degree of liking accorded, McQuail noted a definite link between content and level of response. Three levels of descending popularity were identified. Those plays with the highest level of audience appreciation were likely either to be detection or suspense stories, or alternatively comedies, usually with a romantic basis. At the second level, the moderately liked plays tended to deal with a personal or social problem in a serious way. The third group, the most disliked plays, were distinguishable by their controversial or disturbing character. The continuum along which plays can be judged could be represented as ranging from the most conventional and stylized in form down to the most unexpected and unusual. The principal need that television drama seemed to meet for the audience, McQuail noted, was the need to extend and confirm personal experience through receiving communication. This finding, which emerged as an incidental product of McQuail's investigation, is of the highest importance in the present study—for it largely confirms the theoretical predictions contained in the first five chapters.

The third study from which information is drawn was carried out by the BBC Audience Research Department in December 1964: it deals with *Single Plays on Television* (BBC, 1965). A questionnaire distributed in December 1964 was completed by 1,049 members of the general viewing panel of the BBC. It was designed for completion by those 'interested in viewing plays'; in the event, a question designed to 'filter out' those not interested in plays eliminated only 5 per cent of those who returned questionnaires. The questionnaire was designed to discover viewers' preferences for types of television play. A list of fourteen categories of television play was prepared, the descriptions of the categories couched in language such as might have been used by the ordinary viewer when speaking of a play or in describing its dominant characteristics. Viewers' predispositions were sought from a scale using A, B, C, D, E thus: A = 'usually like very much'; B = 'usually prepared to give them a trial'; C = 'can't say until the play itself is seen'; D = 'usually don't care for them'; E = 'usually dislike them very much'. From this investigation, five categories emerged as being in a very strong 'market' position with at least four out of every five viewers: (a) plays with detective-story plots; (b) plays based on real events in the past; (c) plays dealing with real present-day problems; (d) plays about ordinary nice people; (e) plays meant to be amusing (but not necessarily farcical). Plays coming low on the list (in the last four of the fourteen categories—and with the largest proportion of respondents stating a positive dislike) were: plays with plenty of violent action; plays with strong sex interest; plays relying largely on fantasy; plays relying on ideas with little or no story or plot. This study, which was carried out while McQuail's study was being carried out, and independently from it, largely confirms McQuail's findings.

The fourth study from which information is drawn was also carried out in the BBC. It is a personal analysis carried out by Michael Imison (BBC, 1965), with the title *Drama Audiences in the Sixties*. The first point of interest from Imison's report is that, although audiences praised plays of the 1963/4 season for being 'unusual', and 'up-to-date' and for having 'interesting back-grounds', plays with these qualities received only average or below-average reaction indices (see below for explanation of reaction index). Plays that were frequently criticized, like some 1960 plays, for being 'out of date', 'hackneyed', or 'common-place' get above-average reaction indices. In spite of viewers' apparent preferences, repeats of old stage plays with conventional format were widely appreciated. Secondly, Imison reported that between 1961 and 1964 the share of the time allotted to BBC drama filled by plays more than halved. In the first quarter of 1961, plays filled an average of 71 per cent of the minutes per week allotted to studio drama. If drama on film is included, the plays' share averaged 43 per cent. In the first quarter of 1964, plays filled on average only 33 per cent of studio drama time and only 18 per cent of the time allotted to all drama, including film. Over the same period, the yearly average reaction index for BBC plays fell from 66 to 56. Imison suggests that this fact, coupled with the evidence about audience attitudes, lends strength to a theory that series and serials were biasing audiences against plays (because they offer the same satisfactions for less mental effort). However, he notes that in the last quarter of 1964, when there were fewer plays than ever, their reaction indices actually went up while audiences for series and serials went down. The most credible order of explanatory events seemed to Imison to be:

(i) Less popular type of play done. Reaction index, then size of audience drops.

(ii) Planners reduce play output, increase series and serials as substitute.

(iii) More popular type of play done. Reaction index rises.

(iv) Novelty wears off series/serials. Audience drops. (p. 5)

This explanation of the reduction in the number of plays will be seen to be important in Chapter 7 of this book, when the number of plays available for analysis in the early 1960s is seen to diminish year by year. Thirdly, Imison's report confirms the last two studies mentioned in stressing the popularity of crime and comedy series. Fourthly, Imison confirms that there are no differences in education that seem to affect attitudes to plays. The under-29 age-group liked plays less than the middle-aged; women liked plays more than men. Otherwise, the homogeneity of audience-taste for plays seems to be confirmed.

The fifth study from which information is drawn is *A report on a study of Television Play Viewing* (1965) prepared for the Independent Television Authority by AGB Research Limited and Programme Assessment Limited. This research employed a different method; ten plays were studied in detail through the reactions of a sample group of a hundred viewers. Although the research technique differed from those employed in the previously reported studies, it once again emerged that the most popular types of play are those featuring mystery or crime, comedy, and family situations. To be acceptable to the majority of people, a play must have plenty of action, and a happy, satisfactory ending. Again, the principal dislikes in plays are sex and violence, and plays that 'leave you up in the air'. In this study, play-viewers were asked how interested they were in four different types of entertainment programme on television—feature films, series with different episodes each time, serials, and single self-contained plays. All four types of programme were found to be of very considerable interest to the majority of play-viewers. There was a slight advantage in favour of single self-contained plays. From the point of view of the present study, this is the first important point: it suggests that the choice of single self-contained plays for analysis does in fact do justice to television dramatic output. A second important point to be noted from this ITA study is that of the structure of a drama. It is noted (p. 31) that viewers have a need to discern the logic of what is happening and should feel able to foresee several outcomes that seem logically consistent in a play they are watching. An example of this could be the 'who-dunit', where it is logical that one of the characters introduced in the plot must have committed the murder. Viewers can foresee that the ending of the play will reveal which character was guilty. From comments made during the group discussions, it appeared that viewers were most likely to switch off their sets where no logical outcome could be foreseen in a play. The implication, for the present study, is that some ritualistic quality of a drama is enjoyed. Finally, this ITA study notes that viewers' attitudes to plays are for the most part conservative. Viewers are conservative in two ways: first in moral conservatism—viewers generally dislike seeing the following features in plays: sex, violence, bad language, the ridicule of poverty, old age and mental and physical illness. Secondly, there is literary conservatism. Viewers disliked innovation or unusual subject-matter or methods of production, e.g., free association, the 'direct involvement' technique, flash-backs in non-chronological order, and plays with ambiguous endings.

The sixth and final study from which information is drawn, is one by Television Audience Measurement Limited, *A Special Study on Television Drama* (June 1965). The results of this study are based on replies to questionnaires from about 3,000 viewers in the London, Midlands, and Northern areas during the two weeks ending 22 January, 1965. First, this study confirms that there are no class differences in regularities of viewing. Secondly, respondents were given a list of thirteen different descriptions of plays and asked to say whether they were 'liked very much', 'quite liked', or 'disliked'. Once again, it emerged that the most notable success was the simple 'thriller', which was liked by 60 per cent of the audience and rated well with all sections of the audience, but most of all by men. This was followed by 'a crime story' (46 per cent) and 'domestic comedy' (43 per cent); 'plays about ordinary people', and 'a war story' were next. Low in ratings of 'liked' were 'plays about rich people' (9 per cent), 'costume drama' (11 per cent), and 'plays with a strong love interest' (14 per cent). The highest number of 'dislikes' were for: 'costume drama' (46 per cent), followed by 'historical romance' (36 per cent), 'plays about rich people' (31 per cent) and 'problem plays' (31 per cent).

SUMMARY OF INFORMATION ABOUT AUDIENCES AND THEIR TASTES DERIVED FROM SPECIAL STUDIES: IMPLICATIONS FOR THE PRESENT STUDY OF POPULAR DRAMA

In summarizing this review of special studies, nine points can be made.

(1) Plays as a category of television entertainment are much liked (BBC, 1959, p. 62).

(2) There do not appear to be significant differences between occupational groups/social classes in terms of their tastes for drama or of their appreciation for the drama they see (BBC, 1959, p. 67; McQuail, 1967, p. 126). This conclusion is borne out by several other publications, for example: R. Silvey (1951–1952); J. W. Vrieze (1953); A. P. Runciman (1959).

(3) Older people tend to prefer plays more than do younger people (BBC, 1964, p. 2; BBC, Imison, 1965, p. 6).

(4) Audience size is generally no guide to audience satisfaction (McQuail, 1967, p. 175). But, with BBC plays, there is a connection between audience size and reaction index (BBC, Imison, 1965, p. 2).

(5) There is overwhelming evidence of the massive popularity of crime and comedy dramas (BBC, 1964, p. 5; BBC, Imison, 1965, p. 6; ITA, 1965, pp. 1 and 6). The interest in crime, as reflected by 'market' conditions, is confirmed by the study of D. W. Smythe (1951) for America. Crime and comedy dramas, as has already been argued, are socially integrative.

(6) Aspects of drama disliked are those that are socially disturbing (McQuail, 1967, p. 210; BBC, 1964, p. 5; ITA, 1965, p. 8).

(7) Drama characteristics that are highly favoured are: a good moral or meaning (McQuail, 1967, p. 257), and a clear structure with recognizable logic (ITA, 1965, pp. 2, 7, 31).

(8) Choice of play to be viewed is largely irrelevant as a predictor of satisfaction obtained (McQuail, 1967, p. 200).

(9) Drama for which people state preference exhibits moral and literary conservatism (ITA, 1965).

The implications for the present study of popular drama are as follows:

1. In studying popular drama as a social phenomenon, it is not unreasonable to extrapolate the preferences of one sector of society to the community at large. This will be seen to be important when the substantially middle-class composition of theatre audiences is noted later in this chapter.

2. Evidence from the studies noted above is that people's preference is for drama that is socially reassuring (crime) and for drama that is socially inclusive (comedy). These findings bear out the theoretical predictions about the possible functional similarities between drama and ritual.

3. The findings on the preference for plays with a clear structure—beginning, middle, and end—and an easily recognizable logic, points to a ritualistic quality of drama that is enjoyed.

THE VALUE OF NORMAL TELEVISION AUDIENCE RESEARCH TECHNIQUES IN DETERMINING SATISFACTION WITH DRAMA

During the period 1955–1965, audience research was carried out for the Independent Television Authority by Television Audience Measurement Limited (TAM). An article by R. Shaw (1962) reviews this method and compares it with the audience research techniques of the BBC—which are clearly described in *Audience Research in the United Kingdom: methods and services* (BBC Publications, 1966). It is not possible to compare the findings of TAM research with those of the BBC Audience Research Department, for the two organizations measured different things. TAM research was based upon the use of 'Tammeters'. When attached to a television set, a Tammeter records continuously the times at which the set is turned on and the channels (BBC or ITA) to which the set is tuned. A sample of the population possessing multi-channel receivers in each of the main ITA areas is approached and asked to allow the installation of a Tammeter for an indefinite period. People who agree to have a Tammeter fitted constitute the 'Tam-sample'. As a reward, TAM undertakes to maintain the television set in good repair. Tammeters are read once a week. The combined results from Tammeters are presented in the form of two curves daily for each ITA area. One curve shows the fluctuations from minute to minute in the proportion of sets tuned to the Independent Television programmes; the other curve shows similar information in respect to BBC television programmes. The proportion of the metered sets which were switched on during a given minute is known as the 'Tamrating'. The TAM rating for a broadcast is the average of the TAM ratings for each minute of the broadcast's transmission. The differences between TAM research and BBC research are summarized in the BBC publication on Audience Research (BBC, 1966). Briefly, the differences are that TAM estimates the number of (multi-channel) *'homes'* viewing, whereas the comparable BBC estimate is of the number of *persons* viewing. That is to say, TAM methods give no indication of the actual number of *people* watching the television set at any given moment.

It might, of course, be possible to extrapolate from the known number of persons per household in each ITA area the total number of viewers for any individual programme. But it has been shown that mechanical sets-in-use measures cannot reveal whether anyone is actually *watching* the television set. In his study 'Photographing the T.V. Audience' (1965), C. L. Allen describes the use of a precise photochronographic instrument for measuring television audiences. Four studies with the 'dynascope' were undertaken in 95 homes for a total of 190 weeks. Sequences of still pictures were made from the dynascope at preselected intervals from one-per-minute to one-per-second and provided permanent records of family television-viewing. The dynascope is a quiet, almost silent, instrument. It is unobtrusive, and, as Allen shows, was very rapidly accepted by experimental subjects and did not alter their patterns of viewing behaviour. The test that Allen describes showed that there was 'no audience' (i.e. no one in the normal viewing area) 19 per cent of the set-in-use time—30 per cent of the morning set-in-use time, 25 per cent of the afternoon hours, and 14 per cent of the night-time had no audience. When the 'no audience' and 'inattentive audience only' is combined, it totals 40 per cent of all set-in-use hours; it averaged 52 per cent of set-in-use time in the morning, 47 per cent in the afternoon, and 35 per cent at night. This research alone throws considerable doubt on the value of any audience research method which relies simply on the measurement of homes tuned to a channel.

R. J. Silvey and B. Emmett (1963) report a survey involving interviews with a random sample of 2,000 adults in multi-channel viewing homes. They note: 'confronted with the choice between two television services, some viewers virtually confined their viewing to one (which may be ITV or BBC), and most spend more of their time with one than the other' (p. 14). The enquiry demonstrated that a preference for the programmes of a channel is one of the reasons why people view that channel more. Combined with the evidence cited in the previous section of this chapter, that audience size is no guide to satisfaction, the conclusion to be drawn is that TAM ratings must be discounted as a method of measuring audience satisfaction.

Information is available from 1965 onwards about *appreciation* of ITA programmes. What is called the Tam Tv Q service was produced by Television Audience Measurement Limited, a wholly owned subsidiary of United Broadcast Audience Research Limited—which was owned jointly by the Attwood group of companies and the A. C. Nielsen Company. The Tv Q service in the United Kingdom was operated under licence from the Home Testing Institute of New York. Data was obtained from questionnaires completed by viewers living in representative samples of ITV homes in the TAM areas. Separate questionnaires were completed by each member of a household. The questionnaires list the regular ITV and BBC programmes shown during the course of the week. Each person was asked to rate all programmes listed according to the following scale: 1 one of my favourites; 2 very good; 3 good; 4 fair; 5 poor; N never seen. A so-called 'Tv Q score' represents the percentage of those familiar with the programme who voted it as 'one of my favourites', i.e.

$$\text{Tv Q Score} = \frac{\text{number voting 'one of my favourites'}}{\text{number familiar with programme}} \times 100$$

The possibility of using Tv Q scores was considered—in the hope that it would be possible to include some ITV plays in the present study. But, apart from the fact that little information was readily available, the phrase 'one of my favourites' is a little misleading when applied to one-off, self-contained plays.

For these reasons, ITV plays have been omitted from the present study.

BBC Audience Research methods are currently (September 1970) being extensively reviewed and modified. However, the Audience Research methods in use between 1955 and 1965 provided much valuable information that can be used in the assessment of the 'popularity' of a programme.

The total audience for a given television programme was discovered from interviews (which took place each day) with 2,250 people. Although this is little more than one in every 25,000 of the population, it is sufficient to ensure that the estimates of audience size were subject to no more than a tolerable degree of fluctuation due merely to sampling. The stratified random sample procedure was used. The interviewing included all members of the United Kingdom population over the age of five; an interviewee was only counted in the 'audience' if he actually saw the programme. Informants were not regarded as having viewed a programme if they had viewed less than half of it. A system of aided recall was used (BBC, 1966, pp. 11–12). In an article comparing television Audience Research measures, A. S. C. Ehrenberg (1964) has shown that this is an effective method of Audience Research—even if 7-day recall is used. The BBC technique produced a reliable measure of audience size in terms of those who actually viewed a programme.

However, the really important fact is that the BBC's techniques studied audience *reaction* as well as size. A 'panel' method was used to collect data, i.e., a method that relies upon the co-operation of the same persons (a panel) over a period of time. The BBC1 viewing panel from whom information germane to this study is drawn consisted of 2,000 members. Panel members were recruited either by public appeal or by direct invitation to persons previously interviewed in the course of the survey of listening and viewing. Viewing panel members each served for a fixed period of six months. Evidence suggests that long-continued membership of the panel made very little difference to the nature of the answers the panel members gave to the questions asked.

Once enrolled, viewing panel members received questionnaires each week about all BBC1 and ITV broadcasts. The panel members were asked to continue to view as usual, and not regard panel membership as imposing of itself any duty to view. Only if he saw a television programme under these conditions was a member asked to answer the questionnaire about it. This rule was repeatedly stressed, and its satisfactory operation was reflected in the fact that the larger the broadcast audience, the higher the proportion of the panel that answered the Audience Research questionnaires.

Questionnaires varied in form. The more elaborate questionnaires included questions designed to canvas a panel member's opinion on specific facets of a broadcast. For example, a questionnaire about a play might ask separate questions about acting, production, and script. Questions were usually followed by 'alternative answers' from which panel members selected those that most nearly corresponded to their feelings. Most questions were followed by a 'space for comments' in which those who wished to do so could amplify their replies. Finally, every questionnaire ended with what was called a 'reaction summary' in which the panel member was asked to 'sum up his reactions to the broadcast as a whole'. The simplest forms of questionnaire consisted of no more than this reaction summary (BBC, 1966, pp. 20–21).

The answers to these 'reaction summaries' provided the data for the calculation of the Reaction Index, which represented the sample's *collective* reactions to the broadcast as a whole (or, more accurately, the mean of the reactions of the sample). The panel member summed up his reactions by selecting from a 5-point scale (A+, A, B, C, and C−). In the 'Panel Members' Guide', a booklet sent to panel members on enrolment, a verbal description of these symbols was supplied. Briefly, it suggested that A+ should be selected when the panel member's enjoyment of or interest in the broadcast had been of a quite exceptional kind. At the other extreme, it was suggested that C− was only appropriate in cases of extreme dislike, distaste, or boredom. The panel member was encouraged to regard B as the equivalent of 'normal' enjoyment. In actual use this scale tended to be somewhat distorted. A+ was used much more frequently than it would have been were its connotation of 'exceptional enjoyment' strictly adhered to. This distortion was not, however, a matter of great practical consequence, since the indices were not used as *absolute* measures of reaction but merely a means of comparing the reception of one broadcast with that of others.

A simple formula was used to transform the panel members' answers into the index. A+, A, B, C, and C— were given scores of 4, 3, 2, 1, and 0 respectively, the sum of the points 'scored' then being expressed as a percentage of the maximum that would have been scored if all the panel members participating had selected A+. This was the Broadcast's Reaction Index (BBC, 1966, p. 21).

Reaction reports on audience reactions to individual broadcasts were produced. A Reaction Report contained information derived from the survey of listening and viewing about the broadcasts' estimated audience size. Then followed a statement about the volume and source of the material upon which the rest of the report was based. The Reaction Report dealt with the Reaction Index, not only giving the Broadcast Index, but also its statistical basis, i.e., how the 'reaction summaries' of the sample were distributed over the 5-point scale from A+ to C—. Supplementary material was then provided in the form of a sample of written amplifications of answers to the questionnaire on the particular broadcast.

Reaction Indices were never claimed to be absolute measurements; their value lay in facilitating comparisons between the reactions of audiences to different broadcasts. Clearly, they only had meaning if they compared like with like. For example, it was only meaningful to compare a play with a play, not a play with a football match.

The Reaction Indices have been subjected to much criticism, especially from people inside the BBC. In reviewing its Audience Research techniques, the BBC Audience Research Department is seeking to evolve more sophisticated comparisons between items. In future, panel members are likely to be asked for more detailed information about their views on particular aspects of a programme. For example, they are likely to be asked to indicate their reactions on 'rating scales' to specific qualities that might be found in a play. These qualities might include liveliness/dullness; vulgarity/cleanness; cleverness/stupidity; cheerfulness/depressingness, etc.

Although the Reaction Index in its old form is likely to be abandoned, the Reaction Reports on specific television dramas performed between 1955 and 1965 contain a great deal of useful information, which has been used to assess the comparative popularity of different dramas for the purposes of this study.

SUMMARY OF INFORMATION ON NORMAL TELEVISION AUDIENCE RESEARCH TECHNIQUES AS MEASURES OF AUDIENCE SATISFACTION: IMPLICATIONS FOR THE STUDY OF POPULAR DRAMA

First, size of audience alone is no guide to audience satisfaction with a particular drama. As TAM Audience Research evidence was based only on audience size in the period being considered, it has of necessity been rejected for the purposes of this study. No ITV plays have, therefore, been included in the review described in Chapter 7.

Secondly, BBC Audience Research methods in use between 1955 and 1965 gave detailed information by which plays can be compared one with the other. Audience Research Reports are particularly valuable in this respect. Chapter 7 describes how information derived from Audience Research Reports has been used to select the sample of 'popular' plays for analysis in this study.

It now remains to be seen whether there is any comparable measure of audience size and audience satisfaction for theatre plays.

Theatre Research: Measures of Audience and Audience Appreciation

Very little research has been done on theatre audiences and the satisfaction they experience with the plays they see. Most of the research in Britain has concentrated on audience composition; and, of that research, the major part of it is confidential to commercial organizations, and, therefore, unpublished. Some experimental work has been carried out in America; this will be reported below. However, the research suffers from the limitation of all laboratory-condition research—that one cannot be sure that audiences are responding in the ways in which they would respond under natural circumstances. As the elaborate mechanisms of the American research are not available to the present writer, it has been necessary to argue the case for regarding total audience size as a measure of popularity.

P. H. Mann (1966 and 1967), in one of the very few published pieces of theatre audience research, describes the methodological problems involved in surveying a theatre audience, and, in his second article 'Surveying a Theatre Audience: Findings', reports the results of the work in a provincial theatre. Mann concluded from his survey that for both a special production for young people and for an ordinary production, the Sheffield Playhouse attracted an overwhelmingly middle-class and well-educated audience. Within this audience there were, however, different sorts of people. The Playhouse regulars, who were interested enough to hold seats on permanent bookings, were predominantly middle-aged, middle-class and (from the interview survey indications) 'middle-brow'. Amongst the casuals there was a significant body of University students, younger but still of middle-class origins for the most part. The fact that the students gave support to a traditional play—*Uncle Vanya*—cannot reveal whether they would be more 'avant-garde' in their tastes given different opportunities (p. 89).

In 1964, O. D. Waldorf, with assistance from the BBC Audience Research Department and S. Field Reid, Research Assistant, carried out an Audience Survey for the Aldwych Theatre in London. The response to this survey was less satisfactory than that to P. H. Mann's survey—25 per cent as opposed to 90 per cent. The main conclusion of the Aldwych survey, however, bears out Mann's observations that the Aldwych Theatre audience, like that for the Sheffield Playhouse, was predominantly middle-class and educated. However, the Royal Shakespeare Theatre Company is subsidized, and research into its audience cannot, unfortunately, be extrapolated to the West End theatre as a whole.

Two other major pieces of research into theatre audiences have been carried out in the United Kingdom: in 1964, E. Sweeting, Administrator of the Oxford Playhouse Company, wrote a *Report on the Provincial Audience*. Concentrating on the provinces, this report studies the provision of theatres; the function of repertory theatre; the effect of film and television on audience habits; the effects of design on theatres; the relationships of theatres with schools, local authorities, local industries, charities and trusts. The findings of this report are confidential. Again in 1964, Social Surveys (Gallup Poll) Limited prepared two surveys for the Society of West End Theatre Managers on 'Theatre-going: A study of public attitudes towards West End theatres'. The results of these surveys are, unfortunately, confidential to the Society.

However, it has been argued above (principally from the evidence of D. McQuail's (1967) study) that, regardless of stated preferences, there is very little difference between social classes in their tastes for plays. In terms of their appreciation it will therefore be assumed that audiences—middle-class or otherwise—in West End theatres exhibit tastes substantially the same as those of other members of the population. Theatre *attendance* may be a middle-class habit; *appreciation* of plays shown on stage or on screen does not, however, seem to vary between social classes.

EXPERIMENTAL TESTS OF AUDIENCE APPRECIATION

The principal experimental work on theatre audiences and their appreciation of theatre fare bears out the above statements. Several studies have been carried out with a device installed in the University Theatre, State University of Iowa. This device, the Meier Audience Response Recorder, is described by N. C. Meier (1950). It was used by J. W. Vrieze (1953) in a study of occupation and its influence on audience response in the theatre. It was this experimental study that demonstrated that occupational category did not act as an influence on audience response to dramatic stimuli. A description of the Meier Audience Response Recorder, as used in the theatre, is contained in *An Experimental Study of Comedy* by E. G. Gabbard (1954). (N. C. Meier's article is primarily a technical description of the machine.)

Basically, Meier's machine provides a *continuous* record on waxed tape of an individual observer's interest throughout the entire playing time of a performance. The tape moves through the machine at the rate of a quarter-inch per minute. Each observer indicates the intensity of his interest (very interesting, quite interesting, somewhat interesting, somewhat uninteresting, quite uninteresting, very uninteresting) at every moment of the play. By the time Gabbard produced his study, approximately 3,500 individual records of individual observers had been secured on the Meier machine. Following experiments with the machine as a measurer of *individual responses*, a new assembly of recording instruments was installed in the University Theatre, Iowa, in the summer of 1952 for the purpose of recording *responses of groups*. This new installation, 'the Iowa permanent assembly', consisted of twin Esterline-Angus graphic recorders, a power unit, a sound tape-recorder, and 100 teeter-totter buttons (lever switches) which were attached to seats in the last four rows in the auditorium. The teeter-totter buttons were encased in cloth so that they could be comfortably held in an observer's hand. Slight pressure on one side of the buttons registered favourable response to what was being exhibited on the stage; slight pressure on the other side of the button registered unfavourable response. Pressing of the buttons by observers of the play activated the pens of the recorders. A synchronous motor kept the record charts moving through the graphic instruments at a rate of three-quarters of an inch per minute. The sound tape-recorder, synchronized with the graphic recorders in the projection booth of the theatre, was connected to two microphones, which could be used simultaneously. One microphone was situated to pick up sounds from the stage and also audible reactions of the audience. The other was placed in the projection booth, where at any time the experimenter could make verbal notes required for clarity.

This installation, Gabbard claims, provided the observer with an unobtrusive method of indicating one of two opposite opinions whenever he chose to do so. It provided the experimenter with two charts, which yielded cumulative records of the number of persons simultaneously indicating each of the two opinions. The total number of observers provided for was 100. The synchronization of the charts and the sound tape was such that the time-line running continuously across the two charts provided information as to the total number of persons who liked an incident on the stage, plus the total number who disliked it, plus those who were not moved to indicate any reaction at a particular moment. These three records, if all the observers were in their seats, would total 100. At one moment of time, the charts provided by this machinery revealed the reaction of the group to the line or action on the stage at the moment at which it happened. This elaborate apparatus, Gabbard claimed, eliminated rationalization about a particular incident that might condition an audience member's response.

Despite the elaborate nature of the apparatus, and the evident care taken to test it, it is difficult to imagine an audience responding naturally to a play while holding a teeter-totter button, or alternatively, remembering to press a teeter-totter button while responding naturally.

Apart from the studies based on the Meier Audience Response

Indicator Recorder, no other information on Audience Reactions has been traced. Some theatres keep notes in prompt copies of plays about laughter at particular points. These prompt copies, if obtained by a research worker, could provide valuable material for a future study. However, resources of this sort were not available to me; it is therefore necessary to examine total audience size as an indicator of popularity.

TOTAL AUDIENCE SIZE AS AN INDICATOR OF POPULARITY

Before a play reaches the stage of the West End theatre, it goes through several processes of filtration. First it reaches the hands of a reader of a presenting company. If he deems it a suitable play for performance he sends it to the managers of the presenting company. If the presenting company decides to put the play on, financial support is sought. Then a theatre management is approached (unless the presenting company already owns a theatre), and it is customary for the theatre management to look at the play too. If all these persons decided that the play is worthy of production, its script had to be submitted to the censor. The effects of censorship on what was shown on the stage between 1955 and 1965 will be discussed in the next chapter. The main effect of the filtration process, in the present circumstances of the theatre, is to produce a management bias towards plays with a small cast of actors and with a single set. These factors, of course, determine the cost of the production. Once a production has been decided upon, the management of a presenting company (for example H. M. Tennent Limited) will choose the best possible theatre for the play in the light of their experience. This is a commercial judgement based on wide experience of audience reaction to plays of different types. Occasionally, misjudgements are made. If a theatre turns out to be too big, and audiences are not filling the theatre, a play may be moved to a smaller theatre so that it may be kept in production. Conversely, if a theatre is too small, it may be moved to a larger theatre.

It was agreed by all those with whom I discussed the matter that the principal factor affecting the length-of-run of a play is box-office receipts. When a play is put into production, a 'break-even' figure per week (say takings of £2,000–£3,000) is decided upon. This 'break-even' figure is the necessary minimum figure to be obtained from box-office receipts if presenting company and theatre management (who share receipts) are not to run a play at a loss. The size of this break-even figure, of course, depends upon the size of the production. It is generally agreed that to pay off the original costs of mounting a production, a play would need to run for between 4–6 months, i.e. about 125–200 performances at 8 performances per week. Theatre contracts usually provide that if a play fails to reach its break-even figure for two or three successive weeks, either party to the contract—the presenting company or the theatre management—have the option of taking the play off.

It is now necessary to review briefly the factors that serve to *increase* the length of run of a play, and those that serve to *decrease* it.

It has been known for a theatre management, or a presenting company, to 'nurse a play'. That is to say, a play may be kept going even though it is losing money, to keep actors in employment for a short time or to fill a gap in a theatre's programme before another production is ready to go on stage. But the losses involved in 'nursing a play' if it is losing money are so great that such artificial stimulus to the length of life of a play is very rare, and hardly ever serves to keep a play going for more than two or three weeks—that is to say a maximum of 48 or so performances. The practice of 'nursing a production' is more common with musicals, where the initial costs are very high, than with straight plays. However, musicals are not being considered in the present study.

Secondly, a theatre's reputation may do something to increase the length of life of a play. Following the televising of the Coronation, helped the Whitehall Theatre to become widely known throughout the country. The theatre was seen on millions of television screens as the cameras covered the Coronation procession. The Whitehall Theatre has gained a reputation for providing farces appealing to the family, and it was an observable phenomenon that at times when people were visiting London for large exhibitions, the Dairy Show, the Ideal Homes Exhibition, the Motor Show, receipts at the Whitehall Theatre increased abruptly. This factor must be considered when the frequency of Whitehall productions in the list of plays chosen for analysis in this study is noted later. Again, Agatha Christie's play *The Mousetrap* has become a national institution. Visitors to London are reputed to include it in their programme as a matter of course, together with the Changing of the Guard, the pigeons in Trafalgar Square, and St Paul's Cathedral.

Thirdly, the presence of well-known stars in a production can increase its life. But, in the opinion of London theatre people, it is rarely possible for the presence of a star in a cast to increase the life of a play beyond 300 performances if the play itself lacks appeal. Again, it is not unknown for plays with stars of un-doubted reputation to fold up within a few days of opening.

Fourthly, having an excerpt presented on television has been known to cause box-office receipts at a particular theatre to double for a limited period. In the experience of managements, however, this period of artificial boost is rarely more than eight weeks—i.e. 64 performances. But, conversely, a TV excerpt in which the principal part of the plot of a play is revealed has been known to kill a play stone-dead. Once an audience knows what the play is all about, they see no reason for paying good money to see it on the stage.

Factors tending to *decrease* the length of run must now be considered. In the opinion of theatre people, the influence of critics can kill a play stone-dead. But it cannot sustain a play beyond about 200 performances if the play itself does not have audience appeal. Findings that would bear out this assertion are recorded by M. T. Boaz (1955); reviewing was found not to be responsible for artificially causing a book to become a best seller. In spite of the widespread practice of quoting extracts from favourable criticisms in advertising, it is the opinion of theatre managements that reviews, however good, cannot keep a play going if the audiences do not like it. It is clear that some process of informal communication between those who *have* seen a play and those who *might* wish to see it mediates the effect of critics' opinions. What this process is remains to be researched at a later date; that it is likely to take place can be inferred from the arguments presented in Chapter 5.

Secondly, the life of a play can be artificially limited by the contract made by a management with a star filling a lead part in the play. Nowadays it is rare for a star to sign for the 'run of a play'. Usually, with the financial lure of television and films, stars rarely commit themselves to more than nine months with a play. 'Big name' stars often commit themselves for only limited periods of, say, sixteen weeks—i.e. a total of 128 performances. Although a management may keep a play going even when a star has left, it is a common experience that the loss of a star can damage the life of a play.

Thirdly, theatres that receive subsidies do not need to keep a production going beyond a specified number of performances. For example, the Aldwych, National, and Royal Court theatres all receive subsidies, as does the Hampstead Theatre Club. However, the effect of subsidy is never to put a play into the 'mass popularity' category; it is, inevitably, to limit its length of life. If a play at, say, the Royal Court Theatre is evidently doing well, it may be transferred to a theatre where box-office considerations come into play. This has happened with several productions in the past—for example *Chips with Everything* by Arnold Wesker opened at the Royal Court Theatre on April 27, 1962 and was transferred on June 12 that year to the Vaudeville Theatre. It achieved 334 performances. However, even the initial subsidy of the play did not give it sufficient boost to put it into the group of 'popular' plays considered in this study.

SUMMARY OF REVIEW OF THEATRE RESEARCH: IMPLICATIONS FOR THE CHOICE OF METHOD TO DETERMINE POPULARITY OF THEATRE PLAYS

It was argued in Chapter 5 that controlled laboratory studies have a built-in unreliability in monitoring the real reactions of an audience in a live media-communicating situation. Even if such methods of measuring audience response had been available, they would probably have not been used for the present study. From the information reviewed in this section of Chapter 6, two principal implications follow.

First, total audience sizes can be used as a reasonably reliable measure of audience appeal. If the length of run and the size of the theatre in which the play runs are jointly taken into consideration, the total number of persons estimated to have seen a play can be regarded as a reasonable indicator of the play's success. From the information available on factors mediating the communication process, it may be expected that the longer a play runs the greater will become the importance of inter-personal communication between members of past audiences and members of potential audiences. The implication of this observation is that the longer a play runs, the more likely it is to disentangle itself from factors artificially complicating its length of life—particularly factors artificially sustaining it.

Secondly, this review of theatre practice has demonstrated that plays that *might* be popular with audiences may have been omitted from the study. For example, given a 'free run', plays produced at the Royal Shakespeare Theatre (Aldwych) or at the National Theatre might achieve success comparable to plays covered in the present study. However, and this is the important point, theatrical practice cannot cause a play to reach the dimensions of audience popularity that have been taken as criteria for the present study.

7

The Drama of Reassurance

An adequate theory of the function of popular drama in society should be applicable to all popular drama in all societies. That is to say, if the bounds of the society can be closely defined and if a technique can be devised for isolating the most popular drama in that society, the theory being propounded in this study should be adequate for all situations. To provide some 'experimental' data by which the theory may be tested, this chapter describes an analysis of the social content of popular dramas that could be seen in London between 1955 and 1965. The analysis covers 114 plays —76 television plays and 38 plays presented in the West End theatre—performed between December 31, 1955 and December 31, 1965. The first part of the chapter describes the methods of research that were adopted. Then follows a brief summary of results; detailed results may be found in the thesis upon which this study is based (Goodlad, 1969). Finally, the chapter offers some tentative conclusions about the selection of popular dramas studied. Chapter 8 of the book discusses the findings of this survey in the context of the general theory that the book is exploring. This chapter is, therefore, a self-contained research report.

The Major Assumptions Underlying the Research Methods

Two major assumptions underlie the methods of research employed in this chapter and the conclusions drawn from the results of the research about the popularity of the plays discussed.

First, it is assumed that in terms of their appreciation of plays seen, the British play-viewing public represents a homogeneous community in terms of social class and occupation. Chapter 6 referred to the research findings of D. McQuail on the homogeneity of taste among viewers of television plays in the Leeds area. Although more evidence is needed to substantiate his findings, there is support from the studies carried out on the Meier Audience Response Recorder—particularly as described in the thesis by Vrieze (1953). Again, the BBC study *The Public and the Programmes* (BBC, 1959) lends support to the view that social class and occupation do not substantially influence appreciation of plays. However, the main justification for treating the British public as a homogeneous community in terms of appreciation is that although theatre-going may be a middle-class activity, the appreciation of plays—as noted in the studies by McQuail and Vrieze—is a phenomenon not affected by class. Plays found popular in the London West End theatre are, therefore, dealt with in the same way as plays found popular by television-viewers.

Secondly, the study concentrates on the plays that were found popular—disregarding the restrictions on what is available. There may be serious gaps in what can be known about the functions of popular drama, owing to the processes of control over the supply of drama. However, the assumption upon which the present work is based is that those who control the supply of dramatic material operate within the same social nexus as those who consume it. That is to say, although a series of filtration processes takes place before a play reaches the stage or the television screen, those responsible for the filtration are members of the same community as those who view the final product. It may be that the providers of drama, because of restrictions imposed on them from outside, are unable to provide the public with what they want. The model proposed by M. De Fleur (see Larsen, 1968, pp. 24–29) suggests that social, and more particularly economic pressures, work in the direction of giving the public what it wants. It is, therefore, assumed that the individuals involved in the filtration processes are closely in touch with the values of the play-viewing public. The current controversy about the quantity and quality of violence in American television provides evidence of this process at work. That is to say, the views of the consumers (who do not want violence in their television programmes) and the views of the providers (who have supplied massive quantities of violence) have been publicly explored by means of a government report (USA, 1969) and it is likely that some compromise will emerge.

It has already been noted, in the previous chapter, that before a play reaches the theatre-going public it is subjected to 'commercial' filtration by script-readers, managements of presenting companies, and managements of theatre-owning companies. During the period under review, it also had to pass through the censorship office of the Lord Chamberlain. R. Findlater (1967) reviews the processes of theatre censorship in Britain, listing, for example, the items which the Lord Chamberlain required should be left out of a play if it was to be given a licence for performance. For example, plays must not be indecent; they must not contain offensive personalities; they must not represent on the stage in an invidious manner a living person or any person within fifty years of his death; they must not do violence to the sentiment of religious reverence; they must not be calculated to conduce to crime or vice; they must not be calculated to impair friendly relations with any foreign powers; they must not be calculated to cause a breach of the peace. The censorship office of the Lord Chamberlain has now been abolished; but these restrictions were in force during the period of the dramas reviewed in this study. It may well be that plays which did violence to the sentiments of religious reverence or which were conducive to crime or vice would have been vastly popular with the play-going public, though evidence cited in the previous chapter suggests that the public's taste is for plays that reinforce prevailing morality rather than for plays that challenge it. It is, however, important to note that the filtration/censorship mechanisms may affect the true functioning of drama in society.

J. R. Taylor (1962) in *Anatomy of a Television Play* has described with vivid detail how two ABC Armchair Theatre television plays were produced. His book indicates some of the filtration processes that a play for television has to undergo. Again, a BBC document *Control of Subject Matter in BBC Programmes* (1967) —reprinted from *Report of the Joint Committee on Censorship of the Theatre*—describes (pp. 3–5) how a play reaches the television screen of the BBC channels. The publication demonstrates how responsibility for programme content rests ultimately upon programme staffs. There are, of course, straightforward pointers to action: there is a defined 'code of violence' (p. 7); there are directives on the handling of sexual themes; there is a procedure by which programmes transmitted before 9 o'clock are assumed to be viewable by children, whereas programmes transmitted after 9 o'clock can, and do, include material not limited in that way; there is a practice whereby programmes on subjects known to disturb are openly announced as such, in some cases to the point of deliberate warnings given on the air or in *Radio Times*, or both; there are directives on specific subjects—on drugs, for example, or on the degree of violence permissible in children's programmes. It is noted that in broadcasting there is a constant awareness that the audience consists of family groups quite commonly seeing programmes as groups in their own homes. The whole Audience Research machinery with its reports on programmes underlines this fact incessantly. Again, if a particular programme transgresses the unwritten codes, the BBC switchboard and incoming mail-bags provide sensitive antennae monitoring public opinion. The publication notes that BBC programmes necessarily inhabit a middle ground. Where single plays are concerned, no BBC television production would venture as far towards extremes as would the National Theatre or the Royal Shakespeare Theatre. Neither satire nor documentary realism can go anywhere near as far as the published writing of Norman Mailer or D. H. Lawrence or, indeed, most contemporary novelists.

The document on *Control of Subject Matter in BBC Programmes* emphasizes that control over *subject-matter* is not to be dissociated from control over treatment of a given subject. Treatment is all. *Hamlet* is about incest, murder, revenge, suicide; it is about violence and about sex. It is, however, possible to broadcast *Hamlet*. Conversely, it is also possible to make offensive programmes about innocuous subjects that would prove untransmittable. Again, questions of tone rather than of material constitute the most baffling side of editorial judgements in television. The document concludes (pp. 8–9) that the process of editorial control in television is more akin to similar processes in large newspapers than to the machinery of censorship in the theatre and the film industry. Newspapers act within the laws of libel and obscenity, and are tempered by the necessity to maintain an editorial policy and a relationship with their readers. The BBC acts similarly.

However, the major assumption stands: that those responsible for producing programmes—and editing, controlling, and censoring the content—are members of the same social community as the viewers. They are likely, therefore, to produce material that is broadly acceptable to the community.

METHOD BY WHICH PLAYS WERE SELECTED

TELEVISION PLAYS

'The most popular' television plays were selected as follows:

1. All BBC Audience Research Reports on drama for the period 1955–1965 inclusive were read.

2. Although it was known that there had been a diminution in average Reaction Index over the period in question, it was decided that a single standard of judgement should be applied. Notes were therefore taken on all plays with Reaction Indices over 70. The Audience Research Reports provided information on each play as follows: time; audience size as percentage of the United Kingdom population over the age of five; number in viewing sample—i.e. number of those on viewing panel who returned reports on the play in question; proportion of the total panel expressed as a percentage; percentage distribution of reactions of the audience sample. Apart from giving comments on detailed aspects of a play, all panel members' reports rate a given play according to an index A+, A, B, C, and C−. These ratings are given scores of 4, 3, 2, 1, and 0 respectively, the sum of points 'scored' then being expressed as a percentage of the maximum that would have been scored if all the panel members participating had selected A+. This is the broadcasts' Reaction Index (BBC, 1966, p. 21). It is important to note that the Reaction Index does not, therefore, depend upon the absolute *size* of the audience that saw the play. For example, an audience of 100,000 for a play of limited appeal (say, to intellectuals) might have recorded a Reaction Index the same as that recorded by an audience of, say, 5,000,000. Again, Reaction Indices only indicate *average* appreciation. It is possible, for example, for two plays with widely differing types of appeal to achieve the same Reaction Index. The following example (BBC, 1966, p. 22) of distribution of Reaction Summaries illustrates the point.

The same Reaction Index—in this case 54—could be achieved by widely differing distributions of positions on the reaction rating scale:

	Distribution (i) %	Distribution (ii) %
A+	14	—
A	20	38
B	40	40
C	20	22
C−	6	—
	100	100

3. Although Reaction Indices, particularly in the higher ranges, exhibiting such peculiarities of internal reaction distribution are extremely rare, two additional indices (A and B) were calculated from the information contained in the Audience Research Reports. Although it has been demonstrated (for example by McQuail (1967), p. 175) that audience size is no guide to satisfaction, M. Imison (BBC, 1965, p. 2) noted that there was an association for BBC television plays between size of audience and appeal registered. Because the present study is concerned with *mass* popularity, the two indices were calculated to take account of size of audience. Index A was calculated as follows: the proportion of the population of the U.K. watching the play was multiplied by the proportion of the audience-panel rating the play A+. For example, the play *Never Die*, broadcast on Saturday, January 9, 1960, was seen by 25 per cent of the U.K. population over the age of five; 35 per cent of the panel rated it A+. It therefore scored 875 on Index A. Index B was calculated as follows: the proportion of the population of the UK watching the play was multiplied by the Reaction Index. For *Never Die* the Reaction Index was 79. Index B was therefore 1,975.

4. From the Audience Research reports, and the calculations described in the previous paragraph, three measures of popularity were available. For the first year under consideration, 1956, plays were chosen that met all three of the following requirements: a BBC Reaction Index of 75 or more; an Index A score of 800 or more; an Index B score of 2,000 or more. These indices have no

absolute value; they are merely a rough method for comparing the popularity of plays.

5. It was then necessary to take account of extraneous factors affecting the average size of the audience for BBC television as a whole. In particular, from 1955 onwards Independent Television entered the field as a competitor for viewers. It was therefore deemed necessary to scale Index A and Index B for the years following 1956 to take account of the variation in average audience size. Again from the Audience Research reports, average audience size for each year for plays with Reaction Indices over 70 was calculated. Index A and Index B were then scaled, to take account of audience size, to be *equivalents*—to be measured against the three requirements chosen for plays in 1956. The calculation resulted in the following table.

Year	Average size of audience as % of UK population (5+)	Index A: % of UK population × % of panel giving A+	Index B: % of UK population × BBC Reaction Index
1956	$\dfrac{953}{38} = 25\cdot1\%$	800	2,000
1957	$\dfrac{1,016}{50} = 20\cdot3\%$	647	1,617
1958	$\dfrac{980}{47} = 20\cdot8\%$	663	1,657
1959	$\dfrac{776}{40} = 19\cdot4\%$	618	1,546
1960	$\dfrac{623}{35} = 17\cdot8\%$	567	1,418
1961	$\dfrac{635}{41} = 15\cdot5\%$	494	1,235
1962	$\dfrac{467}{27} = 17\cdot2\%$	548	1,370
1963	$\dfrac{238}{15} = 15\cdot8\%$	503	1,259
1964	$\dfrac{158}{10} = 15\cdot8\%$	503	1,259
1965	$\dfrac{130}{9} = 14\cdot4\%$	459	1,147

6. Following these calculations of proportionality based on average audience size for plays with Reaction Indices over 70, a list of plays was drawn up that met the requirements indicated for

plays of 1956 or the equivalents from the table given above. The plays thus selected are listed in Appendix C, Table C.1.

7. The scripts of the plays thus selected were then read and summarised and subjected to the content analyses outlined in the next section of this chapter. Many of these plays have subsequently been published: a list of plays (for television and for theatre) available in print is given in Appendix C, Table C.2. Summaries of all the BBC plays selected that exist in script form only may be found in the thesis (Goodlad, 1969). The results of the research described in this book are based on plays chosen in this manner.

TV DRAMAS NOT ANALYSED

Two points remain to be made about the selection of television plays for analysis. First, reason must be given why the selection of dramas to be analysed is restricted to single, self-contained plays; secondly, explanation must be given of the absence of 'controls'.

First, single, self-contained plays were chosen to the exclusion of all other types of dramatic television fare so that a homogeneous selection of material could be analysed, which had the minimum number of complicating factors. For example, it is extremely difficult to describe the plot of a serial, which may run on for many episodes. Again, R. W. Stedman (1959) in 'A History of the Broadcasting of Daytime Serial Dramas in the United States' noted that serials which frequently changed characters or stories were singularly unsuccessful. It may be that the appeal of a serial lies not so much in the plot content or theme as in the details of the lives of the characters who appear regularly and become familiar figures. It was deemed wisest, therefore, to omit serials from analysis. Again, series of self-contained episodes involving the same characters—for example 'Z Cars' or 'Maigret' —may introduce similar complications. Musicals introduce the complicating factor of the appeal of the tunes. Films commonly involve elements of sheer spectacle, which are largely absent from plays. Although these alternative forms of drama have been omitted from analysis, it will be necessary later in this study to consider their possible functional equivalence to single, self-contained plays. It was an unfortunate fact that in the period being studied there was a progressive diminution in the number of single plays in favour of serials and series (cf. Imison, BBC, 1965). Because of the lower cost of producing serials and series—where the same 'sets' and actors may be used—it is likely that in the future there will be a preponderance of serials and series over single dramas. However, concentration on single, self-contained plays provides the advantage of comparability on dramatic content and theme.

Secondly, some explanation must be given of the absence of 'controls'. To be a 'control', a play would have to be unpopular with a very large number of people. However, as television writers and producers are painfully aware, if viewers do not like a play, they switch off—often within the first few minutes. It is difficult, if not impossible, therefore, to draw up a comparable list of unpopular plays. The nearest one can get to a comparable list of 'unpopular' plays is to find plays which were viewed, and which achieved a very low Reaction Index. Comments on some such plays are given later in this chapter. In addition, there is the evidence from special studies (cited in Chapter 6) of the known dislikes of television-viewers.

THEATRE PLAYS

The theatre plays included for analysis in the study were selected as follows:

1. Information on West End theatre plays was obtained from the annual editions of the *Stage Year Book*. An edition of this Year Book lists the number of performances achieved by a play by December 31 of the year previous to the publication of the Year Book. Notes were taken on all plays that achieved a length-of-run of 100 or more performances.

2. The size of theatre in which the play ran was also noted from the *Stage Year Book*. To achieve an estimate of box-office popularity, the number of performances of a play was multiplied by the seating capacity of the theatre in which the play ran. For this purpose, it was assumed that all the seats in a particular theatre were occupied for each performance. This, obviously, might not have been the case; but it provided a uniform measure of comparability. This calculation was made necessary because length-of-run alone is not a sufficient measure of popularity. (The measure of popularity used by McGranahan and Wayne (1947) in

their study of popular drama has already been criticized on this score.) For example, the play *Simple Spymen* ran for 1,403 performances in the Whitehall Theatre and was therefore seen by approximately 890,000 persons; whereas *The Reluctant Debutante*, which ran for 752 performances in the Cambridge Theatre, was seen by approximately 952,000 persons. The estimated size of audience—based on these calculations—was rounded to the nearest 1,000; for most theatres this would involve a give-or-take of four or five performances or less.

3. Plays included in the sample for analysis achieved estimated audiences of 400,000 or more and ended their runs in the period beginning December 31, 1955 to December 31, 1965. A full list of plays thus included is given in Appendix C, Table C.1, with details of the number of performances achieved and the estimated total audiences in hundreds of thousands. A few plays have been included in the sample which had already met this stringent requirement of popularity by December 31, 1965 but which had not ended their run. In these cases, the figures given are for the length of run and audience size achieved by the time the play finished its run; or, in the case of *The Mousetrap*, which is still running (September 1970), the number of performances and estimated size of audience achieved by December 31, 1967. The arguments for using box-office success as an indicator of popularity have been presented in Chapter 6.

THEATRE DRAMAS NOT ANALYSED

It was my original intention to concentrate on plays available to persons resident in the London area. It was hoped that information about audience appreciation of ITV plays seen in the London area would be available, so that comparison could be made with plays shown in the West End theatre. Plays which achieved popularity in provincial theatres have not been included.

However, the principal point that needs to be commented upon is once again the absence of 'controls'. Factors tending to increase or decrease the length-of-run of a play have already been mentioned in Chapter 6. It was noted that it is very difficult indeed for factors other than audience appreciation to *extend* the life of a play. However, a wide variety of factors limit the life of a play. A play may have its life artificially limited owing to theatre policy—as for example in the Aldwych Theatre (Royal Shakespeare Company), the National Theatre, the Royal Court Theatre, and the Hampstead Theatre Club. Again, although a play cannot be sustained by praise from critics, bad Press notices can kill a play and cause it to collapse after a very few performances. Theatre people talk (perhaps with some measure of self-justification) of extraneous factors which can ruin a play's chances of success: for example, people are reputed to be reluctant to go to the theatre in very hot weather. Again, the day on which a play opens is believed to have some effect. The time of year in which a play opens is also believed to have some effect—usually disadvantageous. A further reason for not including a 'control' group of 'failed' plays is that the texts of these plays tend not to be published, and it is extremely difficult to get hold of original manuscripts or prompt copies. However, once again, the present chapter notes plays which were performed in the period being studied but which failed to achieve the criteria of popularity being used for the present study.

Texts of all the plays covered in the present study are available; a list of sources is given in Appendix C, Table C.2.

DIMENSIONS OF CONTENT ANALYSIS USED IN THE PRESENT STUDY
I have already outlined the dilemma facing the content analyst—whether to apply a vast range of analytical devices and dimensions to a few plays or a few dimensions of analysis to many. Mention was made of the danger of failing to give an accurate picture of the overall quality of an object by paying too detailed attention to single parts of it. The system of analysis adopted for the present study is inevitably a compromise. It concentrates on those items most likely to validate or refute the theoretical implications and previous observations discussed in the first six chapters of the book.

A limited number of content-analysis dimensions has been adopted in the hope that they will reveal clearly what individual plays are *about* and what the *goals* or *motives* of the characters are in the societies in which they find themselves. Five principal dimensions will be discussed: (a) themes; (b) play types; (c) goals and motives of characters in plays; (d) setting in which play takes place; (e) ending.

In describing how content-analysis dimensions were chosen, it is customary to explain how the dimensions have been pre-tested with independent observers; the purpose of this exercise is to indicate that the dimensions of analysis are in fact suitable ones. The value of the dimensions being used in this study are: first that it is usually not difficult to see what a play is *about* and what the *goals* and *motives* of the characters are. (It is more difficult to rate the sympathetic-unsympathetic, tough–tender, etc., qualities of characters.) Secondly, the principal dimension being used (themes) has been tested already in two studies—that of McGranahan and Wayne (1947) and that of S. W. Head (1954). The six major divisions of theme: love, idealism, power, career, outcast, and morality, have been taken over bodily from the McGranahan and Wayne study. A detailed quotation (chapter 6) outlines how these dimensions are used; the present chapter describes some of the sub-divisions of these major themes that are used in the present study.

Circumstances did not permit me to submit all the plays being studied to the independent judgement of other persons. There is, therefore, a danger of subjectivity in the content-analysis judge-ments being made. This danger cannot be circumvented; it can only be noted. With most plays the dimensions of content analysis being used could be applied with relative ease. In a few cases, for example *Five Finger Exercise*, the independent judgement of other persons was sought. Where any reasonable doubt about the validity of content-analysis dimensions exists in my mind, mention is made in the section recording the results of the analysis.

Dimensions of analysis—especially themes, goals and motives, setting—have only been recorded where they were essential to the structure of a play or where they were present throughout the entire sequence of the play. It is, of course, possible for a play to have several themes simultaneously. Indeed, it will be argued later that some of the most successful plays are probably successful precisely *because* they employ several fundamentally important themes simultaneously. Similarly, a leading character in a play may have a mixture of motives: for example, in competing for the affection of a girl, a man may have the goal of 'getting married' and simultaneously the goal of exercising 'domination' over a competitor for the girl. Again, it is possible for play types to be combined in a variety of ways. For example, detective stories may be presented as thrillers, as comedies, as mysteries, or as psychological explorations of character.

THE ANALYSIS OF THEMES
LOVE THEMES

In plays dealing with love themes, there can of course be a variety of different types of love theme. Some examples will be given of the seven principal categories employed in the present analysis. The numbers in parentheses after the titles of plays refer to the plays thus numbered in Appendix C.

1. *Youthful Love versus Parents.* The typical situation in plays with this theme is that parents either object to the match being made between two people, as happens in *The Orange Orchard* (20), or interfere with the married life of two young people, as happens in *A Fair Cop* (59). To achieve the love the young people wish for, the opposition of parents must be overcome.

2. *True Love versus Unwholesome Love.* In plays with this theme, we are offered a manifest contrast between a clearly desirable love match and, for example, the false allures, or immoral overtures, of some competing person. In *Mother of Men* (45) a young fisherman, Malcolm McDonald, is engaged to be married to a highly desirable local girl, Fiona MacNeil. He is distracted from his duty by the advances of a local beauty, Jessie McCrae, whose sole object is to have power over the young men in Mrs McDonald's family. It is essential to the play that the conflict between Malcolm's 'desirable' love for Fiona and his 'undesirable', 'unwholesome' love for Jessie be resolved.

3. *Love versus Temporary Misunderstanding.* Plays with this theme typically deal with the difficulties of married persons. For example, in *A Chance to Shine* (67) a married woman, Eva, with an honours degree from a university, but no profession, is feeling frustrated now that her children have grown up. She goes to stay with her sister, Midge, and falls in love with Midge's husband. After furious resistance from Midge, the unhappy entanglement is resolved, and Eva returns to her husband.

4. *Love versus Ideals and Higher Values.* In plays with this theme, the clearly desirable love between two individuals is impaired, or obstructed, by the ideals of either or both of the partners. For example, in *The Small Back Room* (44) Sammy lives together with

Susan although they are not married. It is clear that they are deeply in love; however, Sammy, who is a cripple, has not thought himself worthy of her—and has not offered to marry her. The consummation of their love (in marriage) is, therefore, impeded by Sammy's desire to justify himself and show himself worthy of her. Also, Sammy is dedicated to his scientific work in the war effort; he becomes involved in the dangerous operation of de-fusing a bomb—disregarding any possible obligation he may have to the woman he loves.

5. *Idealists' Love versus Social Norms.* In plays with this theme, the love of the hero and/or heroine for another person is contrasted sharply with the standards of the prevailing society. In *Dark Victory* (12) by George Brewer and Bertram Bloch, a distinguished brain surgeon, with a very clear conception of the 'whole' life—which involves treating patients as complete human beings and living among natural beauty—falls in love with a rich and beautiful young patient whom he has treated. The young woman is a member of the 'smart set' of Long Island, New York. When she learns from the surgeon, with whom she has fallen deeply in love, that she only has a few months to live, she rejects his love and throws herself with fanatical energy into the manifestly stale, flat, and unprofitable round of 'society' parties and late-night escapades. However, she gradually realizes the futility of her way of life, particularly as her death is drawing nearer, and joins the surgeon. Although both of them know that she will die within a few months, they live a life of exemplary domestic happiness—in sharp contrast to the type of 'gay' life the young girl has been used to and which is expected of her by her former friends. The surgeon devotes himself to his wife, although he knows that she will soon die, and she devotes herself to him. Having established for herself that the surgeon's love is genuine, and not merely pity for her condition, the young girl agrees with him to lead a 'normal' life until the inevitable death comes upon her. In a tense final scene, she helps him to prepare to go to an urgent case, although she knows that she will die before he returns—having experienced the long-predicted symptoms of her imminent death.

6. *Power Conflicts for Love.* In plays with this theme the 'eternal triangle' is usually the subject. Two persons are in competition for the love of one. This theme occurs in conjunction with the

true-love versus unwholesome-love theme in *Mother of Men* (45) in which two of Malcolm McDonald's brothers are in competition with him for the love of the 'unwholesome' Jessie. Again, in *Desert Duel* (10) a struggle goes on between two Army officers for the love of a woman who is the wife of one of the officers. The two men clearly dislike each other strongly on account of their competing love interest. However, in the event, the husband—who is an idealist—saves the life of his fellow officer.

7. *Love versus Outcast Status*. In plays of this type the typical situation is for a socially abnormal, physically abnormal, or generally 'alienated' character to aspire to love. The outcast may seek love either for its own sake, or so as to change his outcast status and be accepted into a desired society. Norman Wisdom's films typically illustrate the latter. Norman, as, for example, a bumbling and incompetent washer-of-police-cars, aspires to join the police force (desired society) and to win the hand of a beautiful girl in a social class above his own. Norman, by some accidental heroics, simultaneously wins the hand of his desired girl and is accepted into the police force. However, an example of the former type of theme occurs in *Another Man's Life* (19), in which a young man, Simon Chart, takes lodgings in the home of a man who has died trying to save Simon from an ill-judged suicide attempt. Simon's motive is to purge himself of the guilt he feels for destroying the family life of the man who has died. Simon wishes, as an outcast from normal society, to realize himself and to be accepted again. He lives anonymously with the late rescuer's family; he falls in love with his rescuer's widow. Although she is in love with another man, who has been comforting her since the death of her husband, she responds warmly to Simon, who regains his confidence and is accepted (and accepts himself) as a member of the society from which he had sought to escape.

8. *Miscellaneous Love Themes.*

IDEALIST THEMES

9. *Idealist versus External Obstacles*. (Materialists, ideological enemies, mass stupidity, etc.) The typical play showing an idealist battling against external obstacles is the war play in which, for example, officers with a regard for the safety of their men, or for a sane society, sacrifice their own opportunities for promotion or

prestige by battling against impersonal and nonsensical rules, or Nazi ideology. Examples of this type of idealism occur in, for example, *No-man's Land* (7), *Stalingrad* (72), and *The July Plot* (73). However, other types of ideal can be shown in contrast with opposition. For example, in *The Small Back Room* (44), already mentioned, Sammy's devotion to his scientific efforts in the war is shown in sharp contrast to the place-seeking of one of his superiors who has little regard for scientific 'truth'. Again, in *No Deadly Medicine* (43) a brilliant young pathologist's respect for scientific evidence and keenness to do his medical duty is shown to be in sharp contrast to the casualness of his superior.

10. *Idealist versus Internal Obstacles.* (Personal love, loyalty, softness of character, etc.) *Desert Duel* (10), already mentioned, provides an example of a man who fulfils his duty to a brother officer against the internal conflict engendered by the fact that his brother officer is his wife's lover. A familiar story, presented in the stage play *Ross* (94), tells the story of Lawrence of Arabia struggling to maintain his ideal of 'the will' against a personal softness of character, which his enemies succeed in exposing.

POWER THEMES

11. *Power Conflicts in Relation to Idealism.* Power themes typically deal with the struggle for power or domination between two individuals or groups of individuals. The war plays already cited (7, 72, 73) as examples of idealists conflicting with external obstacles in the form of ideological enemies and militaristic stupidity provide convenient examples of this type of theme.

12. *Power Conflict in Relation to Outcast Status.* Two plays provide examples of this type of theme. In *The Caine Mutiny Court Martial* (32) the power struggle has taken place between Lieutenant Maryk and Captain Queeg. Maryk has taken over command of the ship *Caine* from Captain Queeg during a typhoon. The play centres on the court-martial of Maryk, in which both men are trying to justify their behaviour. Maryk's defence counsel succeeds in demonstrating that Captain Queeg suffers from a form of paranoia; Queeg is, therefore, psychologically abnormal and, according to the criteria being used to define outcasts, an outcast from normal society. In *Moving On* (74), a young soldier, Taffy Thomas, has accidentally killed one of his friends with a Bren gun in the Korean War. In the detention centre to which he

is sent, he comes under the control of a sadistic sergeant, Tucker. Tucker, by systematic cruelty, tries to make Taffy admit that he *deliberately* killed his friend. The play is a psychological power struggle between the two men, in which the outcast (Taffy), who is technically a criminal, engages in a battle of will with Tucker. He finally kills Tucker, having been driven beyond the limits of human endurance. Both of these plays involving power conflicts in relation to outcast status end unhappily for the outcast. However, it is clearly possible for the outcast to win and for the play to end on a different note.

13. *Miscellaneous Power Conflicts*. Plays with miscellaneous power conflicts cover all power struggles other than those covered in the two previous categories. For example, *Plunder* (21) shows a power struggle between two men for some jewels. Power conflicts for love are included under the love theme; however, there can be struggles for power for a variety of other objectives—for example, wealth, prestige, political advancement, a coveted job, position, etc. All such conflicts are included in this category.

OUTCAST THEMES

14. *Physically Abnormal Person versus Normal Society*. The clearest example of a play containing this theme is *The Weeping Madonna* (1), in which Tina, a lonely little girl with a dislocated hip, is an 'outcast' from the normal society of her physically unhandicapped friends. She is also rejected by her parents, who are preoccupied with other activities—including playing a cynical confidence trick. In the play, by an 'accident'—or was it a miracle?—the little girl's hip is cured and she is also accepted by her parents. Again, in *The Orange Orchard* (20), the central character is an old lady, Mrs Martha Blanchard, who lives with her daughter Maude and her son-in-law Tom White. Because of her age and apparently failing health, she is regarded as a nuisance by her daughter and son-in-law. In the small society shown to us, she is an outcast.

15. *Criminal or other Socially Abnormal Person versus Normal Society*. Plays that examine the reasons for the criminality of a criminal, and explore psychologically the nature of his alienation from society, are included in this category; plays that deal with illegal, immoral, or sinful behaviour by ordinary persons are normally included under the morality-theme categories. An

example of the criminal outcast is *The Case of Private Hamp* (48), which explores the reasons why a private soldier in the First World War deserted from his unit. The emphasis is not on the wickedness of desertion by a normal person, but on understanding *why* this particular young man, Hamp, deserted. Again, *The Caine Mutiny Court Martial* (32) combines the power conflict in relation to outcast status with an exploration of the outcast nature of Queeg. The play is therefore classified under both headings. The well-known play *Pygmalion* is to be classified under this heading; Eliza Doolittle, as a vulgar, working-class girl with an appallingly grating voice, is 'outcast' from upper-middle-class and upper-class society, to which she vainly aspires. The play concentrates on the transformation of Eliza from being a socially unacceptable 'outcast' to being a society lady.

CAREER THEMES

16. *Career Themes*. There are no sub-categories of these themes. In career themes, the central character is attempting to win personal success in his occupation, to make money, create a work of art, or advance his professional status. The goal is personal achievement, not the success of an ideal, system, way of life, nation or other super-individual institution. Various obstacles block the path to success. Among the plays studied, there are no examples of this particular theme. The emphasis in *No Deadly Medicine* (43) is quite clearly on a power conflict in relation to idealism. The young pathologist who comes into conflict with the old pathologist of casual ways is clearly interested in his own professional advancement. However, the play does not centre on the young pathologist's career; this is only mentioned in the closing scene. The emphasis is entirely on the struggle between the two men over the way in which the pathology laboratory should be run.

MORALITY THEMES

17. *Conflicts resulting from Immoral Love*. Plays which deal with the temporary straying from the straight and narrow path by a clearly sympathetic character who gets entangled with another woman and then returns to his lawful wife are typically classified under the love theme. However, the emphasis in some plays is on the evil that results from misdirected, or immoral, love. In

Something to Hide (70) a complicated detective-thriller play is built upon the unlawful doings of Howard Holt, who has been having an affair with a girl Julie Grant and has tried to keep his wife ignorant of the fact. In a different style, *The White Falcon* (5) tells the story of King Henry VIII and Ann Boleyn. Anxious, at any cost, to have a son and heir, Henry ruthlessly arranges the annulment of his marriage to Catherine of Aragon. In thus pursuing his 'love impulse' he overthrows the law of the land, the law of God, and the bounds of common human decency.

18. *Immoral Parents versus Youthful Love.* The sort of situation that might be involved in, for example, *The Skin Game* (40) would be one in which the legitimate aspirations to love (and possibly, thereafter, marriage) of two young people was thwarted by parents whose motives were not merely obstructive—in which case the play would be classified as 'Youthful Love versus Parents'—but were evil, involving some sort of dark-dealing and law-breaking.

19. *Law or Honest Folk versus Criminals.* Into this category fall all plays whose themes concentrate on detecting, thwarting, punishing, etc., the unlawful, sinful deeds of otherwise normal persons. The bank robbers in *A Fair Cop* (59) or the corrupt judge in *The Seat of the Scornful* (9) and the villains tracked down in numerous detective stories point to the presence of this theme.

20. *Ordinary Citizens versus the Law.* Although law-breaking appears in many of the morality-theme plays, a distinction must be drawn between the law-breaking of persons who are clearly criminals and the understandable (if not justifiable) law-breaking of ordinary citizens. For example, in *Hour of the Rat* (34) a young Treasury official sets out to murder a Japanese war criminal who has so far escaped arrest. Although we can understand the motives of vengeance in the mind of the young Treasury official, he is still breaking the law. Again, in *Murder on the Agenda* (42) five ex-soldiers have sworn to avenge the death of one of their comrades by killing the man who betrayed him to the Nazis and who was, therefore, ultimately responsible for his subsequent mental breakdown. Again, although we can understand to a certain extent the motives of the ex-soldiers, their action is clearly unlawful and unjustified. This distinction between two types of situation in which law-breaking takes place will prove useful

when the stresses in social structure that might tempt ordinary citizens to criminal behaviour are noted.

CLASSIFICATION OF TYPES OF PLAY

For the purposes of this study, the type of play is much less important than the *theme* of the play and the *goals/motives* of the characters involved. However, it will be important to note the manner in which a theme is *treated*; therefore, a rough classification of play types has been adopted. Plays have been placed into one of the following eleven categories according to the manner of treatment of the subject-matter: (1) farce, (2) straight/psychological, (3) comedy, (4) war setting (any), (5) detective story, (6) thriller, (7) documentary style, (8) mystery, (9) science fiction, (10) fantasy, (11) relying on ideas. In addition, a subcategory was demarcated of plays involving murder—actual, supposed, or planned. These categories are not intended to be mutually exclusive; indeed, several plays involve a combination of types. For example, several different types of play may be presented as 'thrillers': the detective story *Something to Hide* (70) is presented as a thriller; *You're a Long Time Dead* (27) is a comedy-thriller; *The Small Back Room* (44) is primarily a psychological study, though the climax of the play, which can be foreseen from the first scene, is an episode in which the hero defuses a bomb of a type that has killed several persons earlier in the play; *The Critical Point* (23) presents some fairly deep psychological study in the form of a science-fiction thriller. Typically, however, the thriller involves an intrinsically frightening episode, such as a murder. The murder can be one that we would earnestly like to see thwarted—as in *A Woman of Property* (16), in which cruel persons systematically starve to death and ill-treat a mentally retarded woman in order to get her property. Again, our sympathy may be with the killer, and we inwardly hope that the murder will take place—as in *Hour of the Rat* (34), already mentioned. Or the thriller can involve straightforward terror—as for example in *Shut out the Night* (26), in which a young girl is left alone in a house with a man we gradually realize to be a pathological sex-killer.

A word of explanation may be in order about one or two of the categories which are not self-explanatory. The category 'straight/psychological' deals with plays that concentrate on a systematic penetration of motives and states of mind. *The Caine Mutiny Court Martial* (32) is an example of this, involving, as it does, the analysis of the states of mind and motives of the two persons in conflict. Again, *The Weeping Madonna* (1) gives a vivid portrayal of the loneliness of the crippled child. *Moving On* (74) presents the mental torture of the young soldier who is being ill-treated by the sadistic sergeant in a detention centre. *Another Man's Life* (19) is a straightforward treatment of the outcast theme—exploring the alienation of Simon Chart as he tries to remove the guilt he feels for causing the death of the man who tried to rescue him from his suicide attempt. The power struggle between the two pathologists in *No Deadly Medicine* (43) is dealt with in straightforward analytical terms. War plays can be treated in a variety of ways simultaneously—occasionally as comedies, or, as with *Reluctant Heroes*, as farces; but commonly they involve a straight psychological approach to the states of mind of the characters involved. This is particularly the case when an idealist is involved —struggling against external forces (for example Nazism) or against his internal desire to forget his military duty (as happens in *Desert Duel* (10), for example).

The distinction between farce and comedy is sometimes difficult to draw. In both cases the characters involved must have some degree of credibility. However, farces commonly portray stereotyped characters whose actions involve much slapstick humour and rushing in-and-out of doors, beds, windows, etc. Comedies, on the other hand, present characters in a little more depth, though their motives are either assumed or explicit. It is possible for a comedy to be combined with a straight/psychological approach; but comedies of manners, in which no penetrating analysis of characters takes place, and situation comedies, in which the humour is based on the complicated and difficult situation in which characters find themselves, are clearly different from farce. The language tends to be realistic, the situation more probable (if not completely so) than that in farce, and the humour verbal rather than physical.

Detective stories can, of course, be combined with other types of play. The combination of detective story with thriller has already been noted. Detective stories can also be presented as 'Why-' rather than 'Whodunits'. They can also be presented as comedies or as straightforward documentary-style plays.

The category 'documentary style', again, overlaps with several other styles. It is used primarily for plays in which events of distant or recent history are dealt with in a realistic fashion, with emphasis on historical accuracy. The technique is usually used for war plays—as for example in *Stalingrad* (72); *The July Plot* (73); *The Joel Brandt Story* (76); it is also used for *The White Falcon* (5).

The category 'mystery' is used for plays in which the supernatural occurs—whether or not an explanation of the supposedly supernatural phenomenon is given. 'Fantasy' is used to describe plays that involve either surrealistic techniques of presentation or subject-matter that cannot clearly be regarded as science fiction. An example is *Trilby* (39), a melodrama dealing with the hypnotic powers of Svengali over a young girl whom he turns into a singer of fame. Plays by G. B. Shaw would commonly appear in this category—perhaps in combination with another category. A play like *The Chairs* by Ionesco—a fantasy built upon an idea—or *The New Tenant* or *The Bald Primadonna*, by the same author, would go in this category along with another category. Again, Arnold Wesker's *Chips with Everything* would be noted in this category, along with another category.

From this brief description, it will be seen that the classification of play types is primarily a convenient method of sorting types of treatment; it is not intended to be a definitive method of systematizing the content of plays.

ANALYSIS OF GOALS/MOTIVES

The goals or motives of the principal characters in a play are obviously of considerable interest. Clearly, there can be a similarity of goals/motives between heroes and heroines and their opponents (villains)—particularly in plays that involve a straight struggle for power. In the presentation of results, the goals/motives of heroes and heroines and their opposition (and villains if the two are coincidental) will be dealt with separately. However, the main categories of analysis are as follows.

Success. This category is used to describe goals involving the seeking of prestige, upward social mobility, professional advancement, etc. The central character (sympathetic/hero) may have such a goal/motive. However, it is commonly those opposed to central/sympathetic characters, or the villains, who have success of this kind as their goal. For example, in *No Deadly Medicine* (43) it is clear that the idealistic young pathologist wishes to succeed in his profession. However, his interests in the pathology laboratory are clearly different from those of his opponent—the old doctor who simply wishes to maintain a position of power and prestige. In *The Small Back Room* (44) Sammy's opponents in the scientific research laboratory seek political advantage rather than usable scientific results. In *Heart to Heart* (69), a television interviewer is involved in a confrontation with a people's politician whose sole desire is for political power. The success motives of opposition characters need not be sinister, though they may be unfeeling; for example, Professor Higgins in *Pygmalion* is primarily interested in bringing to a successful conclusion his experiment in training Eliza Doolittle for life in high society; he is largely indifferent to the personal happiness of Eliza. Again, in *Wednesday's Child* (68) the parents of an unmarried mother are more interested in maintaining a façade of middle-class respectability and in upward social mobility than in the personal problems of their daughter.

Power. Power goals or motives aim at achieving a super-ordinate position. Frequently, idealists are in direct conflict with villains. For example, the war plays previously mentioned (*The July Plot* (73), *The Joel Brandt Story* (76), *Stalingrad* (72)) show men of ideals in conflict with Nazis. In *Moving On* (74) the main characters are involved in a power struggle for domination in a tense psychological situation—the young soldier Taffy (who seeks justice and self-justification) in direct power conflict with Sergeant Tucker (who is dominated solely by sadism).

Money, Jewels, Wealth, etc. The goals of either hero or villain may be simply gain. In *Plunder* (21), the hero wants money that is the rightful due of his fiancée, on her behalf; the villain wants the same money for personal gain.

Protection, Rescue. These goals include those aimed at the rescue or protection of the self or other people. The hero of *Plunder* (21) is seeking to protect his fiancée from the machinations of evil persons. Again, Joel Brandt, the hero of the play of that name (76), is an idealist whose aim is to protect his fellow Jews from Eichmann.

Affection, Love, Marriage. These goals may be those of the hero or of the villain. Again, in *Plunder* (21) both the hero and his opponent/accomplice want to get married—fortunately to different persons. Power struggles can be involved with the desire of the conflicting characters to get married. Frequently, specially in comedies, two young people simply want to get married; they have to struggle against the opposition of others.

Preservation of Marriage, Love. For those who are already married, a goal may be a successful married life, settled, happy, secure. Some circumstances in the play may interrupt the comfortable and happy state of affairs. The preservation of marriage may be presented as the goal of the central character, as in *Desert Duel* (10) for example, or of an opposition character—as for example in *A Chance to Shine* (67) in which a young teacher, Midge, resists the heroine's attempts at self-realization, which would in fact have involved the bearing away of Midge's husband!

Self-realization. In the last-mentioned example, *A Chance to Shine*, Eva is a frustrated, middle-class, university-educated woman whose children have grown up; she feels a sense of desolation, and wants to do something to bring back her sense of being needed. Again, in *The Small Back Room* (44) Sammy is trying to 'realize himself' not only as a scientist of integrity but also as a *man* worthy of the love of Susan. In *Cross of Iron* (61) a conflict develops between a German officer with a strong sense of personal honour and other officers, who maintain that he has betrayed his trust by letting a U-boat be captured. So strong is the hero's sense of honour that he refuses to take the easy way out of the difficult situation he is in. In *Another Man's Life* (19) Simon Chart is trying to re-orient himself in the society from which he has tried to escape by suicide. In *Heart to Heart* (69) David Mann, a television 'inquisitor', is drinking heavily; he knows that his fame is based on an inner lie. He is keen to be doing something he considers worth while; the play concentrates on his re-discovery of what *is* worth while, and his consequent self-realization.

Revenge. Revenge may be a motive of hero or villain. With heroes, sympathetic characters, the desire for revenge is one with which the audience can sympathize. The revenge taken by Taffy in *Moving On* (74) against the sadistic Sergeant Tucker is understandable. Again, the young Treasury official in *Hour of the Rat* (34) has a reasonable motive for killing the notorious Japanese war criminal. In contrast, the revenge motives of villains on the opposition tend to be unreasonable. In *Something to Hide* (70)

Karen Holt kills her husband for revenge—a rather extreme act in the circumstances. In the detective play *The Body of a Girl* (31) the killer of the schoolgirl turns out to be a farmer who was jilted by the girl and who has murdered her out of a desire for revenge.

An Ideal. The goals of heroes are frequently idealistic—common sense, the 'good' society, honour, professional integrity, etc. The central character of *Mother of Men* (45) wants to bring up a family worthy of her late fisherman husband. The idealist heroes of the war plays (7, 72, 73) are struggling for the safety of their troops, or for a rational society, against the unreasonable or insane instructions of ideological or militarist bigots. Ideals of professional integrity figure largely in *The Small Back Room* (44) —scientific integrity; in *The Critical Point* (23)—scientific discovery; in *No Deadly Medicine* (43)—medical thoroughness; in *The Intervener* (57)—the upholding of the law regardless of injury and humiliation to the self. Occasionally the unsympathetic character may be shown as having some sort of ideal—in *The White Falcon* (5) King Henry VIII's immoral love impulses are combined with an almost fanatic desire to bear a son to be heir to the English throne.

Thrills. These goals include sexual thrills, a 'good time', and general excitement for its own sake. The desire for thrills may be understandable and, in its outcome, relatively innocent. In *You're a Long Time Dead* (27) the hero is an educated person married to a vulgar, working-class wife whose brash ways constantly offend his sensitivity. He seeks the thrill of emotional entanglement with a beautiful and educated young woman with whom he shares a common interest in photography. He is tempted to poison his wife partly to gratify his desire to 'have' the educated young woman; however, he comes to realize that the young woman cares nothing for him—she only shares his interest in photography. On the other hand, opposition characters (villains) use their desire for thrills damagingly. In *The Critical Point* (23) the bored wife of a young scientist humiliates him in front of his superior simply for 'kicks'. Again, Jessie in *Mother of Men* (45) distracts Malcolm McDonald from his fiancée, Fiona, simply for the fun of it. In more sinister vein, the murderer in *Shut out the Night* (26) seeks to satisfy an insane urge to kill young women.

Acceptance into Desired Society. This is commonly the goal of the outcast. Eliza in *Pygmalion* wants to become a 'lady'; old Mrs

Blanchard in *The Orange Orchard* (20) wants to be accepted into the family of her daughter. Again, this type of acceptance can be the goal of hero or of villain. More commonly, however, it is the goal of the hero.

Justice. This is commonly the goal of detectives and other law-enforcement persons in competition with rogues in morality-type plays. It can, however, be the shared motive of opposition characters in a power conflict—as, for example, in *The Caine Mutiny Court Martial* (32) in which both central characters (Maryk and Queeg) seek justice. In *The Case of Private Hamp* (48) the military court martial—which represents the opposition to the outcast character—desires justice by the letter of the law; in this case, our sympathies are entirely on the side of the unfortunate Hamp. In *The White Falcon* (5) some of the characters in opposition to the wishes of King Henry VIII desire justice—for example, Archbishop Cranmer.

Illicit Love. This goal is almost exclusively the goal of villains in plays where conflicts arise from immoral love-impulses.

These categories represent the principal ways in which the goals of heroes and heroines and their opponents are classified.

CLASSIFICATION OF PLAY SETTING

Plots can of course be isomorphic regardless of setting. However, it will be of some interest to see whether the setting in which a play takes place represents the setting in which the majority of the play's audience spend their lives. Four main categories are used as follows: (i) upper/upper-middle-class settings; (ii) middle-class settings; (iii) lower-middle/working-class settings; (iv) other settings—including for example war. A note has also been made of the number of plays involving a court scene at some point or other, regardless of whether or not the overall setting fits one of the other four categories. To be deemed as fitting into one of the first three settings, the principal action of the play must take place in an environment clearly associated with the social characteristics of the principal characters. For example, the designation 'upper/ upper-middle-class setting' is given to plays that take place in the homes of higher professional persons or rich and leisured persons, or in upper-middle-class hotels. The designation 'middle-class setting' is given to plays that take place in the homes of, for example, a schoolmaster (*The Body of a Girl* (31)). *A Chance to*

Shine (67) also takes place mainly in the home of a school-teacher. *Wednesday's Child* (68) is set in a middle-class suburb. The designation 'lower middle-class/working-class setting' is used when the play takes place primarily in the home of a lower middle-class or working-class person. For example, *A Fair Cop* (59) takes place in the new home of a humble police constable with eminently working-class parents interfering all the time. *Another Man's Life* (19) takes place in a working-class home. *Mother of Men* (45) is set in a Scottish fisherman's cottage. Some plays, especially detective plays or war plays, may involve the hunt for a villain in a variety of settings. The fourth category is used for these plays. Similarly, the revenge play *Hour of the Rat* (34), although dealing with the activity of an obviously middle-class person, is set in a variety of places—in the homes of several of the hero's former prisoner-of-war-camp colleagues.

CLASSIFICATION OF ENDINGS

Four categories are used to describe the endings of plays: (a) happy; (b) unhappy/tragic; (c) ambiguous/unresolved; (d) just—whether happy or otherwise. The first three categories are self-explanatory. However, several plays—particularly detective stories or revenge plays in which the hero (with whom we sympathize) is in fact convicted for his revenge—can hardly be described as happy (if the hero has been sent to prison) nor can they be described as unhappy (if the murderer has been discovered in a detective story). Plays of this kind are frequently 'resolved' and we are left with the feeling that things are as they should be. The designation 'just' is used for plays where a resolution of conflict has taken place, where a crime has been unravelled, where somebody has been brought to justice, but where the other descriptions of ending would be inappropriate.

Summary of Results

A detailed description of the social content of the 114 popular plays may be found in the thesis upon which this study is based (Goodlad, 1969). The following paragraphs give a brief summary of the principal findings. They are not startling, and anyone familiar with the West End theatre or with television drama will feel himself on familiar ground.

1. Plays containing either morality themes or love themes or both account for 79 per cent of all plays. Morality themes are the most frequent, occurring in 52·6 per cent of all plays. Love themes occur in 43·9 per cent of plays. There is then a considerable drop to outcast themes, which occur in 26·3 per cent of the plays.

2. The morality plays deal with transgressions against society. Most commonly the transgressors are motivated by a desire for more than reasonable power (social control), a desire for money, the wish for revenge for some (supposed) wrong, and illicit sex. Nearly half the morality plays (43·3 per cent) involved murder and 10 per cent of them involved court scenes. The typical morality format is a detective story, often also a thriller, with a clear-cut ending involving a just solution to the social problem involved.

3. The love plays deal with problems raised by monogamy. Nearly a third of the love plays are concerned with misunderstandings that arise within marriage. Of the remainder, 24 plays deal with the problem of getting a spouse (nearly half the total of love plays) and 9 (18 per cent) deal with the assimilation of an outcast into society through love and affection. Love themes characteristically appear in comedies or farces and have happy outcomes. When they appear in comedies they are often also given straight/psychological treatment—that is to say, motives are not taken for granted but are dealt with sensitively.

4. Outcast themes occur in more than a quarter of all the popular plays (26·3 per cent). The most frequent pattern is for the social outcast (who is occasionally physically abnormal too) to be accommodated in the desired society. More than half the outcast themes receive straight/psychological treatment and a third of them occur in comedies; there is overlap in this.

5. A small cluster of plays (15·8 per cent of the total 114) involve idealists. These plays tend to be war plays with unhappy endings involving the death of the hero. The ideal followed by the hero is not vainglorious: it is pre-eminently social. These plays typically present characters of high moral virtue who are attempting to save or protect other members of their society regardless of personal cost.

6. No plays with career themes occurred in the sample. There were no mystery plays (dealing with the supernatural) and no

plays based primarily on ideas (political, religious, metaphysical, etc.). There were only two science-fiction plays.

7. The plays in the sample were skewed upwards in their settings—upper-class, upper-middle-class, and middle-class settings being over-represented with reference to the actual population of the United Kingdom. But there was no marked pattern of class association with theme. Comedies had a tendency to be set in lower-middle or working-class settings and detective stories in middle-class ones. Ten plays (8·8 per cent) had court scenes. Six of these were concerned with murder.

8. Eleven categories of play type were used for the analysis. For the 114 plays under consideration, 164 types were noted (the eleven categories occurring singly or in combination). The most popular type of treatment was straight/psychological (24·4 per cent). This was followed by comedy (23·2 per cent), thriller (16·5 per cent), detective story (11 per cent), farce (10·4 per cent). The most important association of play types with themes was in the case of farces, which most frequently contained morality themes: sixteen out of seventeen, i.e. 94·1 per cent of farces, did so. Farces often also contained a love theme: ten out of seventeen, i.e. 58·8 per cent, did so. The majority of comedies (71·1 per cent) contained love themes. Detective stories were almost exclusively morality plays: seventeen out of eighteen, i.e. 94·4 per cent. Thrillers, which were frequently in combination with detective stories, contained morality themes on twenty-four out of twenty-seven occasions, i.e. 88·9 per cent. No less than 33 (28·8 per cent) of plays involved murder. The majority of these murder plays (87·9 per cent of them) dealt with morality themes.

9. The most frequent hero-goals were affection, love, getting married, and the preservation of love. Protection/rescue came second, with the pursuit of an ideal third. However, it is the goals/motives of the villains/opposition that give the best indication of the social forces with which the plays deal and which may or may not be socially contained in the drama. The most frequent goal of opposition characters was the exercise of power-for-its-own-sake. The second villain-goal was an excessive desire for money, jewels, and wealth (another form of social power). Thirdly, villains were frequently seeking success, prestige, upward mobility. Their success-seeking was usually presented as unwholesome—a breach of what society could tolerate.

Fourthly, villains were found to be seeking (unreasonable) revenge on virtuous persons who had supposedly done them wrong. Finally, villains were found to be seeking illicit love. In plays with love themes, 'opposition' characters—who could hardly be described as villains—were often seeking affection, love, marriage. What was usually involved was a misunderstanding between a couple (often associated with supposed unfaithfulness), which was happily resolved by the end of the play.

10. The majority of play endings (79·5 per cent) were either happy or just, or both happy and just. In only ten plays were plots left ambiguous or unresolved.

Discussion of the Findings

In her article 'Human Values in Drama', A. H. Cooke (1958) argues that there is today no body of drama that constantly holds before us a common faith or symbol. Although we do have a record of contemporary man's life and problems, these are not, she argues, organized around any standard set of values, simply because this age does not have any organized set of virtues or values pervading it. The findings recorded above point to an opposite conclusion. The popular plays analysed for the present study are overwhelmingly moral in outlook.

A play, almost by definition, deals with some moral issue, showing a conflict between alternative types of social behaviour. But it can do so in a way subversive of traditional morality or by showing the 'hero' alienated and adrift in an apparently hostile and meaningless universe. The morality discussed, and by and large upheld, in the plays reviewed is straightforward, conventional, and simple, even if slightly crude. For the reasons outlined earlier, it is not possible to compare the plays analysed in this study with 'control' plays that were unpopular. However, mention may be made of some of the plays that did not achieve sufficient popularity to be included in the sample.

PLAYS THAT WERE NOT POPULAR
A wide variety of factors other than theme may account for the relative unpopularity of particular plays on television. Complexity of characterization, difficulty of dialogue, unfamiliarity of format

may be possible reasons. However, it is noteworthy that the following selection of plays in the period being studied achieved BBC Reaction Indices of 35 or under:

1958	*The Cherry Orchard*	Chekhov
1961	*Waiting for Godot*	Beckett
1963	*Krapp's last Tape*	Beckett
1963	*The bald Prima Donna*	Ionesco
1964	*The Room*	Pinter

Apart from the fact that these plays are highly intellectual, it is interesting to note that they are all disturbing plays. *The Cherry Orchard* shows an ineffectual upper-middle-class family about to leave their home, which is the centre of their lives. The amusing and weirdly inconsequential dialogue serves only to emphasize the acute pathos of this small disintegrating society. The two tramps in *Waiting for Godot* pass their time at a crossroads in a featureless desert, unsupported by any recognizable society, alone, frightened, pathetic. Krapp is shown alone with his tape-recorder, surrounded by darkness and once again detached from any recognizable society. He is reviewing the pathetic remnants of his past life as recorded in his tape-diary; he is trying to think of something suitable to say on his last tape, but has apparently lived out the best years of his life. As the curtain falls, he is seen staring blankly out into the auditorium as one of his earlier tapes finishes a description of former bliss and then rolls on in silence on the machine with Krapp unable to contribute any more. The typically English middle-class family of *The bald Prima Donna* reduce the very fabric of social existence to incoherence by destruction of language in their meaningless recital of stock phrases. Most frightening of all is Pinter's *The Room*, in which the central character seems to cherish her room as a last refuge from an unintelligible and largely terrifying outside world. Her sanctuary is invaded by characters of singular menace. It does not require physical violence and visible chaos for a society in disintegration to be portrayed; the subtle disintegration portrayed in these plays is much more alarming.

During the period being reviewed, the West End stage of London witnessed a revolution (cf. J. R. Taylor, 1963). *Look Back in Anger* opened on May 8, 1956, heralding a wave of 'new' drama. During the period, important works by Wesker, Pinter, Osborne, Arden, and Behan were produced, together with revivals of Shaw and Ibsen, and London productions of plays by writers whose main work comes from overseas—Beckett, Ionesco, Genet, Sartre, Tennessee Williams. In the Appendix to his book (1963), Taylor noted that out of a total of 71 productions in the main bill of the Royal Court Theatre only 13 plays covered their running expenses. Among those to fail thus were *Platonov* by Chekhov; *Requiem for a Nun* by Faulkner; *The Chairs* and *The Lesson* by Ionesco; *End Game* and *Happy Days* by Beckett; *The Good Women of Setzuan* by Brecht; *The Lion in Love* by Delaney; *The Blacks* by Genet; *The American Dream* by Albee; *Sergeant Musgrave's Dance* by Arden; *Jacques* by Ionesco; *Cock-a-doodle-Dandy* by O'Casey; *Epitaph for George Dillon* by Osborne and Creighton; *Nekrassov* and *Altona* by Sartre; *Major Barbara* by Shaw; *Chips with Everything* by Wesker; and *Orpheus Descending* by Williams.

The following list shows the approximate audience sizes achieved by some plays of widely recognized artistic merit.

	Play	Author	Theatre	No. of Performances	Est. Audience Size
1964	*John Gabriel Borkman*	Ibsen	Duchess	36	18,000
	Carving a Statue	Greene	Haymarket	52	47,000
	The Father	Strindberg	Queen's	38	38,000
	The Seagull	Chekhov	Queen's	90	89,000
	Hedda Gabler	Ibsen	St Martin's	98	54,000
1963	*The Life of Galileo*	Brecht	Mermaid	33	16,000
1960	*Rhinoceros*	Ionesco	Strand (tr. from R. Court)	105	114,000
	A Passage to India	Forster	Comedy	267	211,000
	Rosmersholm	Ibsen	Comedy	86	68,000
1959	*The Long and the Short and the Tall*	Hall	New	205	219,000
	Long Day's Journey into Night	O'Neill	Globe	301	273,000
	Roots	Wesker	Duke of York's	52	44,000
1958	*Cat on a Hot Tin Roof*	Williams	Comedy	132	105,000
1957	*A View from the Bridge*	Miller	Comedy	220	170,000
1956	*The Quare Fellow*	Behan	Comedy	79	63,000
	Waiting for Godot	Beckett	Criterion	226	148,000
	The Family Reunion	Eliot	Phoenix	100	103,000
	The Wild Duck	Ibsen	Saville	68	82,000

Even the most successful of the plays listed achieved barely half the audience of those included in the sample used in this study.

When an adequate theory to account for the popularity of popular drama has been achieved, it may then be possible to account for the relative unpopularity of these plays.

THE FINDINGS IN THE LIGHT OF THE THEORETICAL PREDICTIONS
Theoretical predictions were made in the first four chapters about the likely content of popular drama. Chapter 2 reviewed the way in which folk tales, ritual, and myth—and drama as a descendant of these social phenomena—focus attention on elements of stress in society. Myths and rituals were found to deal with the items of social experience least amenable to rational control. In social experience, items least amenable to rational control are likely to be those potentially disruptive of the moral order of society. It was suggested that in popular drama characters would be found whose social status, and anticipated activity, could be readily identified so that the inter-relationship between characters within social structure could be contemplated. It was predicted that emphasis in characterization was likely to be on stereotypes rather than on the individuality of particular persons. Stereotyped characters were not universally found; but in the plays with the strongest morality interest—i.e. farces—stereotypes prevail. It is interesting to note that of the top ten stage plays (for which the clearest method of comparison between plays exists), three were farces. Although stereotyping of characters was not a universally-found phenomenon, the presence of the major moral themes—morality and love—was discovered in nine out of the top ten plays. Six had morality themes and four had love themes; only one play, *The Teahouse of the August Moon*, had other themes.

It has yet to be demonstrated which matters are most widely found to offer problems of rational control. However, the evidence from the 114 popular plays is that the following items are problematical: in plays with morality themes, the aspirations of characters requiring social control were principally for an 'unreasonable' amount of control over a society; for money; for revenge for some real or imagined wrong; for illicit sexual intercourse. In the second most popular category, plays with love themes, the problems of monogamy were stressed. There are evident strains in the one-man-one-woman ratio prevalent in our society. If sex could be indulged in without social constraint, there would be no problem about getting married, and similarly there would be no problem about containing sex within monogamous marriage.

The third prediction from Chapter 2 was that if popular drama continues the function of ritual as a method of social control, it is likely to be conservative in outlook. Although moral and social conservatism may be largely a feature of the commercial milieu in which drama is produced, it is noteworthy that none of the plays in the sample offered any serious, fundamental challenge to prevailing morality and social conditions. Apart from *An Inspector Calls* (58), which is mildly Socialist, no play offers any such social criticism as the dramas of Wesker, Osborne, or Arden, or even, for that matter, Ibsen.

In Chapter 3, which discussed theories of roles and their implications for the study of popular drama, it was suggested that the function of popular drama may be to sharpen consciousness of roles. The evidence in this study is not sufficient to support or refute this proposition. It is not possible to tell simply from the *content* of popular dramas why people enjoy *watching* them. The delineation of roles in their relationship to each other may be irrelevant in providing enjoyment. However, two points deserve comment. First, the social-class setting of plays over-represented the upper end of the social scale. This phenomenon may simply be due to the fact that many writers are middle-class persons who are more familiar with middle- and upper-middle-class environments than they are with lower-middle-class or working-class environments. It is, however, possible that upper- and upper-middle-class persons are taken as moral references in society. Again, comedies over-represented both upper and lower ends of the social scale in comparison with the sample of plays as a whole. Comedy typically provides opportunity for social commentary and for contrast between the 'manners' of different sections of the community. Comedy may owe its wide popularity in the sample studied to the contrast between social roles that it offers. Secondly, note has been made of the singular popularity of farces as a category of drama. Role-reversal and transvestism are typical devices of farce—they occur in six of the farces in the sample: (36), (59), (66), (85), (86), and (105). As techniques for emphasizing the distinctiveness of particular social roles, role-reversal and transvestism have a long and distinguished history.

The second prediction of Chapter 3 was that the emphasis in popular drama was likely to be on social duty and social integration rather than on demonstrations by characters of existential independence from social obligations. In this respect it is of interest that career themes did not occur in any of the plays in the sample. Again, there were no plays dealing with purely personal or private problems. For example, there were no plays dealing with the way in which individuals have to cope with private agonies or accidental disasters such as sickness, bereavement, or natural catastrophe. The reason for this may be that there are other social mechanisms for dealing with such matters. The important point here, however, is that the problems of individuals that are dealt with in popular plays are concerned with the relationship of individuals to their society. The most popular forms of play were found to be those with morality themes in which social deviance is censured.

In Chapter 4 it was suggested that dramatic stylization might be a method by which rationality could be brought to bear on items of experience likely to be socially disruptive. The potentially disruptive items of experience have already been noted. Social disruption resulting from the undisciplined pursuit of private goals commonly involves violence. Evidence from television research has been cited in Chapter 6 showing that television viewers *dislike* violence in drama. But it is to be noted that the most popular forms of play involve the ultimate violence—murder. Nearly a third of all the plays in the sample (33) involved murder; nearly half the morality plays involved murder. But the treatment is not one in which violence is directly portrayed; typically, violence is assumed to have happened or to be likely to happen, and the emphasis is intellectual—violence is dealt with in a detective story, for instance. The unpleasant fact of violence, and the unruly motives which give rise to it, can be contemplated in detective stories without the viewer having to become emotionally involved in the portrayal of violent and socially disruptive situations. Again, it is noteworthy that violence is almost invariably 'contained' in the plays in the sample. The overwhelming majority of plays have happy and/or just endings.

Secondly, Chapter 4 outlined how moral order can be asserted through the demonstration of disorder. If a function of popular drama is to provide the viewer of the drama with a feeling of the moral coherence of society (or even to control by example the participation of members in their society), the singular popularity of morality themes is of the highest importance. Durkheim's views (*The Division of Labour in Society*, 1893) were that the concept of crime was a product of group feeling, and that group feeling was enhanced by the contemplation of crime.

> As soon as the news of a crime gets abroad, the people unite, and although the punishment may not be predetermined, the reaction is unified. In certain cases, indeed, the people themselves executed the sentence collectively as soon it had been pronounced. . . . The nature of collective sentiments accounts for punishment, and, consequently, for crime. Moreover, we see anew that the power of reaction which is given over to governmental functionaries, once they have made their appearance, is only an emanation of that which has been diffuse in society since its birth. The one is only the reflex of the other. The extent of the first varies with that of the second. (p. 104)

It is difficult to believe that the beholder of a morality play in which a court trial features (and 10 per cent of the morality plays in the sample involved court scenes) is simply 'being entertained'. The singular popularity of morality plays, and the frequency within that category of crime dramas, seems to bear out the theoretical hypothesis that people may watch drama to increase their awareness of the moral norms of the social group of which they are members.

Thirdly, Chapter 4 predicted that if the function of drama is primarily to express or control social cohesion, the most popular forms of drama will be those in which social integration takes place. The research findings support this hypothesis. Happy and just endings are in the majority. In the category of plays with 'outcast' themes (26·3 per cent of the total) the dominant pattern is one of social inclusion.

Fourthly, Chapter 4 predicted that when social ideals are the subject of drama (as opposed to social norms) it was likely that the dramas would deal with the total or almost complete total disruption of society. The evidence from the sample of plays is that 'idealist' themes occur most frequently in war plays. Ideals are upheld by being shown as difficult of achievement. Something very close to a sacrificial ritual appears to be occurring in these plays in which heroes of high moral stature die in the support of notably social ideals.

Chapter 5 reviewed some of the characteristics of the media of mass communication. Evidence was cited that the mass media in general tend to reinforce rather than change opinion and that they tend to reflect social norms—in both ways acting as conservative forces. The value of this evidence, it was suggested, is that it points to the likely content, and possible functions and effects, of drama as a form of mass communication. It may be argued that drama owes its socially supportive content to its nature as a mass medium of communication and to that alone. Because those who provide mass drama depend for their livelihood upon an accurate intuition of what the public wants, it is highly likely that what is enjoyed in the mass media will be very closely in line with what is provided. That is to say, it is not surprising that the drama that has proved to be popular reflects that which is provided. Further, because drama is a popular form of mass-media provision (compared with the other fare offered on, for example, television), it is to be expected that drama as a form of mass communication will exhibit to a heightened extent all the principal functional characteristics of mass media. If mass media in general tend to reinforce opinion and to reflect social norms, it is to be expected—and in the event this has proved to be the case—that drama will be the archetypal form of mass communication.

It is interesting to note that the findings of this survey of popular drama are similar to those of the independent studies cited in Chapter 6. The two principal forms of drama found to be popular by methods differing substantially from those used in the present study were crime and comedy dramas.

Conclusions to be Drawn from the Survey of Popular Drama, 1955–1965

The analysis of the social content of popular drama, 1955–1965, presented in this chapter of the book supports the hypotheses cited earlier:

1. That popular drama is a technique (expressive or instrumental) of organizing social experience;
2. That popular drama informs about social structure—

particularly the moral relationships between individuals in a society upon which the structure of that society depends for its existence;

3. That popular drama expresses emotion at items of private experience (goals/motives) that must be repressed in the interests of social order.

Over and over again, the popular drama reviewed in this study shows potential social problems being resolved and discord turned to harmony. In brief, it is the drama of reassurance.

8

Towards a Theory of the Functions of Popular Drama in Society

Drama and its Possible Functional Equivalents

This book has dealt with single self-contained plays that achieved popularity in the West End theatre of London and on BBC television. There is evidence (for example in M. Imison's study (BBC, 1965) and in the *Report on a Study of Television Play Viewing* (ITA, 1965)) that television series and serials are similar in appeal and content to single, self-contained plays. In the following discussion, it is reasonably safe to assume that the words 'popular drama' could be applied not only to single plays but to fictive series and serials. But they cannot normally be applied to films and musicals, which are complicated by the scenery and the music respectively.

The theory being proposed in this book is that although people watch drama 'to be entertained', popular drama fulfils functions other than those of mere entertainment. It has already been argued (in Chapter 5) that the concept of 'escape' is frequently used too loosely in connection with entertainment. When people watch drama, it is unlikely that they are indulging in the same sort of escape as they do when they sleep, take drugs, or drink alcohol. The likelihood is that they are not escaping *from* their social obligations, but escaping *into* an understanding of society, which is necessary to them for their participation in society.

The principal objective consequence for members of a community in watching drama is likely to be an ordering and organization of their social experience with reference to what is permitted or appropriate behaviour in the community. This ordering of experience may be an expressive aspect of culture—an indicator or monitor of morality, or it may be an instrumental aspect of culture—a technique of control by which a community informs its members about desirable behaviour. If drama has assumed the social functions at one time fulfilled by myth, folk tale, and ritual, it may now be acting as a method of social control.

If this theory is correct, three principal features should be discoverable in all forms of genuinely *popular* drama: first, the drama should inform the community about social structure— particularly about the moral rules (as opposed to detailed legal codes) necessary for the smooth running and survival of the community.

Secondly, popular drama will contain expression of emotion at repressed items in a culture. Where individual goals, motives, lusts, aspirations pull against the conformity required for social stability, drama will deal with these goals and motives in a form of social argument. In the United Kingdom in the period 1955–1965, it appears that the principal items of conflict between individuals and their society were those concerning the degree of social control an individual may have; money; the desire to take violent revenge when wishes are thwarted; the desire for illicit sex; and, closely related to that, the strain set up by the institution of monogamy.

Thirdly, whatever the apparent conflicts in the popular dramas may be, it is likely that the latent conflicts will be those present in the real life of the community. For example, private citizens may not undergo the dramatic tribulations of the characters in Westerns, or detective stories; but the conflicts in those fictions are likely to result from the same anti-social impulses as those encountered by the viewers in their social lives.

Although evidence for the United Kingdom is limited (it is principally taken from the studies by McQuail (1967) and the British Broadcasting Corporation (BBC, 1959)), it can tentatively be proposed that the unit functionally subserved by the popular drama surveyed in this study is the United Kingdom population as a whole excluding those under the age of five. From a practical point of view, it might be wise to consider the population over the age of twelve and under the age of sixty-five. There appears at present to be no evidence of a difference in taste for particular types of drama between persons of different sex, social class, or occupation. However, in the testing of the theory to be proposed in the next section of this chapter, it will be necessary to define the social units subserved by popular drama a little more closely.

The functional needs that drama is likely to meet are those for an understanding of how society is organized (cognitive), for reassurance that this organization is just (affective), and for a mechanism through which emotion may be expressed at elements of social structure that are fundamentally confusing or irritating. For example, it is suggested that people feel a need to contain the irrational within a recognizably rational framework—to contemplate it without being directly and personally involved with it. Violence that breaks out when the processes of rational discussion have been exhausted is fundamentally disturbing; it is likely that any society will need a cultural mechanism with which to contemplate violence and analyse (intuitively) the conditions in which resort to violence is appropriate. It is suggested that popular drama fulfils this functional need by providing a mechanism for social argument.

It is always difficult in functional analysis to *prove* that an item under discussion does in fact fulfil the functions imputed to it. Perhaps all that can be hoped for is that functional analysis can propose a theory, which experimental work can then attempt to *disprove*. The more satisfactory the functional theory, the clearer the specification of functional equivalents. Single, self-contained plays, dramatic series and serials have characteristics in common with several other items of entertainment, and indeed with other cultural items. For example, *conflict* may be the fundamentally appealing aspect of drama. Straightforward conflict can be found in spectator sports, for example, boxing or football. Indeed, in providing the individual with the feeling that he belongs to a community, football-watching may be functionally more effective than the watching of drama. If, as some theory has it, an individual's social identity is closely related to the territory he inhabits, it is not improbable to consider spectator team-sports (such as football, rugby, etc.) as a ritual form of territoriality.

Secondly, plays have plots: *interesting things happen*. The satisfaction of pure, naked curiosity may be the source of appeal in drama. In this respect, drama may be functionally equivalent to news broadcasts. Indeed, news broadcasting, as will be shown below, may be a major functional equivalent to drama.

Thirdly, interest in *character* may be the dominant source of appeal in drama. Novels, documentary films, paperback books on psychology and sociology, gossip with neighbours, etc., may all be functional equivalents for drama if people are simply interested in character.

Fourthly, the element of *mimesis* may be the source of drama's appeal. This appeal may be functionally replicated in circuses, where apes imitate human beings by dressing in clothes and drinking tea and human beings imitate apes by swinging on trapezes; vaudeville shows in which comic actors imitate well-known personalities; night clubs in which transvestite homosexuals dance with clients, may all satisfy needs of individual members of a community to understand social roles and to enjoy the mere act of imitation.

Fifthly, there is inevitably an element of *spectacle* even in the barest drama. It is possible that people simply want to know what other places look like. To this extent, travelogue films, actual travel, and visiting of other people's homes may provide functional equivalents to drama.

Sixthly, it is possible that the simple *control of basic instinct* in socially approved activity may itself be fundamentally interesting to people. Ballroom dancing, as the socially regulated expression of sexual urges, may provide for some members of a community a satisfactory substitute for drama.

Seventhly, characters in plays speak *language*. It is possible that there is a fundamental satisfaction simply in hearing one's native tongue spoken clearly and fluently by competent speakers. 'It does not matter what is said provided it is said beautifully' (Pater). There is for many people an undoubted appeal in the flowery passages of some Shakespeare plays, in the mellifluous recitation of bus routes and the names of household articles in Harold Pinter's plays, in the fluent wit and logic of Bernard Shaw. At a lower level, the verbal vignettes of Peter Cook and Dudley Moore may provide a satisfaction similar to that found in much drama.

Finally, the *themes* of drama may have functional equivalents. There may be alternative ways in a community of learning about social structure, expressing emotion at repressed items, and discussing points of conflict. The following short table indicates some of the principal possible functional equivalents:

	Informing about social structure	Expressing emotion at repressed items	Discussing conflict points
Newspapers, broadcasts	×	×	×
Legal trials	×	×	×
Jokes and joking	×	×	×
Religion	×	×	×

Newspapers and news broadcasts may be very similar to drama in fulfilling the functions specified. Indeed, it is significant that the BBC Survey (1959) found that news broadcasts were second only to drama in popular appeal. The presence in plays of court scenes has already been commented upon. It is interesting that legal trials have many ritual features savouring of stage drama—a special place for the 'audience' to sit in; special clothes for the participants; special language; and a similar concern with morality. If legal trials could take place at times convenient to the general public, could be limited in length, and could sustain moral discussion to the same extent as a play by Agatha Christie, it is highly likely that popular morality-drama and legal trials could be functionally interchangeable. Jokes and joking, which sometimes form a subsidiary element of drama, may, for communities that do not have access to drama, be functionally similar in regulating an individual's awareness of what is and is not appropriate in social behaviour. Finally, religion may be a functional equivalent for drama. It has been argued at length, in Chapter 2, that drama is associated in its origins with religious ritual. It is possible that in particular communities participation in religious activity, particularly where there is explicit discussion of social behaviour (through sermons, homilies, prayers-for-the-souls of deviants, etc.), may be a functional alternative to the consumption of popular drama.

While these items may be the more obvious possible functional equivalents, it is extremely difficult to limit the range of functional equivalents. Should popular songs, for example, be included? Some of the items listed are likely to be purely incidental to the fundamental experience of enjoying popular drama—conflict to a certain extent is unnecessary, for some popular dramas do not contain any conflict worthy of the name; spectacle is likely to be irrelevant; mimesis *per se*, divorced from any social commentary, is also likely to be of peripheral importance. However, in specifying a suitable range of functional equivalents to be included in experimental tests of the hypothesis, it is likely to be safe in practice to limit possible equivalents to those which inform about social structure, which express emotion at repressed items, and which offer a discussion of points of possible conflict between the individual and the community.

To be complete, a functional theory of the place of popular drama in society must include a concept of dynamic and change. If the principal objective measurable consequence of watching popular drama is to provide for a community an ordering and organization of social experience, it is necessary to specify what social conditions are likely to be prevailing when popular drama is no longer found. The following hypothesis is suggested. If a subject ceases to be a principal feature in popular drama, either (a) it is no longer a subject of conflict in the society, or (b) concern about the item is being expressed elsewhere. For example, it is to be expected that a war, when in progress, would be widely covered in news broadcasts, would be the subject of ritual activity, popular marches, 'sit-ins', public discussion, jokes, prayers in church, etc. It is, therefore, highly unlikely that a community would need to discuss war in its popular drama during the conduct of the war. However, it is possible that when a war is over, and when public discussion of the war has waned, some form of recollection in the media will be necessary so that people can organize into social coherence the profound feelings they experienced at the time. For example, war plays, series, and films, are likely to continue for some years after a war has ended. After social upheaval, it is probably necessary for the members of a community to convince themselves retrospectively that they were justly engaged in social behaviour (violence and killing) that they are normally trained to regard as abhorrent. Again, when after a war it becomes necessary to resume normal social relations with persons of another country—for example with Germans and with Japanese for the British—it may be necessary for some plays to portray virtuous qualities of opposition persons. This may be the explanation for the popularity of such plays as *Cross of Iron* (61), *No Man's Land* (7), *Stalingrad* (72), *The July Plot* (73), which appear in the sample of plays reviewed in this study.

It has been noted previously that plays dealing with religion are unusual, and unpopular. It may well be that those who find a need for religious information, discussion, and integration, find adequate provision in the existing rituals of churches.

It is now necessary to suggest possible experiments that may validate or refute some of the theoretical predictions made in this section. The present study has simply identified, by content analysis, the subject-matter of popular drama in a particular community over a period of ten years. To achieve a more comprehensive theory of the function of popular drama in society it is necessary to specify experiments that would compare communities in the presence or absence of drama.

Possible Experiments to Test the Functional Theory of the Place of Popular Drama in Society

At the level of individual psychology, abundant evidence is available about the general functions of the mass media of communication. For example, there is evidence that 'escape' fare on television is likely to function positively for the individual in providing fantasy gratification, compensation for loneliness, a feeling of social integration, etc. Conversely, there is no adequate evidence that television drama is dysfunctional at the individual level. There is, for example, no adequate evidence yet of the much-feared 'narcotizing dysfunction', nor is there adequate evidence that violence in the media is damaging to the individual psyche, though there is evidence that it is not liked. Validation of a functional hypothesis at the social level is, however, much harder to achieve.

As in the choice of dimensions for content analysis, the research worker is faced with a dilemma. He can either collect a great deal of information about a relatively small population, or he can collect cruder information about a large population. Statistical techniques permit a reasonable generalization from limited populations to larger ones. However, in considering the functions of drama in a society, it may not be possible—for practical reasons of time and expense—to apply the most sensitive instruments of social-psychological analysis to a very large group. Thematic apperception, verbal association, and controlled laboratory testing is expensive and time-consuming. Again, the processing of large quantities of information about individuals is difficult and complicated—although computers now increase possibilities enormously. The principal difficulty may be in collecting sufficient information from individuals to differentiate groups of individuals satisfactorily along lines that are likely to be relevant to their supposed functional requirements for drama. However, one can speculate about what is desirable even if its achievement may lie a long way in the future.

Freidson's insistence (1953) that members of the mass audience be considered as members of a social nexus has been noted already. Research in the United Kingdom on the popularity of drama has, to date, ignored the processes of social filtration to which drama is subjected before it reaches the consciousness of individuals and as individuals react to it. The first requirement of research would be to identify in a community those people who are the opinion-leaders, and the social nexus to which individual audience members belong. It would be valuable to discover to what extent individual reactions to particular dramatic fare correspond to those of opinion leaders, for example family members or peer-group leaders. It might, for example, be possible to run controlled tests of drama appreciation with selected groups who are either denied the mediating processes by which they can catch opinions from opinion leaders, or who are changing their group allegiances. It might, for example, be interesting to test the types of drama appreciated by a sample of individuals recruited to a particular organization with its own ethos before they join the organization, and immediately after-wards, and after a period of membership. Videotape-recordings of plays of known social dimensions could be shown to, say, army or police recruits shortly before they join the service, and plays of similar social content could be shown to them when they have had time to find new opinion-leaders in their new communities.

Secondly, it would be interesting to compare the responses of a randomly sampled cross-section of the population matched by age, sex, social class, intellectual ability, occupation, with a sample of members of radical organizations who exhibit discontent with the social order. There is a complicating possibility that manifest reaction *against* social order is latent longing *for* social order. But, with the necessary precautions, it would be interesting to test whether those who are in explicit revolt from the prevailing social order differ in their responses to drama from those who by their actions profess acceptance of it.

Thirdly, it would be interesting to compare with a random

sample of the population a stratified random sample deliberately designed to include minority groups. My wife is German; she reacts strongly against slapstick comedies in which Germans are made to look ridiculous. But, by identifying and mocking a former enemy group, these comedies would seem to function in strengthening the group solidarity of the home community. It would be necessary to choose fairly carefully plays that might be supposed to increase the feelings of group solidarity of the main population by the dramatic technique of excluding members of the minority one. A complicating feature is likely to be the phenomenon that immigrant groups frequently, like religious neophytes, are more vigorous in their championing of the beliefs of the community to which they have migrated than are the old residents. Even American Indians have been seen shouting with glee at Western films as 'another redskin bites the dust'!

Fourthly, the most valuable tests of all would be inter- or cross-cultural comparisons of drama preference. The evidence cited in the present study (Chapter 7) suggests that the nuclear family and the institution of monogamy produce singular stresses in British society. It would be valuable to devise comparable methods for assessing the popularity of dramas in societies with different social institutions. It would then be possible to compare the popular dramas, popular myths, and popular rituals of polygamous, polyandrous, and extended-family societies. Duncan (1962) has suggested that a society is determined by the communication of significant symbols (p. 438); significant symbols might provide indicators of the fundamental social structures of a particular society. The following short table lays side by side the results of the study by McGranahan and Wayne (1947) and the results of the present study, which was based on McGranahan and Wayne's system of classifying play themes.

Although the method by which McGranahan and Wayne selected the 'most popular' plays performed in America in 1927 and in Germany in 1927 has been called in question, the difference between countries in results suggests that there is a fruitful avenue of research here.

Fifthly, it would be extremely valuable to carry out a widespread study of the pattern of consumption by members of a community of items which may be deemed functional equivalents and which order social experience. The total time spent in the

Basic Themes : Percentage occurrences		
McGranahan and Wayne		This study U.K. plays 1955-65
U.S. plays 1927	German plays 1927	
Love 60	31	44
Morality 36	9	53
Idealism 4	44	16
Power 2	33	20
Outcast Nil	18	26
Career 11	9	Nil
Unclassified 13	2	1

consumption of popular drama (on stage, in films, on television, etc.), in the reading of fiction, in the reading of newspapers, in the reading about or in attendance at legal trials, in religious behaviour, in active membership of social groups, etc., taken together for the average individual, might represent a constant, K. This constant could then be used as a diagnostic instrument in sociological investigation. In view of the considerable amount of time apparently spent by Britons consuming media fiction—especially in the form of popular television drama—such an elaborate project with all the necessary interviewing and data-processing would not necessarily be an extravagance. It would be valuable to include in the investigation some tests of felt or actual social alienation. If the functional theory proposed in this book is correct, the more alienated an individual feels himself to be, the more need he is likely to feel for one or other of the functional equivalents. Studies (referred to in Chapter 5) have already been made of addiction to individual types of mass communication. But the important point is that cultural items (among which mass-media drama may be numbered) may be interchangeable. It might, therefore, be expected that even the alienated individual would have a constant, K, in terms of *total* consumption of the cultural items that are deemed functionally equivalent. His *pattern* of deviation from the norm might then be illuminating.

In view of the known results of social alienation, such as

suicide, delinquency, depression, etc., it is of the greatest possible interest to identify those cultural items that give the individual a feeling of social integration. The evidence adduced in this study is that popular drama is not only a monitor of a community's morality, but that it—or its functional equivalents—is the very mechanism by which a society maintains its moral integrity and coherence. In areas of the country where symptoms of social alienation were high—for example high suicide or delinquency rates—it might be desirable to provide an increased supply of the cultural items deemed functionally equivalent. This is hardly a revolutionary suggestion, because churches, social clubs, etc., are already being introduced into areas otherwise unsupplied with opportunities for communal behaviour. The point of this suggestion is, however, that a theatre or cinema providing a regular menu of the dramas known to be popular with the members of a community—possibly with a café in which they could discuss what they had seen—might be a suitable alternative to clubs and churches, which may not fit the cultural patterns of the community for which they are provided.

Summary of Principal Conclusions

This book has sought to provide the prolegomena for a thorough sociological investigation into the place of popular drama in society. To provide a basis of systematic experimental investigation, the characteristics—in terms of social content—of 114 self-contained plays were examined. This analysis revealed the nature of 'popular drama' for the period 1955–1965. Because the analysis of these plays only has meaning in the light of the discussion of literature presented in the first six chapters, this summary of conclusions is divided into two parts. The first part summarizes the conclusions that can reasonably be drawn from the literature reviewed in the book; the second part summarizes the conclusions to be drawn from the 'experimental' part of the study in so far as it substantiates the points argued from the literature.

SUMMARY OF CONCLUSIONS DRAWN FROM THE REVIEW OF LITERATURE IN CHAPTERS 2–6

Chapter 2 argued that drama is associated in its origins with ritual and myth, and has similarities in content to both, and to much folk-lore. The principal conclusions reached from the survey of literature are:

1. Myth, ritual, and folk-lore frequently perform a cognitive function in informing the members of a community about social structure and about the behaviour expected from individual members of the community if social structure is to be preserved.

2. Myths and rituals are frequently vehicles for the expression of emotion at matters of tension in social structure.

3. The conflicts forming the themes of popular myths are likely to be those experienced in real life by the members of the community in which the myths are current.

4. As an instrumental element of culture, myth, ritual, and folk tale have the latent (and often manifest) function of exercising social control.

5. As an expressive element of culture, myth, ritual, and folk tale are likely to be conservative in content.

Chapter 3 argued that because drama portrays roles and because role-theory uses terminology borrowed from drama, information about the conscious or intuitive use made of roles by members of a community may suggest some possible functions of drama in society. The principal conclusion drawn from the review of literature on roles was that:

6. The awareness of behaviour appropriate to a particular role is used, consciously or intuitively, by members of a community to organize their experience of social relationships and to structure their participation in relationships.

Chapter 4 reviewed the opinions of non-sociological commentators (mainly literary critics) about the possible social functions of drama. From this review it was argued that a probable function of popular drama in society is to provide a monitor of morality, a technique by which the moral order underlying social structure can be identified by contrast with its opposite—immorality, disorder. This argument finds support in the writings of social commentators (for example Durkheim 1893, Douglas 1966) and may be stated as a tentative conclusion as follows:

7. Popular drama draws attention to social order by contrasting it with disorder, to morality by contrasting it with immorality.

Chapter 5 reviewed the nature and effects of certain types of mass communication, arguing that popular drama, as a form of mass communication, is likely to exhibit in its particulars the characteristics of mass communication in general. From this review of literature, the following conclusions are tentatively proposed:

8. By virtue of its nature as a form of mass communication, popular drama is likely to reinforce prevailing opinion and belief rather than change it and, in its content, to reflect prevailing social norms.

9. There is, at present, insufficient evidence to support the proposition that violence in mass-media dramatic fictions is dysfunctional for the majority of people. It is, however, possible that the repeated portrayal of violence on television may adversely affect young children who have not yet learned norms of behaviour and who may not be able to 'selectively perceive' the material with which they are confronted.

10. Evidence on the social uses of 'escape' fare in the mass media of communication (popular drama being an example of 'escape' fare) suggests that this fare functions positively—principally as a social lubricant.

11. There is insufficient evidence to support the proposition that mass media exercise a 'narcotizing dysfunction'. That is to say, there is insufficient evidence to suggest that television drama distracts viewers from more worth-while types of social activity.

Chapter 6 justified the techniques of research applied to the study of the social content of popular drama in this book. Evidence from previous studies was cited which is sufficiently important to be restated in the form of conclusions. Evidence was cited from the BBC Audience Research Report *The Public and the Programmes* (1959) in support of the general conclusion that:

12. Plays were one of the favourite categories of television fare with the British viewing public in the period considered in this book.

Important negative evidence was drawn from the study by D. McQuail (1967 and 1970) about the homogeneity of the television audience in terms of tastes for and appreciation of different types of drama. Although more evidence is required before sociological theory can be built upon the proposition, it can be tentatively concluded that:

13. Although there are some differences between members of

different occupational and educational groups and different social classes in terms of their tastes for particular types of television drama, there are no significant differences between them in their appreciation of what they see.

Review of Audience Research techniques used in the period being studied revealed the important point that:

14. The size of the audience for a television play is not, taken by itself, a sufficient guide to audience satisfaction.

For this study, the above conclusion meant that evidence drawn from the employment of 'tammeters' was inadequate in defining a scale of popularity and that plays produced on Independent Television had to be omitted from the study.

Plays presented on the stage of London West End theatres, unlike television plays, are subject to 'market' conditions over relatively long periods. There is time for such social processes as 'opinion leadership' (known from mass communication research) to intervene between the publicity of the theatres, the comments of the critics, and the decisions of members of the public to attend the plays. The estimated number of attendances at a play has, therefore, been used in this study as a measure of popularity, and it is proposed as a tentative conclusion that:

15. Where free 'market' conditions prevail, the estimated total audience for a theatre play may be used as a measure of popularity.

SUMMARY OF CONCLUSIONS DRAWN FROM CHAPTER 7 AND FROM THE STUDY AS A WHOLE

The content analysis of popular drama presented in Chapter 7 indicates the types of drama apparently most enjoyed by the British public (in the London area) in the period 1955–1965. Supporting evidence was cited in Chapter 6 from studies carried out by the BBC (1964 and 1965), for the Independent Television Authority (ITA, 1965), and by D. McQuail (1967 and 1970). From all this evidence, it may be concluded that:

16. In the period 1955–1965, single, self-contained plays finding greatest favour with the British public were those with strongly moral themes—either detective stories (frequently presented as thrillers) or romantic comedies.

The content analysis of Chapter 7 revealed that a large proportion of the popular television and stage plays dealt with areas in which the aspirations/goals/motives of individuals were at odds with prevailing moral codes. If it is assumed that the themes of popular drama, like those of popular myths and other folk-lore, are subjects of conflict in the real life of the community, it may be concluded from the present study that:

17. It is a testable sociological proposition that popular drama deals with the areas of social living in which members of a community find it most difficult to comply with the moral requirements necessary for the survival of the prevailing social system.

In the period 1955–1965, Britons would seem to have had most difficulty with: the institution of monogamy; judgement of the social power that an individual may be permitted to exercise; desire for money and other types of wealth; desire for revenge for real or imagined wrongs suffered; the wish to use violence in pursuing private goals.

The principal task of this study has been to establish the nature of popular drama as a first step in the construction of a theory of the place of popular drama in society. It might be prudent to limit the conclusions to the seventeen listed so far. There are obvious hazards in drawing conclusions about *why* people watch drama from analysis of the *content* of the drama they seem to like. But the discussion in the first part of this chapter, although speculative, points to two important propositions about the possible functions of popular drama in society. With the proviso that these conclusions are speculative and that adequate exploration of functional equivalents is required (particularly newspapers, news broadcasts, jokes and joking, legal trials, and religious activities), the final conclusions of the study may be stated as follows:

18. It is a testable sociological proposition that people watch drama in order to organize and confirm their experience of society, particularly with reference to socially approved behaviour. In a given culture, popular drama will function expressively as a monitor or indicator of morality, particularly those aspects of morality in which there is a tension between the instincts of individuals and the requirements of society.

19. Secondly, it is a testable sociological proposition that in a given culture popular drama and its functional equivalents are used instrumentally, deliberately or intuitively, directly or through mediating processes of social intercourse, to disseminate

and probably determine the moral values upon which prevailing social structure depends. Popular drama, therefore, is likely to function not only as an expressive element of culture (monitoring morality) but as an instrumental aspect of culture (determining the prevailing morality).

9

Speculative Tailpiece

The description that this book has given of the possible social functions of popular drama has, so far, tried to avoid value judgements. The student of drama may be infuriated that the study has ignored the subtleties and individuality that make good plays refreshing artistic experiences. Again, there is a clear implication in much of what has been written that popular drama, especially drama on television, may be fulfilling many of the functions traditionally fulfilled by religion. A few comments are, therefore, needed.

Underlying this functionalist study of popular drama, there has been, inevitably, a model of society. The model of society is an 'engineering' one based upon the idea of equilibrium. Much of the discussion in the foregoing chapters assumes the existence of a sort of moral equilibrium in society upon which the stability of society's structure depends. Differences between individuals in terms of social class, education, income, occupation, etc., can be readily described and provide convenient ways of describing the relationships between one part of society and another. However, a society would not exist at all as an organic whole unless there were some consensus of opinion about what behaviour is or is not permissible. A great deal of a society's beliefs about permitted behaviour is codified in law. But to be effective, law must be credible and acceptable. It must express beliefs about behaviour which the individual members of the community accept. Individuals must be persuaded to submit their instincts for power, sex, wealth, approbation, etc., to the overall needs of the organism —society. That is to say, the competing instincts of individual members of a community will be in dynamic tension. The theory outlined in this book, put crudely, is that popular dramas offer to the sociologist the equivalent of the engineers' strain gauges. The themes of the popular dramas reveal the places where interlocking forces produce potential instability—they 'express' an aspect of the overall culture. Not only do they function expressively in this way; it has also been suggested that popular dramas may function instrumentally by teaching the behaviour needed from individuals if society is to stay in existence. In addition, they may help to hold society together by giving individuals an opportunity to express emotion at requirements of social living that they find irritating. Popular dramas may provide people with cues for discussing alternative types of behaviour. For example, a man may have an almost overwhelming desire to take somebody else's large motor car. He may also want to be convinced that his inhibition *against* stealing the car is right. Popular drama may function—like law courts or reports in local newspapers of mischief—in confirming him in his feeling that it would in fact be wrong to take the car. Popular drama has, therefore, been called the drama of reassurance.

But drama is obviously one of the highest artistic activities of man. There is a saying that 'science reassures, art disturbs'. This is of course a ridiculous oversimplification. But the suggestion is that science, which offers a systematic description of physical phenomena, bringing more and more of experience within the grip of reason, feeds our belief that we are in control of our environment, 'understand' it, and can agree about it. This is reassuring. Art, on the other hand, disturbs. Experimental art, almost by definition, challenges order by extending—through the eyes of the artist—the range of perceptions upon which our intuition of order is based. New art is usually misunderstood—because old categories of thought are used when we try to comprehend it. Frequently it is regarded as subversive—particularly so when the traditional assumptions that it challenges are moral ones.

How then can drama be instrumental in preserving the *status quo* in society? It is at this point that the distinction becomes crucial between the drama of mass popularity and the drama that excites critical discussion. Television writers and producers have been known to react with fear and hostility to the activities of Audience Research departments. They are hostile because mass popularity is hardly a measure of artistic merit. They are probably afraid that controllers, with an eye on the box office or on the ratings, will only favour the types of drama known to have mass appeal. Clearly, it would be disastrous if controllers of television output, and of theatre, did not encourage experiment. Indeed, with the increasing expense of mounting drama, it is highly desirable that some theatres receive Government subsidy so that artistic innovation can take place. In terms of social acceptability, and artistic originality, there are clearly different types of drama.

An organism survives by adapting to changes in its environment. Functionalist sociology maintains that society survives by adapting its institutions to changing social requirements. For institutions to change, social debate must take place. Where better than in drama, which is a form of social argument? Drama is certainly effective in stimulating discussion—theatres have been wrecked in the past by angry audiences, and even modest changes in theatre practice (the most recent example is that afforded by *Oh! Calcutta!*) can still bring shrieks of protest. For society, conceived of as an organism, to survive, changes of moral belief are clearly required. But because change breeds insecurity, it is unlikely, in normal circumstances, for drama that preaches change to be popular with the mass of the people. Conceivably during a revolution it might be. But what is more likely is that one type of drama—the drama of reassurance—will reassure most of the people most of the time that the morality they live by is good; another type of drama—The Theatre of Revolt, The Theatre of the Absurd, The Theatre of Cruelty, Epic Theatre—will excite critical discussion and social debate and will meet another equally important need. It will also be presented as 'entertainment' (this is where confusion arises between the different types of 'entertainment') but it will disturb social equilibrium by varying experience, challenging assumptions, and generally overthrowing the complacent routine on which one bases one's day-to-day existence. Like reassurance, disturbance may be necessary to the survival of an organism.

It is one of the paradoxes of the human condition that part of oneself requires comfort and a minimization of disturbance (from part of the person comes the pressure to minimize disturbance, to maximize creature comforts, to reduce effort, to avoid problems, to seek the cabbage-life of ease), while another part of the person requires change, variety, effort, disturbance, etc. People deprived of external stimuli go mad and die. Unexercised muscles turn flabby, unused organs rot, and unexercised bodies die of heart disorders. When it is possible to see a good view from an aeroplane or helicopter, people still climb mountains. When it is possible to stay in buildings at an even temperature of 68° F people still expose themselves to the elements in pursuits of pleasure. Intellectuals take off their white collars and put on old clothes to enjoy manual work in their gardens; manual workers indulge in intellectually complicated intricacies of betting. While there is an evident individual need for reassurance and pap, there is an equal need for strong meat and challenge. The popular drama reviewed in this book may, if the theory proposed is correct, fulfil one social need; there may be an equally powerful social need for a different type of intellectual stimulation.

It is common experience that an individual may enjoy different types of drama at different times. Personally, I thoroughly enjoy mind-stretching experimental drama such as is provided by the Royal Court Theatre. However, at other times and in other places I also enjoy a good detective play or a Western. This is not evidence of schizophrenia. It is important to draw this distinction between the different types of satisfaction, because much confusion arises from the confounding of the two separate activities. Once the distinction between the different types of need is clearly understood, much fruitlessly polemical literary criticism may become unnecessary. Once the function of popular drama is fully understood and appreciated, it may well come to be recognized that Agatha Christie possesses a singular expertise in devising the modern equivalent of complex religious ritual. This expertise is quite different from the dramatic expertise that produces an extension of consciousness. There may, of course, be many common characteristics—a dramatist must at least be technically competent. But the murderer caught in *The Mousetrap* offers a reassuring type of dramatic experience; Ionesco's *New Tenant*, overwhelmed by the flood of his own possessions crushing him to death before our eyes upon the stage, is offering a completely different type of dramatic experience. Both are valid; both are valuable; both are enriching; but in different ways.

But what of the theological implications of the drama of reassurance? It has been suggested that church attendance in

America in the 1960s was inversely proportional to the frequency of Westerns on area television. At first sight, this may seem to be a ludicrous social contrast. But may there not be an interesting observation here? The popular dramas surveyed in this study are fundamentally about the Commandments—thou shalt do no murder; thou shalt not steal; thou shalt not commit adultery; thou shalt not covet; thou shalt not bear false witness; etc. Indeed, the ordinariness of the moral messages may dismay students of drama. However, if it is true that people need to be repeatedly reassured of a moral framework (just as children need the security of discipline), may they not be finding all they want in the popular drama of theatre and television? Is it not possible that popular drama has assumed one of the major functions in the Western world of church services?

Again, Durkheim would argue that one of the chief values of communal worship for the worshipper is the experience of being part of a community. The television and radio serials—'Coronation Street', 'The Archers', etc.—may provide a substitute community for modern man. There is evidence (cited in Chapter 5) that people use the mass media in this way. Again, many people nowadays work in large organizations that give structure to their social relationships—'the firm' may be the expression of belief in community which a church previously expressed. If it is necessary to feel linked to one's fellow mortals in an organization whose activities have recognizable purpose—the trade union, the factory, the football team, the supporters' club, etc.—secular manifestations of group solidarity may exhaust most people's capacity for communal activity.

Even those with unconventional moral feelings springing from consciences sensitive to the needs of their fellow-men may find adequate secular outlets—sit-ins, marches of protest, Oxfam Fund-walks, etc.—which unite them in refreshing and spiritually uplifting activity with those who want to change the *status quo*.

Sensitive souls like Pascal may have been terrified onto their knees by the infinite spaces of the universe. Sartre may experience cosmic chaos in confrontation with a root. Beckett's Krapp may reveal the utter aloneness of man as his last tape runs out. But most of us comfortably avoid contemplating the infinite. The rites of passage help us over the crevasses so that we can avoid ever contemplating the philosophic structure of our lives. Death, as Gorer (1966) has shown, is lavishly provided with secular as well as with religious rites. Although it contained religious activity, the Churchill funeral was a vast secular ritual accommodating the community to the death of one of the most human of our species. Other matters of ultimate concern with which churches traditionally deal are less amenable to 'public' treatment —the salvation of individual souls through Confession, Absolution, Communion, prayer, etc. Is it surprising that, if mass-media popular drama and secular ritual can satisfy the principal needs for the experience of community in society, church attendance is low?

This may be a travesty of the truth; but why should manifest religious activity be at a relatively low ebb while vast numbers of people watch dramas, with evident satisfaction, for many hours of their lives?

APPENDIX A:

Primary Bibliography

(Works cited in the book)

Albert, R. S., 'The Role of Mass Media and the effect of aggressive film content upon children's aggressive responses and identification choices', *Genetic Psychology Monographs*, 1957, **55**, pp. 221–285

Albrecht, M. C., 'Does literature reflect common values?', *American Sociological Review*, 1956, **21**, pp. 722–729

Allen, C. L., 'Photographing the Television Audience', *J. of Advertising Research*, 1965, **5**, pp. 2–8

Alpert, H., *Emile Durkheim and his Sociology*, Russell & Russell, New York, 1961

Amis, K., *The James Bond Dossier*, Cape, London, 1965

Arons, L. and May, M. A. (eds), *Television and Human Behaviour: Tomorrow's Research in Mass Communication*, Appleton-Century-Crofts, New York, 1963

Ballard, E. G., *Art and analysis: An essay toward a theory in Aesthetics*, Martinus Nijhoff, The Hague, 1957

Bandura, A., 'The Influence of Models' Reinforcement Contingent on the acquisition of Imitative Responses', *J. of Personality & Social Psychology*, 1965, **1**, pp. 589–595

Bandura, A. and Menlove, F. L., 'Factors determining vicarious extinction of avoidance behavior through Symbolic Modeling', *J. of Personality & Social Psychology*, 1968, **8**, pp. 99–108

Bandura, A., Grusec, J. E. and Menlove, F. L., 'Observational learning as a function of Symbolization and Incentive', *Child Development*, 1966, **37**, pp. 499–506

Bandura, A., Grusec, J. E. and Menlove, F. L., 'Vicarious extinction of Avoidance Behavior', *J. of Personality & Social Psychology*, 1967, **5**, pp. 16–23

Bandura, A., Ross, D. and Ross, S. A., 'Transmission of Aggression through imitation of aggressive models', *J. of Abnormal & Social Psychology*, 1961, **63**, pp. 575–582

Bandura, A., Ross, D. and Ross, S. A., 'Imitation of film-mediated aggressive models', *J. of Abnormal & Social Psychology*, 1963, **66,** pp. 3–11

Banton, M., *Roles: An introduction to the study of social relations,* Tavistock, London, 1965

Barbu, Z., 'The Sociology of Drama', *New Society*, 1967, **9,** 227, pp. 161–164

Barcus, F. E., *Communication Content: Analysis of the Research,* 1900–1958, Ph.D. Dissertation, University of Illinois, 1959 (*Dissertation Abstracts* 1959, **20,** 3279. Microfilm: 60–143)

Barker, W. J., 'The Stereotyped Western Story', *Psychoanalytic Quarterly,* 1955, **24,** pp. 270–280

Bascom, W., 'The myth-ritual theory', *J. of American Folklore,* April–June 1957, **70** (276), pp. 103–114

Bell, R. H., *A study of the image of American Character as presented in selected network television dramas,* Ph.D. Dissertation, The Ohio State University, 1961 (*Dissertation Abstracts,* 1961, **22,** 2242–2243. Microfilm: 61–5070)

Belson, W. A., 'Measuring the Effects of Television; a description of method', *Public Opinion Quarterly,* 1958, **22,** pp. 11–18

Belson, W. A., 'New developments in audience research methods', *J of American Sociology,* 1958 39, **64,** pp. 174–179

Belson, W. A., 'Effects of television on the interests and initiative of adult viewers in Greater London', *British J. of Psychology,* May 1959, **50** (2), pp. 145–158

Belson, W. A., *The Impact of Television,* Crosby Lockwood, London, 1967

Bentley, E., 'The psychology of farce', *New Republic,* 1958, **138,** pp. 11–19

Bentley, E., *The Life of the Drama,* Methuen, London, 1965

Berelson, B., *Content Analysis in Communication Research,* The Free Press, Glencoe, Illinois, 1952

Berelson, B., 'The State of Communication Research', *Public Opinion Quarterly,* 1959, **23,** 1, pp. 1–15. (Reprinted in Dexter & White, 1964)

Berkowitz, L., 'The expression and reduction of hostility', *Psychological Bulletin,* 1958, **55,** pp. 257–283

Berkowitz, L., 'Cognitive Dissonance and Communication Preferences', *Human Relations,* 1965, **18,** pp. 361–372

Berkowitz, L., Corwin, R. and Heironimus, M., 'Film violence and subsequent aggressive tendencies', *Public Opinion Quarterly,* 1963, **27,** pp. 217–229

Berkowitz, L. and Geen, R. G., 'Stimulus Qualities of the target of aggression: a further study', *J. of Personality & Social Psychology,* 1967, **5,** pp. 364–368

Berkowitz, L. and Rawlings, E., 'Effects of film violence on inhibitions against subsequent aggression', *J. of Abnormal & Social Psychology*, May 1963, **66** (5), pp. 405–412

Bloom, S. W., 'A Social Psychological Study of Motion Picture Audience Behavior: a case study of the negro image in mass communication', *Dissertation Abstracts*, 1956, **16**, p. 1187

Blum, A. F., 'Popular Culture and the image of Gesellschaft', *Studies in Public Communication*, 1961, **3**, Summer, pp. 145–148

Boaz, M. T., 'A qualitative analysis of the criticism of Best Sellers: a study of the reviews and reviewers of best selling books from 1944 to 1953', *Dissertation Abstracts*, 1955, **15**, p. 596

Bodkin, M., *Archetypal Patterns in Poetry*, Oxford University Press, London, 1934 (Paperback edition, 1963)

Bogart, L., 'Adult talk about newspaper comics', *American J. of Sociology*, 1955, **61**, pp. 26–30

Breed, W., 'Mass Communication and Sociocultural Integration', *Social Forces*, 1958, **37**, pp. 109–116

Brehm, J. W. and Cohen, A. R., *Explorations in Cognitive Dissonance*, J. Wiley, New York, 1962

British Broadcasting Corporation, *The Public and the Programmes:* a study of Listeners and Viewers, the Time they devote to listening and viewing, the Services they patronize, their selectiveness and their tastes (an Audience Research Report), BBC, 1959. VR/59/332

British Broadcasting Corporation, *Single Plays on Television:* Audience Research Bulletin, BBC, 1965. VR/65/31

British Broadcasting Corporation, *Drama Audiences in the Sixties*, A report prepared for internal circulation by M. Imison, 1965

British Broadcasting Corporation, *Audience Research in the United Kingdom: Methods and Services*, BBC Publications, London, 1966

British Broadcasting Corporation, *Control of Subject Matter in BBC Programmes*, BBC Publications, London, 1967

Byrne, D., 'The relationship between humour and the expression of hostility', *J. of Abnormal & Social Psychology*, 1956, **53**, pp. 84–89

Carter, R. E. Jr., 'Communication Research and the Social Sciences', *American Behavioural Scientist*, 1960, **4**, pp. 8–13

Cassirer, E., *The Philosophy of Symbolic Form*, Volume 1, Yale University Press, New Haven, 1953. Volume 2, Yale University Press, New Haven, 1955

Cooke, A. H., 'Human Values in Drama', *J. of Human Relations*, 1958, **6**, 3. Spr., pp. 70–81

Davis, K., *Human Society*, Macmillan, New York (17th ed.), 1964

Davison, W. P., 'On the effects of Communication', *Public Opinion Quarterly*, 1960, pp. 344–360. (Reprinted in Dexter & White, 1964)

De Fleur, M. L., 'Occupational Roles as portrayed on television', *Public Opinion Quarterly*, 1964, **28,** pp. 57–74

De Fleur, M. L., 'Mass Communication and social change', *Social Forces*, 1966, **44,** pp. 314–326

Dexter, L. A. and White, D. M. (eds), *People, Society, and Mass Communications*, Free Press of Glencoe, New York, 1964

Dienstfrey, H. D., 'Doctors, Lawyers, and other TV Heroes', *Commentary*, 1963, **35,** 6 (June), pp. 519–524

Douglas, M., *Purity and Danger: An analysis of concepts of pollution and taboo*, Routledge & Kegan Paul, London, 1966

Duncan, H. D., *Communication and Social Order*, The Bedminster Press, New York, 1962

Durkheim, E., *The Division of Labour in Society* (1893), translated by G. Simpson, Free Press of Glencoe, Illinois, 1960

Durkheim, E., *Suicide* (1897), translated by G. Simpson and J. A. Spalding, Routledge & Kegan Paul, London, (Reprint) 1963

Durkheim, E., *Elementary Forms of the Religious Life* (1912), translated by J. W. Swain, Collier Books, New York, 1961

Ehrenberg, A. S. C., 'A comparison of TV audience measures', *J. of Advertising Research*, 1964, **4,** pp. 11–16

Ehrle, R. A. and Johnson, B. G., 'Psychologists and Cartoons', *American Psychologist*, 1961, **16,** pp. 693–695

Elkin, F., 'The psychological appeal of the Hollywood Western', *J. of Educational Sociology*, 1950, **24,** pp. 72–86

Elkin, F., 'The value implications of popular films', *Sociology and Social Research*, 1954, **38,** pp. 320–322

Emery, F. E., 'Psychological Effects of the Western Film: A study in television viewing', *Human Relations*, 1959, **12,** 3, pp. 205–232

Ennis, P. H., 'The Social Structure of communication systems: a theoretical proposal', *Studies of Public Communication*, 1962, pp. 120–144

Esslin, M., *The Theatre of the Absurd*, Eyre & Spottiswoode, London, 1964

Evans-Pritchard, E. E., *Theories of Primitive Religion*, Clarendon Press, Oxford, 1965

Fearing, F., 'Influence of the movies on attitudes and behaviour', *Annals of the American Academy of Political and Social Science*, 1947, **254,** pp. 70–79

Feshbach, S., 'The Effects of aggressive content in television programmes upon the aggressive behaviour of the audience', in Arons and May (eds.), *Television and Human Behaviour*, 1963

Feshbach, S., 'The Stimulating versus Cathartic Effects of Vicarious Aggressive Activity', *J. of Abnormal & Social Psychology*, 1961, **63,** pp. 381–385

Festinger, L., *A Theory of Cognitive Dissonance*, Harper & Row, New York, 1957

Festinger, L., *Conflict, Decision, and Dissonance*, Stanford University Press, California, 1964

Findlater, R., *Banned: A review of theatrical censorship in Britain*, MacGibbon & Kee, London, 1967

Fischer, J. L., 'The socio-psychological analysis of folktales', *Current Anthropology*, June 1963, 4 (3), pp. 235–295

Forsey, S. D., 'The influence of family structures upon patterns and effects of family viewing' in Arons and May (eds.), *Television and Human Behaviour*, 1963

Frankfort, H. and H. A., *Before Philosophy* (Introduction and Chapter 1), Penguin Books, London, 1964 edn

Freidson, E., 'Communication Research and the concept of the Mass', *American Sociological Review*, 1953, 18, pp. 313–317

Frye, N., *Anatomy of Criticism*, Princeton University Press, 1957

Gabbard, E. G., *An Experimental Study of Comedy*, Ph.D. Dissertation, State University of Iowa, 1954 (*Dissertation Abstracts*, 1954, 14, p. 2437. Microfilm: 10–212)

George, A. E., *Propaganda Analysis: A study of inferences made from Nazi Propaganda in World War 2*, Published for the Rand Corporation by Row, Peterson, & Co., New York, 1969

Gerbner, G., 'Toward a general theory of communication', *Audio-Visual Communication Review*, 1956, 4, pp. 171–199

Gerbner, G., 'On Content Analysis and critical research in Mas Communication', *Audio-Visual Communication Review*, 1958, 6, pp 85–108. (Reprinted in Dexter & White, 1964)

Gerson, W. M., 'Mass Media Socialization Behaviour: Negro-White Differences', *Social Forces*, 1966, 44, pp. 40–50

Goffman, E., *The Presentation of Self in Everyday Life*, Allen Lane, The Penguin Press, London, 1969 (First published in Anchor Books USA, 1959)

Goodlad, J. S. R., *An analysis of the social content of Popular Drama, 1955–1965*, Ph.D. Dissertation, University of London, 1969

Goodrich, H., *Man and Society in Mass-Media Fiction: The pattern of life in the Mass Media as revealed by Content-Analysis Studies*, Ph.D. Dissertation, University of Illinois, 1964 (Microfilm: 65–819)

Goody, J., 'Religion and ritual: the definitional problem', *British J. of Sociology*, June 1961, 12 (2), pp. 142–164

Goranson, R. E., *Mass Media and Violence*, see United States of America

Gorer, G., *Death, Grief, and Mourning in Contemporary Britain*, London 1966

Grace, H. A., 'Charlie Chaplin's Films and American Cultural Patterns', *J. of Aesthetics and Art Criticism*, June 1952, **10**, 4, pp. 353–363

Grace, H. A., 'A Taxonomy of American Crime Film Themes', *J. of Social Psychology*, 1955, **42**, pp. 129–136

Greenwald, A. and Albert, S. S., 'Observational Learning: A technique for elucidating S-R Mediation Processes', *J. of Experimental Psychology*, 1968, **76**, pp. 267–272

Hall, S. and Whannel, P., *The Popular Arts*, Hutchinson, London, 1964

Hallman, R. J., *Psychology of literature: a study of alienation and Tragedy*, Philosophical Library, New York, 1961

Halloran, J. D., *The Effects of Mass Communication: with special reference to Television*, Television Research Committee, Working Paper No. 1, Leicester University Press, 1964

Harrison, J. E., *Themis: A study of the social origins of Greek religion* (First published by Cambridge University Press, 1912), Merlin Press, London, 1963

Harvey, J., 'The Content characteristics of Best-Selling novels', *Public Opinion Quarterly*, 1953–54, **17**, pp. 91–114

Head, S. W., *Television and Social Norms: An analysis of the social content of a sample of television dramas*, Ph.D. Dissertation, New York University, 1953. (*Dissertation Abstracts*, 1953, **13**, p. 808. Microfilm: A53–991)

Head, S. W., 'Content Analysis of Television Drama Programs', *Quarterly of Film, Radio, and Television*, 1954, **9**, pp. 175–194

Hicks, D., 'Short- and Long-term retention of affectively varied Modeled Behavior', *Psychonomic Science*, 1968, **11**, pp. 369–370

Himmelweit, H. T., Oppenheim, A. N., and Vince, P., *Television and the Child: An empirical study of the effect of television on the young*, published for the Nuffield Foundation by the Oxford University Press, London, 1958

Homans, P., 'Puritanism Revisited: An analysis of the contemporary screen-image Western', *Studies of Public Communication*, 1961, **3** (Summer), pp. 73–84

Hoy, C., *The Hyacinth Room: an investigation into the nature of comedy, tragedy and tragic-comedy*, Chatto & Windus, London, 1964

Hubert, H. and Mauss, M., *Sacrifice: Its nature and function*, translated by W. D. Halls, Cohen & West, London, 1964

Independent Television Authority, *A report on a study of Television Play Viewing*, prepared for the ITA by AGB Research Ltd & Programme Assessment Ltd, April 1965 (Confidential to ITA)

James, E. O., *Origins of Sacrifice*, John Murray, London, 1933

James, E. O. (1957A), *Prehistoric Religion: A study in prehistoric archaeology*, Thames & Hudson, London, 1957

James, E. O. (1957B), 'The nature and function of myth', *Folklore* (London), December 1957, **68** (4), pp. 474–482

Janis, I. L. and King, B. T., 'The influence of role-playing on opinion change', *J. of Abnormal & Social Psychology*, 1954, **49**, pp. 211–218

Janowitz, M., 'The application of sociological knowledge to mass communication', *World Congress of Sociology*, 1959, **3**, pp. 129–159

Jones, D. B., 'Quantitative Analysis of Motion Picture Content', *Public Opinion Quarterly*, 1950, **14**, pp. 554–558

Karp, E. E., 'Crime Comic Book Role Preferences', *Dissertation Abstracts*, 1955, **15**, pp. 638–639

Katz, E., 'Communication Research and the image of society: convergence of two traditions', *American J. of Sociology*, 1960, **65**, pp. 435–440

Katz, E. and Foulkes, D., 'On the use of Mass Media as "escape": clarification of a concept', *Public Opinion Quarterly*, 1962, **26**, 3 (Fall), pp. 377–378

Katz, E. and Lazarfeld, P. F., *Personal Influence: the part played by people in the flow of Mass Communication*, Free Press of Glencoe, Illinois, 1955

Kazin, A., 'Psychoanalysis and literary culture today', *Partisan Review*, 1959, **26**, 1 (Winter), pp. 44–55

Klapper, J. T., *The Effects of Mass Communication*, Free Press of Glencoe, Illinois, 1960

Kluckhohn, C., 'Myths and Rituals: A general theory', *Harvard Theological Review*, 1942, **35**, pp. 44–78

Koestler, A., *The Act of Creation*, Hutchinson, London, 1964

Kracauer, S., 'National types as Hollywood presents them', *Public Opinion Quarterly*, 1949, **13**, pp. 53–72

Kracauer, S., 'The challenge of qualitative content analysis', *Public Opinion Quarterly*, 1952–3, **16**, pp. 631–642

Kracauer, S., *Theory of Film: the redemption of physical reality*, Oxford University Press, New York, 1960

La Farge, C., 'Mickey Spillane and his Bloody Hammer', *Saturday Review*, 6 November 1954, pp. 11–12, 54–59. (Reprinted in Rosenberg & White, 1963)

Larsen, O. N. (ed), *Violence and the Mass Media*, Harper & Row, New York, 1968

Lattimore, R., *Story Patterns in Greek Tragedy*, Athlone Press, University of London, 1964

Lazarfeld, P. F., 'Audience research in the movie field', *Annals of the American Academy of Political and Social Science*, 1947, **254**, pp. 160–168

Lazarfeld, P. F. and Merton, R. K., 'Mass Communication, Popular Taste and Organized Social Action', in Rosenberg & White, *Mass Culture*, 1963, pp. 457–473

Levonian, E., 'Opinion Change as mediated by an audience-tailored film', *Audio-Visual Communication Review*, July–August 1963, **11**, 4, pp. 104–113

Lovass, O. I., 'Effect of exposure to Symbolic Aggression on Aggressive Behavior', *Child Development*, 1961, **32**, pp. 37–44

Lowenthal, L., 'Popular Culture: a humanistic and sociological concept', *International Social Science Journal*, 1960, **12**, 4, pp. 532–542

Maccoby, E. E., 'Why do children watch television?', *Public Opinion Quarterly*, 1954, **18**, pp. 239–244

Maccoby, E. E. and Wilson, W. C., 'Identification and observational learning from films', *J. of Abnormal and Social Psychology*, 1957, **55**, pp. 76–87

Mann, P. H., 'Surveying a theatre audience: methodological problems', *British J. of Sociology*, 1966, **17**, 4

Mann, P. H., 'Surveying a theatre audience: findings', *British J. of Sociology*, 1967, **18**, 1

Manser, A., *Sartre: A Philosophic Study*, Athlone Press, University of London, 1966

Mass Media and Violence; *see* United States of America, 1969

Meier, N. C., 'The Meier Audience Response Recorder', *American J. of Psychology*, 1950, **63**, 1, pp. 87–90

Mendelsohn, H., 'Listening to Radio', in Dexter & White, 1964, pp. 240–248

Merton, R. K., *Social Theory and Social Structure*, Free Press of Glencoe, Illinois, 1957

Meyerson, L., *The effects of filmed aggression on the aggressive responses of high and low aggressive subjects*, Ph.D. Dissertation, University of Iowa, 1966

Miller, A., 'The Family in Modern Drama', *Atlantic*, 1956 April, **197**, pp. 35–41

Moreno, J. L., *Psychodrama* (Vol. 1), Beacon House, New York, 1946

Mott, F. L., *Golden Multitudes*, Macmillan, New York, 1947

Munden, K. J., 'A contribution to the psychological understanding of the origin of the cowboy and his myth', *American Imago*, 1958, **15**, pp. 103–148

Murray, G., 'Excursus on the ritual forms preserved in Greek Tragedy' in Harrison, J., *Themis* (2nd edn 1927), Merlin Press, London, 1963

Mussen, P. and Rutherford, E., 'Effects of aggressive cartoons on children's aggressive play', *J. of Abnormal & Social Psychology*, 1961, **62**, pp. 461–464

McCormack, T., 'Social Theory and Mass Media', *Canadian J. of Economic and Political Science*, 1961, **27**, 4 November, pp. 479–489

McGranahan, D. V. and Wayne, I., 'German and American Traits reflected in popular drama', *Human Relations*, 1947, **1**, pp. 429–455

McManus, J. T. and Kronenberger, L., 'Motion pictures, the theater, and race relations', *Annals of the American Academy of Political and Social Science*, 1946, **244**, pp. 152–158

McPhee, W. N. and Meyerson, R., *Futures for Radio*, Bureau of Applied Social Research, Columbia University, 1955

McQuail, D., *Factors Affecting Public Interest in Television Plays*, Ph.D. Dissertation, University of Leeds, 1967

McQuail, D., 'The Audience for Television Plays' in Tunstall, J. (ed.), *Media Sociology*, Constable, London, 1970, pp. 335–350

Nussbaum, M., 'Sociological Symbolism of the "Adult Western" ', *Social Forces*, 1960, **39**, 1, October, pp. 25–28

Olsen, M. E., 'Motion picture attendance and social isolation', *Sociological Quarterly*, April 1960, **1** (2), pp. 107–116

Orwell, G., 'Raffles and Miss Blandish', reprinted in Rosenberg & White (eds.), *Mass Culture*, 1957, pp. 154–163

Parker, E. B., 'The functions of television for children', *Dissertation Abstracts*, 1960, **21**, pp. 2813–2814

Pearlin, L., 'Social and personal stress and escape television viewing', *Public Opinion Quarterly*, 1959, **23**, 2 (Summer), pp. 255–259

Pederson-Krag, G., 'Detective Stories and the Primal Scene', *Psychoanalytic Quarterly*, 1949, **18**, pp. 207–214

Pickard-Cambridge, A. W., *Dithyramb, Tragedy, and Comedy*, Oxford University Press, 1927

Pickard-Cambridge, A. W., *Dramatic Festivals of Athens*, Oxford University Press, 1953

Pool, I. de S. (ed.), *Trends in Content Analysis*, University of Illinois, Urbana, 1959

Potter, S., *The Theory and Practice of Gamesmanship* (1947), Penguin, London, 1962

Potter, S., *Some notes on Lifemanship* (1950), Penguin, London, 1962

Potter, S., *One-upmanship* (1952), Penguin, London, 1962

Potter, S., *Supermanship* (1958), Penguin, London, 1962

Powdermaker, H., 'An anthropologist looks at the movies', *Annals of the American Academy of Political and Social Science*, 1947, **254**, pp. 80–87

Radcliffe-Brown, A. R., *The Andaman Islanders*, Cambridge University Press, 1933

Riesman, D., *The Lonely Crowd*, Yale University Press (paperback ed.), 1961

Riley, M. W. and J. W., 'A sociological approach to Mass Communications Research', *Public Opinion Quarterly*, 1951, **15**, pp. 443–460

Rolo, C. J., 'Simenon and Spillane: the metaphysics of murder for the millions' in Rosenberg & White (eds.), *Mass Culture*, 1957, pp. 165–175

Rosenberg, B. and White, D. M., *Mass Culture: the popular arts in America*, Free Press, New York, 1957

Rossiter, A. P., *English Drama from Early Times to the Elizabethans: Its Background, Origins, and Developments*, Hutchinson, London, 1950

Runciman, A. P., 'Selected social psychological factors related to viewers of television programs', *Dissertation Abstracts*, 1959, **20,** p. 4746

Sartre, J.-P., *Being and Nothingness*, translated by H. Barnes, Methuen, London, 1957

Sartre, J.-P., *Existentialism and Humanism*, translated by P. Mairet, Methuen, London, 1965 ed

Schramm, W., Lyle, J. and Parker, E. B., *Television in the lives of our children*, Stanford University Press, California, 1961

Schumaker, W., *Literature and the irrational: a study in anthropological backgrounds*, Prentice-Hall, Englewood Cliffs, New Jersey, 1960

Scotch, N. A., 'The Vanishing Villains of Television', *Phylon*, 1960, **21,** 1 (Spring), pp. 58–62

Shannon, L. W., 'The opinions of Little Orphan Annie and her friends', *Public Opinion Quarterly*, 1954–55, **18,** pp. 169–179

Shaw, R., 'The verdict of us all', *Contrast*, Autumn, 1962

Siegel, A. E., 'The effect of film-mediated fantasy-aggression on strength of aggressive drive in young children', *Dissertation Abstracts*, 1956, **16,** p. 154

Silvey, R. J., 'Methods of Viewer Research employed by the BBC', *Public Opinion Quarterly*, 1951–2, **15,** pp. 89–104

Silvey, R. J., 'Because it's free', *Contrast*, Spring 1962

Silvey, R. J. and Emmett, B., 'What makes television viewers choose?', *New Society*, 14 March 1963, **24,** pp. 11–14

Smythe, D. W., 'An analysis of television programs', *Scientific American*, 1951, **184,** 6, pp. 15–17

Smythe, D. W., 'Reality as presented by television', *Public Opinion Quarterly*, 1954–55, **18,** pp. 143–156

Society of West End Theatre Managers, *Theatre Going: A study of public attitudes towards West End theatres*, Two surveys prepared by Social Surveys (Gallup Poll) Ltd, October 1964 (Confidential to the Society)

Spence, L., *Myth and ritual in dance, game, and rhyme*, Watts, London, 1947

Spiegelman, M., Terwilliger, C. and Fearing, F., 'The Content of comic strips: a study of mass medium communication', *J. of Social Psychology*, 1952, **35,** pp. 35–57

Spiegelman, M., Terwilliger, C. and Fearing, F., 'The content of comics: goals and means to goals of characters', *J. of Social Psychology*, 1953, **37**, pp. 189–203

The Stage Yearbook, issues for 1956–1966 inclusive, published by Stage & Television Today, London

Stedman, R. W., 'A history of the broadcasting of daytime serial dramas in the United States', *Dissertation Abstracts*, 1959, **20**, pp. 803–804

Steiner, G. A., *The People look at Television: a study of audience attitudes*, Knopf, New York, 1963

Strickland, J. F., 'The effect of motivation arousal on humour preferences', *J. of Abnormal & Social Psychology*, 1959, **59**, pp. 278–281

Sturcken, J. W., 'An historical analysis of live network television drama from 1938–1958', *Dissertation Abstracts*, 1960, **21**, p. 269

Sweeting, E., *Report on the Provincial Audience*, 1964, Stencilled (refer to Miss E. Sweeting, Administrator, Oxford Playhouse Co.)

Tannenbaum, P. H. and Greenberg, B. S., 'Mass Communication', *Annual Review of Psychology*, 1968, **19**, pp. 372–373

Taylor, J. R., *Anatomy of a Television Play*, Weidenfeld & Nicolson, London, 1962

Taylor, J. R., *Anger and After: a guide to the new British drama*, Penguin Books, London (revised edn), 1963

Television Audience Measurement Ltd, *Special TvQ Enquiry into viewers' opinions of the TV play 'The Other Man'*, 1964

Television Audience Measurement Ltd, *A Special study on television drama*, June, 1965

Thomson, G., *Aeschylus and Athens: a study in the social origins of Drama*, Lawrence & Wishart, London, 1941

Timasheff, N. S., *Sociological Theory: its nature and growth*, Random House, New York (3rd edn), 1967

Tiryakian, E. A., *Sociologism and Existentialism*, Prentice-Hall, Englewood Cliffs, New Jersey, 1962

Tunstall, J. (ed.), *Media Sociology*, Constable, London, 1970; see McQuail

United States of America, *Mass Media and Violence*, Vol. XI (*sic*). A report to the National Commission on the Causes and Prevention of Violence, by D. L. Lange, R. K. Baker, and S. J. Ball, November 1969

Van Gennep, A., *The Rites of Passage*, translated by M. B. Vizedom and G. L. Caffee, Routledge & Kegan Paul, London, 1960

Vrieze, J. W., 'An experimental study of Occupation and its influence on audience response in the theater', *Dissertation Abstracts*, 1953, **13**, 3, p. 132

Waldorf, O. D., *Aldwych Theatre Audience Survey*, prepared for the Royal Shakespeare Theatre Company with assistance from the BBC Audience Research department and S. Field Reid, 1964 (Confidential: Royal Shakespeare Theatre Co.)

Wall, W. D., 'The responses of adolescent groups to certain films', *British J. of Educational Psychology*, 1951, **21**, pp. 81–88

Warner, W. L. and Henry, W. E., 'The Radio day-time serial: a symbolic analysis', *Genetic Psychology Monographs*, 1948, **37**, pp. 3–71

Warshow, R., 'The gangster as tragic hero', *Partisan Review*, February 1948, pp. 240–244

Warshow, R., 'Movie chronicle: the Westerner', *Partisan Review*, 1954, **21**, pp. 190–203

Weston, J. L., *From Ritual to Romance*, (Cambridge University Press, 1920) Doubleday Anchor Books, New York, 1957

Wiley, C. G., *A study of the American woman as she is presented in the American drama of the 1920's*, Ph.D. Dissertation, University of New Mexico, 1957. (Microfilm: 22–931)

Williams, R., *The Long Revolution*, Chatto & Windus, London, 1961

Williams, R., *Communications*, Chatto & Windus, London (revised edn), 1966

Willis, Lord, 'Television and the dramatist', *J. of the Royal Society of Arts*, July 1965

Wilson, E., 'Who cares who killed Roger Ackroyd', reprinted in Rosenberg & White (eds.), *Mass Culture*, 1957, pp. 149–154

Wolfenstein, M. and Leites, N., 'An analysis of themes and plots', *Annals of the American Academy of Political and Social Science*, 1947, **254**, pp. 41–48

Wright, C. R., 'Functional analysis and mass communication', *Public Opinion Quarterly*, 1960 (Winter), **24** (4), pp. 605–620

APPENDIX B:

Secondary Bibliography

(Relevant (supportive) material not cited in the book)

Arnheim, R., 'The world of the daytime serial', in Lazarfeld, P. F. and Stanton, F. N. (eds.), *Radio Research*, 1942–43, Duell, Sloan, & Pearce, New York, 1944

Asheim, L., 'From Book to Film: mass appeal', *Quarterly of Film, Radio, and Television*, 1952, 6, pp. 258–273

Askew, M. W., 'Classical Tragedy and psychotherapeutic catharsis', *Psychoanalysis and the Psychoanalytic Review*, 1960, 47 (3), pp. 116–123

Bailyn, L., 'Mass media and children: a study of exposure, habits, and cognitive effects', *Psychological Monographs*, 1959, 73, pp. 1–48

Bandura, A., Ross, D. and Ross, S. A., 'Vicarious Reinforcement and Imitative Learning', *J. of Abnormal & Social Psychology*, 1963, 67, pp. 601–607

Bandura, A., and Walters, R. H., *Social Learning and Personality Development*, Holt, Rinehart, and Winston, New York, 1963

Barron, M. L., 'A content analysis of inter-group humour', *American Sociological Review*, 1950, 15, pp. 88–94

Bentley, E., *What is Theatre?*, Beacon Press, Boston, Mass., 1956

Bentley, E. (ed.), *The Theory of the Modern Stage*, Penguin Books, London, 1968

Bogart, L., *The Age of Television: a study of viewing habits and the impact of television on American life*, F. Ungar, New York, (2nd edn) 1958

Campbell, D. T., 'The indirect assessment of social attitudes', *Psychological Bulletin*, 1950, 47, pp. 15–38

Chambers, E. K., *The Medieval Stage*, Oxford University Press, 1903

Cooper, R. E. and Dinerman, H., 'Analysis of the film "Don't Be a Sucker": a study in communication', *Public Opinion Quarterly*, 1951–2, 15, pp. 243–264

Cornford, F. M., *The origin of Attic comedy*, Arnold, London, 1914

Cripps, T. R., 'The death of Rastus: Negroes in American films since 1945', *Phylon*, 1967, 28, 3 (Fall), pp. 267–275

Cunningham, R. P., 'A sociological approach to aesthetics: an analysis of attitudes towards the motion picture', *Dissertation Abstracts*, 1954, **14**, pp. 2423–2424

Currie, R. H., 'The stylization of the dramatic television image', *Dissertation Abstracts*, 1962, p. 4439

De Charms, R. and Moller, E. R., 'Values expressed in American children's readers, 1800–1950', *J. of Abnormal & Social Psychology*, 1962, **64**, pp. 136–142

De Fleur, M. L., *Theories of Mass Communication*, D. McKay, New York, 1966

Defries, A., 'Origins and social significance of Harlequin and the Commedia dell' Arte', *Sociological Review*, 1927, **19**, pp. 289–296

Doris, J. and Fierman, E., 'Humour and Anxiety', *J. of Abnormal & Social Psychology*, 1956, **53**, pp. 59–62

Douglas, Mary, *Natural Symbols: explorations in cosmology*, Barrie & Rockcliff, The Cresset Press, London, 1970

Dudek, F. J., 'Relations among television rating indices', *J. of Advertising Research*, 1964, **4**, pp. 24–28

Dudek, F. J. and Thoman, E., 'Scaling preferences for television shows', *J. of Applied Psychology*, 1964, **48**, pp. 237–240

Duncan, H. D., *Symbols in Society*, Oxford University Press, New York, 1968

Duncan, H. D., *Symbols and Social Theory*, Oxford University Press, New York, 1969

Dysinger, W. S. and Ruckmik, C. A., *The Emotional Responses of children to the motion picture situation*, Macmillan, New York, 1933

Eastman, R. M., 'Drama as psychological argument', *College English*, 1959, **19**, pp. 327–332

Eliasberg, W., 'The stage thriller: sociometric interpretation of the relationship between the stage, the play, and the audience', *J. of Social Psychology*, 1944, **19**, pp. 229–239

Emery, E., Ault, P. H. and Agee, W. K., *Introduction to mass communications*, Dodd, Mead, New York, 1960

Eron, L. D., 'The relationship of TV viewing habits and aggressive behaviour in children', *J. of Abnormal & Social Psychology*, 1963, **67**, pp. 193–196

Esslin, M., *Brief Chronicles*, Temple Smith, London, 1970—especially, pp. 272–284, 'Contemporary English Drama and the Mass Media'

Feshbach, S., 'The drive-reducing function of fantasy behaviour', *J. of Abnormal and Social Psychology*, 1955, **50**, pp. 3–11

Feshbach, S., 'The catharsis hypothesis and some consequences of interaction with aggressive and neutral play objects', *J. of Personality*, 1956, **24**, pp. 449–462

Freidson, E., 'The relation of the social situation with contact to the media in mass communication', *Public Opinion Quarterly*, 1953, **17**, pp. 230–238

Gamberg, H., 'The modern literary ethos: a sociological interpretation', *Social Forces*, 1958, **37**, 1 October, pp. 7–14

Glick, I. O. and Levy, S. J., *Living with Television*, Aldine, Chicago, 1962

Goldsen, J. M., 'Analysing the Content of Mass Communication: a step toward inter-group harmony', *International J. of Opinion and Attitude Research*, 1947

Goldstein, B. and Perrucci, R., 'The TV Western and the modern American Spirit', *Southwestern Social Science Quarterly*, 1963, **43**, pp. 357–366

Goldstein, N. S., 'The effect of animated cartoons on hostility in children', *Dissertation Abstracts*, 1957, **17**, p. 1125

Gray, S., 'Confessions of a television playwright', *The Times Literary Supplement*, 19th September 1968, pp. 1042–1043

Gundlach, R., 'The Movies: Stereotypes or Realities', *J. of Social Issues*, 1947, **3**, pp. 26–32

Halloran, J. D., Brown, R. L. and Chaney, D. C., *Television and Delinquency*, Television Research Committee, Working Paper No 3, Leicester University Press, 1970

Herzog, H., 'What do we really know about daytime serial listeners' in Lazarfeld & Stanton (eds.), *Radio Research*, 1942–43, 1944

Harvey, B., 'Nonresponse in Television Meter Panels', *J. of Advertising Research*, 1968, **8**, 2, pp. 24–27

Hausdorf, D. M., 'Depression laughter: magazine humor and American Society', *Dissertation Abstracts*, 1963, **25**, p. 1913

Henry, W. E., *The Analysis of Fantasy*, J. Wiley, New York, 1956

Hirsch, K. W., 'Television program selection as a function of prestige', *Audio-Visual Communication Review*, 1960, **8**, 284

Hoban, C. F., 'Determinants of Audience Reaction: Status', *Audio-Visual Communication Review*, 1953, **1**, pp. 242–251

Huaco, G. A., 'Toward a sociology of film art', *Berkeley J. of Sociology*, 1962, **7**, 1 (Spring), pp. 63–84

Hyman, S. E., 'The Ritual view of Myth and the Mythic', *J. American Folklore*, 1955, **68** (270), October–December, pp. 462–472

Jacobson, H. B., 'The concepts and function of Mass Communication in Society', *Indian Journal of Social Research*, 1962, **3**, 1 (January), pp. 97–108

Jakes, F. H. Jr, 'A study of the standards imposed by four leading television critics with respect to live television drama', *Dissertation Abstracts*, 1960, **21**, p. 991

Johns-Heine, P. and Gerth, H. H., 'Values in mass periodical fiction, 1921–1940', *Public Opinion Quarterly*, 1949, **13**, pp. 105–113

Katz, E., 'The functional approach to the study of attitudes', *Public Opinion Quarterly*, 1960, **24**, pp. 163–204

Kenny, D. T., 'The contingency of humor appreciation on the stimulus-confirmation of joke-ending expectation', *J. of Abnormal and Social Psychology*, 1955, **51**, pp. 644–648

Kitto, H. D. F., *Form and Meaning in Drama*, Methuen, London, 1956

Kluckhohn, C., 'Recurrent themes in myths and mythmaking', *Daedalus*, 1959, **88** (2), Spring, pp. 268–279

Kluckhohn, C., 'Notes on some anthropological aspects of communication', *American Anthropologist*, 1961, **63**, pp. 895–910

Kronenberger, L., 'Highbrows and the Theater Today', *Partisan Review*, 1959, **26**, 4 (Fall), pp. 560–574

Lazarfeld, P. F. and Stanton, F. N. (eds.), *Radio Research*, 1942–43, Duell, Sloan and Pearce, New York, 1944

Levi-Strauss, C., 'The structural study of myth', *J. of American Folklore*, 1955, **68** (270) October–December, pp. 428–444

Lichty, L. W., ' "The real McCoys" and its audience: a functional analysis', *J. of Broadcasting*, 1965, **9**, 2 (Spring), pp. 157–166

Lindsley, O. R., 'A behavioural measure of television viewing', *J. of Advertising Research*, 1962, **2**, pp. 2–12

Maccoby, E. E., 'Television: its impact on children', *Public Opinion Quarterly*, 1951, **15**, pp. 421–444

Malpass, L. F. and Fitzpatrick, E. D., 'Social facilitation as a factor in reaction to humor', *J. of Social Psychology*, 1959, **50**, pp. 295–303

Martel, M. U. and McCall, G. J., 'Reality-orientation and the pleasure principle: a study of American mass-periodical fiction (1890–1955)', in Dexter & White (eds.), 1964

Mayer, A., 'Myths, Movies, and Maturity', *Saturday Review*, 1956, **39**, pp. 7–8

Mercey, A. A., 'Social uses of the Motion pictures', *Annals of the American Academy of Political and Social Science*, 1947, **250**, pp. 98–104

Meyersohn, R. B., 'Social Research in Television' in Rosenberg & White (eds.), 1967, pp. 345–357

Monaghan, R. R., 'Television preference and viewing behaviour', *Dissertation Abstracts*, 1965, **25**, p. 6831

Montani, A. and Pietranera, G., 'Psychoanalysis and aesthetics of Motion pictures', *Psychoanalytic Review*, 1946, pp. 177–196

More, D. M. and Roberts, A. F., 'Societal Variations in Humor responses to cartoons', *J. of Social Psychology*, 1957, **45**, pp. 233–243

Mott, F. L., 'Is there a best-seller formula' in Rosenberg & White (eds.), 1957, pp. 113–118

Myers, L. Jr, 'An examination of television audience methods and application of sequential analysis to the telephone interview method', *Dissertation Abstracts*, 1956, **16**, pp. 1955–1956

MacDonald, D., 'A theory of mass culture', *Diogenes*, 1953, **3**, pp. 1–17, reprinted in Rosenberg & White (eds.), 1957

McLeod, J., Ward, S. and Tancill, K., 'Alienation and uses of the mass media', *Public Opinion Quarterly*, 1965, **29**, pp. 583–594

McQuail, D., 'Uncertainty about the audience and the organisation of mass communications', *The Sociological Review*, 1969. Monograph No. 13, pp. 75–84

McQuail, D., *Towards a Sociology of Mass Communications*, Collier-Macmillan, London, 1969

Nafziger, R. O. and White, D. M., *Introduction to mass communication research*, Louisiana State University Press, Baton Rouge, 1963

Norbeck, E., *Religion in Primitive Society*, Harper & Row, New York, 1961

O'Connell, W. E., 'The adaptive function of wit and humor', *J. of Abnormal and Social Psychology*, 1960, **61**, pp. 263–270

Parker, D. W., 'A descriptive analysis of "The Lone Ranger" as a form of popular art', *Dissertation Abstracts*, 1955, **15**, p. 2600

'Politics and the Theatre', *The Times Literary Supplement*, 28 September 1967, pp. 879–880

Powdermaker, H., *Hollywood, the Dream Factory*, Little, Brown & Co., New York, 1951

Raglan, Lord, 'Myth and Ritual', *J. of American Folklore*, 1955, **68** (270) October–December, pp. 454–461

Ricutti, E. A., 'Children and Radio: a study of listeners and non-listeners to various types of radio programs in terms of selected ability, attitudes, and behaviour measures', *Genetic Psychology Monographs*, **44**, pp. 69–143

Riley, J. W. and Cantwell, F. V., 'Some observations on the social effects of television', *Public Opinion Quarterly*, 1949, **13**, pp. 223–234

Rosen, J. C., 'The effect of the motion picture "Gentleman's Agreement" on attitudes toward Jews', *J. of Psychology*, 1948, **26**, pp. 525–536

Roucek, J. S., 'The Sociology of literature', *Indian J. of Social Research*, 1961, **2**, 2, July, pp. 22–30

Sargent, S. S. and Saenger, G., 'Analysing the content of mass media', *J. of Social Issues*, 1947, **3**, pp. 33–38

Scott, E. M., 'Personality and movie preference', *Psychology Reports*, 1957, **3**, pp. 17–19

Schramm, W. (ed), *The Process and Effects of Mass Communication*, University of Illinois Press, Urbana, 1954

Schramm, W. (ed), *The science of human communication: new directions and findings in communication research*, Basic Books, New York, 1963

Seeman, M., 'On the meaning of Alienation', *American Sociological Review*, 1959, **24**, pp. 783–791

Squires, S. I., 'The construction and evaluation of a test designed to measure aesthetic perception of televised drama', *Dissertation Abstracts*, 1957, **17**, p. 307

Stephenson, W., *The Play Theory of Mass Communication*, University of Chicago Press, Chicago & London, 1967

Stoddard, G. D., *Getting Ideas from the Movies*, Macmillan, New York, 1933

Thayer, J. R., 'The relationship of various audience composition factors to television program types', *Dissertation Abstracts*, 1962, **24**, p. 437

Telberg, I., 'Heroes and villains of Soviet Drama', *American Sociological Review*, 1944, **9**, pp. 308–311

Thompson, D. (ed), *Discrimination and Popular Culture*, Penguin, London, 1965

Topping, M. C., 'The cultural orientation of certain "Western" characters on television: a content analysis', *J. of Broadcasting*, 1965, **9**, 4 (Fall), pp. 291–304

Turner, V. W., *The Ritual Process*, Routledge & Kegan Paul, London, 1970

Warshow, R., *The immediate experience: movies, comics, theatre, and other aspects of popular culture*, Doubleday, New York, 1962

Warshow, R., 'The Gunfighter as a moral hero', *Hibbert J.*, 1963, **61**, pp. 172–176

Wilensky, H. L., 'Social Structure, Popular Culture, and Mass Behavior: Some Research implications', *Studies in Public Communication*, 1961, **3**, pp. 15–22

Wright, C. R., *Mass Communication: a sociological perspective*, Random House, New York, 1966

Additional bibliographical material may be found in the thesis (Goodlad, 1969) upon which this book is based. A tertiary bibliography in the thesis lists other works germane to the present study but which are peripheral in their main concern. In addition, the thesis contains a list of the principal bibliographical sources used for the thesis.

APPENDIX C

Table C1 Appreciation Indices

TELEVISED PLAYS

Play Number	Title	Author	BBC R.I.	Index A	Index B
1956					
1.	*The Weeping Madonna*	Iain MacCormick	75	841	2,175
2.	*Pygmalion*	G. B. Shaw	81	1,240	2,511
3.	*The Corn is Green*	Emlyn Williams	77	1,089	2,541
4.	*Love in a Mist*	Kenneth Horne	85	1,581	2,635
5.	*The White Falcon*	Neilson Gattey and Jordan Lawrence	79	952	2,212
6.	*Manhandled*	Stuart Ready	79	930	2,370
7.	*No Man's Land*	William Fairchild	80	1,040	2,080
8.	*Haul for the Shore*	Jean McConnell	83	1,504	2,656
9.	*The Seat of the Scornful*	Ted Allen	74	840	2,220
10.	*Desert Duel*	Colin Morris	78	1,000	1,950
11.	*Murder Mistaken*	Janet Green	83	1,333	2,573
12.	*Dark Victory*	George Brewer and Bertram Bloch	78	1,170	2,340
1957					
13.	*The Dashing White Sergeant*	Charles Gairdner and R. Pilcher	76	725	1,900
14.	*Laburnum Grove*	J. B. Priestley	79	792	1,896
15.	*Jane Steps Out*	Kenneth Horne	81	1,000	2,025
16.	*A Woman of Property*	Michael Voysey	78	864	1,872
17.	*Edward My Son*	Robert Morley and Noel Langdon	85	1,078	1,870
18.	*The Amazing Dr Clitterhouse*	Barre Lyndon	81	920	1,863
19.	*Another Man's Life*	Philip Guard	77	693	1,617
20.	*The Orange Orchard*	Eden Phillpotts	83	1,008	1,743
21.	*Plunder*	Ben Travers	78	960	1,872
22.	*The Hasty Heart*	John Patrick	84	1,125	2,100
23.	*The Critical Point*	Evelyn Frazer	83	882	1,743
24.	*Wishing Well*	Eynon Evans	78	777	1,638
1958					
25.	*The Man Upstairs*	Patrick Hamilton	75	682	1,650
26.	*Shut Out the Night*	Roy Rigby	76	841	2,204
27.	*You're a Long Time Dead*	Elaine Morgan	78	1,044	2,262
28.	*Background*	Warren Chetham-Strode	84	1,081	1,932

Play Number	Title	Author	BBC R.I.	Index A	Index B
29.	My Flesh, My Blood	Bill Naughton	82	1,025	2,050
30.	Ladies in Retirement	Edward Percy and Reginald Denham	75	704	1,650
31.	The Body of a Girl	Michael Gilbert	76	899	2,204
32.	The Caine Mutiny Court Martial	H. Wouk	87	1,254	1,914
33.	Suspect	Edward Percy and Reginald Denham	80	1,080	2,160
34.	Hour of the Rat	John M. White	82	1,034	1,804
35.	Yesterday's Enemy	Peter R. Newman	79	864	1,896
36.	Wanted—One Body	Raymond Dyer	81	1,288	2,268
37.	A Cuckoo in the Nest	Ben Travers	76	858	1,976
38.	So Many Children	Gerald Savory	83	1,100	1,826
1959					
39.	Trilby	George du Maurier	75	651	1,575
40.	The Skin Game	John Galsworthy	76	682	1,672
41.	Skeleton in the Sand	Kenneth John	80	1,260	2,400
42.	Murder on the Agenda	Eynon Evans	78	924	2,184
43.	No Deadly Medicine	Arthur Hailey	75	640	1,500
44.	The Small Back Room	J. Hopkins	76	651	1,596
45.	Mother of Men	Ada G. Abbott	84	1,050	1,764
46.	Beside the Seaside	Leslie Sands	79	1,075	1,975
(8.)	Haul for the Shore (Repeat: see 1956)		76	700	1,520
47.	Sleeping Partnership	Kenneth Horne	80	1,380	2,400
48.	The Case of Private Hump	James L. Hodson	79	1,134	2,133
49.	Through a glass darkly	Helen McCloy	78	651	1,638
1960					
50.	Never Die	Stewart Marshall	79	875	1,975
51.	Dear Octopus	Dodie Smith	80	819	1,690
52.	Is your honeymoon really necessary?	E. V. Tidmarsh	78	1,305	2,262
53.	The return of Peggy Atherton	Malcolm Stewart	77	682	1,694
54.	Doctor in the House	Ted Willis/R. Gordon	75	950	1,875
55.	Reluctant Heroes	Colin Morris	77	1,271	2,387
56.	Your Obedient Servant	Diana Morgan	75	660	1,500
1961					
57.	The Intervener	Donald Wilson	81	760	1,620
58.	An Inspector Calls	J. B. Priestley	78	884	2,028
59.	A Fair Cop	Christopher Bond	70	899	2,030
60.	The Winslow Boy	Terence Rattigan	75	629	1,275
(22.)	The Hasty Heart (Repeat: see 1957)		79	555	1,185
61.	Cross of Iron	Lukas Heller	77	697	1,309
62.	The Barretts of Wimpole Street	R. Besier	88	1,121	1,672
63.	Will Any Gentleman	Vernon Sylvaine	75	780	2,250
1962					
64.	This Happy Breed	Noel Coward	79	666	1,422
65.	Dial M for Murder	Frederick Knott	75	550	1,650
66.	See How They Run	Philip King	77	984	1,848
67.	A Chance to Shine	Elaine Morgan	78	646	1,326
68.	Wednesday's Child	Denis Constanduros	74	690	1,702
69.	Heart to Heart	Terence Rattigan	82	1,372	2,296
70.	Something to Hide	Leslie Sands	74	550	1,628

Play Number	Title	Author	BBC R.I.	Index A	Index B
1963					
71.	The Affair	Ronald Millar/ C. P. Snow	82	864	1,476
72.	Stalingrad	Claus Hubalek	76	648	1,368
1964					
73.	The July Plot	Roger Manvell	75	608	1,425
1965					
74.	Moving On	Bill Mellen	76	612	1,368
75.	The Brides of March	John Chapman	72	714	1,512
76.	The Joel Brandt Story	Heinar Kipphardt	77	540	1,155

THEATRE PLAYS

Play Number	Title	Author	Number of Performances	Est. Aud. (Thousands)
77.	The Mousetrap	Agatha Christie	6,270 (at 31.12.67)	2,840
78.	Boeing-Boeing	Marc Camoletti	2,036	1,397
79.	Teahouse of the August Moon	John Patrick/ V. Sneider	964	1,216
80.	Sailor Beware	Philip King and Falkland Cary	1,082	1,174
81.	The Amorous Prawn	Anthony Kimmins	903	1,067
82.	Roar Like a Dove	Lesley Storm	1,006	1,034
83.	Witness for the Prosecution	Agatha Christie	460	1,024
84.	The Reluctant Debutante	William Douglas-Home	752	952
85.	Dry Rot	John Chapman	1,475	935
86.	Simple Spymen	John Chapman	1,403	890
87.	The House by the Lake	Hugh Mills	928	789
88.	The Lovebirds	Basil Thomas	516	785
89.	One for the Pot	Ray Cooney and T. Hilton	1,223	775
90.	Billy Liar	Keith Waterhouse and Willis Hall	582	737
91.	The Right Honourable Gentleman	M. Bradley-Dyne	572	721
92.	A Severed Head	Iris Murdoch	1,100	719
93a.	Separate Tables. Table Number Seven	Terence Rattigan	726	690
93b.	Separate Tables. Table by the Window			
94.	Ross	Terence Rattigan	762	686
95.	Come Blow Your Horn	Neil Simon	582	663
96.	The Spider's Web	Agatha Christie	577	647
97.	Goodnight, Mrs Puffin	Arthur Lovegrove	800	630
98.	The Chalk Garden	Enid Bagnold	663	597
99.	Nude With Violin	Noel Coward	617	560
100.	Watch it Sailor	Philip King and Falkland Cary	604	541
101.	The Gazebo	Alec Coppel	479	537

Play Number	Title	Author	Number of Performances	Est. Aud. (Thousands)
102.	*Signpost to Murder*	Monte Doyle	420	532
103.	*Bell, Book, and Candle*	John van Druten	486	500
104a.	*The Private Ear* ⎫ Given at one	Peter Shaffer	547	496
104b.	*The Public Eye* ⎭ performance	Peter Shaffer	547	496
105.	*Chase Me Comrade*	Ray Cooney	772	489
106.	*Five Finger Exercise*	Peter Shaffer	610	483
107.	*Waltz of the Toreadors*	Jean Anouilh	700	457
108.	*Romanoff and Juliet*	Peter Ustinov	379	429
(71.)	*The Affair* (included in TV list)		379	411
109.	*Who's Afraid of Virginia Woolf*	Edward Albee	426	404
110.	*The Masters*	Ronald Millar/ C. P. Snow	256	402
111.	*The Tunnel of Love*	J. Fields and P. de Vries	503	400
112.	*Hostile Witness*	J. Roffey	444	400

Table C2

Availability of Play Texts

The majority of plays included in the present study are available in book form. This appendix lists the sources of texts and states when and where particular plays were presented. All Television plays appeared on BBC1; where no printed text exists, the word 'Summary' indicates that the play of this number is summarized in Goodlad, 1969. The majority of play texts are published by four publishing houses, which will be referred to in abbreviation as follows:

H. F. W. Deane & Sons Ltd, London = Deane
English Theatre Guild Ltd, London = ETG
Samuel French Ltd, London = French
Evans Brothers Ltd, London = Evans

TELEVISED PLAYS

Play Number	Title	Date of Presentation	Time	Source
1.	*The Weeping Madonna*	Sun. 8 Jan. 1956	8.15– 9.45	Summary
2.	*Pygmalion*	Sun. 15 Jan. 1956	8.15– 9.45	(Hamlyn, London, 1965)
3.	*The Corn is Green*	Sun. 22 Jan. 1956	8.30–10.00	(Heinemann, London, 1938)
4.	*Love in a Mist*	Sun. 29 Jan. 1956	8.15– 9.45	(French, 1942)
5.	*The White Falcon*	Sun. 5 Feb. 1956	8.15– 9.45	Summary
6.	*Manhandled*	Sun. 12 Feb. 1956	8.15– 9.45	Summary
7.	*No Man's Land*	Thur. 23 Feb. 1956	8.30–10.00	Summary

Play Number	Title	Date of Presentation	Time	Source
8.	Haul for the Shore	Sun. 26 Feb. 1956	8.45–10.15	(Deane, 1953)
9.	The Seat of the Scornful	Sun. 15 Apr. 1956	8.15– 9.45	Summary
10.	Desert Duel	Sun. 10 June 1956	8.15– 9.45	Summary
11.	Murder Mistaken	Thur. 18 Oct. 1956	8.10–10.00	(Evans, 1953)
12.	Dark Victory	Sun. 18 Nov. 1956	8.30–10.00	(ETG, 1939)
13.	The Dashing White Sergeant	Tue. 26 Mar. 1957	8.30–10.00	(Evans, 1955)
14.	Laburnum Grove	Sun. 14 Apr. 1957	8.30– 9.30	(French, 1935)
15.	Jane Steps Out	Sun. 28 Apr. 1957	8.00– 9.30	(French, 1945)
16.	A Woman of Property	Thur. 2 May 1957	8.30–10.00	Summary
17.	Edward, My Son	Sun. 23 June 1957	8.00– 9.45	(French, 1945)
18.	The Amazing Dr Clitterhouse	Sun. 7 July 1957	8.00– 9.30	(French, 1938)
19.	Another Man's Life	Sun. 21 July 1957	8.00– 9.30	Summary
20.	The Orange Orchard	Thur. 8 Aug. 1957	8.00– 9.30	Summary
21.	Plunder	Sun. 11 Aug. 1957	8.00– 9.30	Summary
22.	The Hasty Heart	Thur. 29 Aug. 1957	8.00– 9.30	(Dramatic Services Inc., N. York, 1945)
23.	The Critical Point	Thur. 5 Dec. 1957	8.02– 9.30	Summary
24.	Wishing Well	Tue. 17 Dec. 1957	8.02– 9.30	(French, 1946)
25.	The Man Upstairs	Sat. 4 Jan. 1958	9.00–10.30	(Constable, London, 1954)
26.	Shut Out the Night	Thur. 30 Jan. 1958	9.00–10.30	Summary
27.	You're a Long Time Dead	Thur. 13 Feb. 1958	8.30–10.00	Summary
28.	Background	Thur. 27 Mar. 1958	8.30–10.00	(French, 1951)
29.	My Flesh, My Blood (Published as Spring and Port Wine)	Sat. 29 Mar. 1958	9.15–10.30	(French, 1958)
30.	Ladies in Retirement	Sat. 12 Apr. 1958	9.00–10.35	(ETG, 1940)
31.	The Body of a Girl	Sun. 27 Apr. 1958	8.30–10.00	Summary
32.	The Caine Mutiny Court Martial	Sun. 1 June 1958	8.30–10.20	Summary
33.	Suspect	Wed. 3 July 1958	8.30–10.00	(French, 1937)
34.	Hour of the Rat	Tue. 23 Sept. 1958	8.30– 9.30	Summary
35.	Yesterday's Enemy	Tue. 14 Oct. 1958	8.00– 9.30	Summary
36.	Wanted—One Body	Sun. 26 Oct. 1958	8.00– 9.25	(ETG, 1961)
37.	A Cuckoo in the Nest	Sun. 21 Dec. 1958	8.00– 9.30	(French, 1938)
38.	So Many Children	Sat. 27 Dec. 1958	9.05–10.35	(French, 1959)
39.	Trilby	Sat. 17 Jan. 1959	8.40–10.10	Summary
40.	The Skin Game	Sun. 18 Jan. 1959	8.30–10.00	(Duckworth, 1920)
41.	Skeleton in the Sand	Tue. 10 Feb. 1959	8.00– 9.25	Summary
42.	Murder on the agenda	Sat. 14 Feb. 1959	8.35–10.09	Summary
43.	No Deadly Medicine	Sun. 15 Mar. 1959	8.30–10.00	Summary
44.	The Small Back Room	Sun. 5 Apr. 1959	8.00– 9.00	Summary
45.	Mother of Men	Thur. 4 June 1959	8.45–10.00	Summary
46.	Beside the Seaside	Sun. 2 Aug. 1959	8.05– 9.35	(ETG, 1956)
47.	Sleeping Partnership	Sun. 25 Oct. 1959	8.45–10.15	(ETG, 1952)
48.	The Case of Private Hamp	Tue. 24 Nov. 1959	9.00–10.20	Summary
49.	Through a glass darkly	Sat. 19 Dec. 1959	8.35– 9.55	Summary
50.	Never Die	Sat. 9 Jan. 1960	8.45–10.15	Summary

51.	Dear Octopus	Sun.	10 Jan. 1960	8.00– 9.30	(French, 1938)
52.	Is your honeymoon really necessary?	Sun.	21 Feb. 1960	8.00– 9.30	(Deane, 1947)
53.	The return of Peggy Atherton	Sat.	27 Feb. 1960	8.40–10.00	(Deane, 1950)
54.	Doctor in the House	Sun.	5 June 1960	8.35–10.10	(Evans, 1957)
55.	Reluctant Heroes	Sun.	11 Sept. 1960	8.20– 9.50	(ETG, 1951)
56.	Your Obedient Servant	Sat.	19 Nov. 1960	8.35–10.10	(Evans, 1960)
57.	The Intervener	Sun.	12 Feb. 1961	8.45–10.15	Summary
58.	An Inspector Calls	Sun.	19 Feb. 1961	8.45–10.15	(French, 1945) (Heinemann, 19)
59.	A Fair Cop	Sun.	2 Apr. 1961	8.15– 9.45	Summary
60.	The Winslow Boy	Sun.	20 Aug. 1961	7.55– 9.25	(French, 1946)
61.	Cross of Iron	Sun.	17 Sept. 1961	7.45– 9.10	Summary
62.	The Barretts of Wimpole Street	Sun.	24 Dec. 1961	8.50–10.30	(Gollancz, 1930)
63.	Will Any Gentleman	Tue.	26 Dec. 1961	8.05– 9.35	(French, 1952)
64.	This Happy Breed	Sun.	1 Apr. 1962	8.35–10.05	(French, 1945)
65.	Dial M for Murder	Sun.	5 Aug. 1962	8.45–10.05	(French, 1952)
66.	See How They Run	Mon.	6 Aug. 1962	6.45– 8.15	(French, 1946)
67.	A Chance to Shine	Fri.	2 Nov. 1962	9.25–10.40	Summary
68.	Wednesday's Child	Fri.	23 Nov. 1962	9.25–10.25	Summary
69.	Heart to Heart	Thur.	6 Dec. 1962	8.30– 9.25) 9.35–10.35)	Summary
70.	Something to Hide	Sun.	16 Dec. 1962	9.00–10.00	(Summary
71.	The Affair	Fri.	12 Apr. 1963	8.15–10.00	(French, 1962)
72.	Stalingrad	Wed.	4 Dec. 1963	9.10–10.45	Summary
73.	The July Plot	Wed.	9 Dec. 1964	9.25–11.05	Summary
74.	Moving On	Wed.	24 Mar. 1965	9.25–10.45	Summary
75.	The Brides of March	Sat.	30 Oct. 1965	7.25– 8.55	(ETG, 1951)
76.	The Joel Brandt Story	Tue.	14 Dec. 1965	9.00–10.40	Summary

THEATRE PLAYS

77.	The Mousetrap	Ambassadors, 25/11/52–31/12/67 (Still running—Mar. 1971)	(French, 1954)
78.	Boeing-Boeing	Opened at Apollo, 20/2/62 Duchess, 10/5/65 to end	(Evans, 1967)
79.	The Teahouse of the August Moon	Her Majesty's, 22/4/54–11/8/56	(Heinemann, 1952)
80.	Sailor Beware	Strand, 16/2/55–22/2/58	(French, 1955)
81.	The Amorous Prawn	Opened Saville, 9 Dec. 1959 Piccadilly, 23/1/61–17/2/62	(French, 1960)
82.	Roar Like a Dove	Phoenix, 26/9/57–5/3/60	(French, 1957)
83.	Witness for the Prosecution	Winter Garden, 28/10/53–29/1/55	(French, 1954)

84.	*The Reluctant Debutante*	Cambridge, 24/5/55–9/3/57	(Evans, 1957)
85.	*Dry Rot*	Whitehall, 31/8/54–15/3/58	(ETG, 1954)
86.	*Simple Spymen*	Whitehall, 19/3/58–9/7/61	(ETG, 1960)
87.	*The House by the Lake*	Duke of York's, 9/5/56–15/2/58	(Evans, 1956)
88.	*The Lovebirds*	Adelphi, 20/4/57–1/3/58	(Evans, 1958)
89.	*One for the Pot*	Whitehall, 2/8/61–4/7/64	(ETG, 1963)
90.	*Billy Liar*	Cambridge, 13/9/60–3/2/62	(Evans, 1960)
91.	*The Right Honourable Gentleman*	Her Majesty's, 28/5/64–9/10/65	(French, 1966)
92.	*A Severed Head*	Criterion, 27/6/63—end	(French, 1964)
93a.	*Separate Tables*	St. James's, 22/9/54–30/6/56	(French, 1955)
94.	*Ross*	Haymarket, 12/5/60–10/3/62	(French, 1960)
95.	*Come Blow Your Horn*	Prince of Wales, 27/2/62–25/5/63	(French, 1951)
96.	*The Spider's Web*	Savoy, 14/12/54–3/11/56	(French, 1956)
97.	*Goodnight, Mrs Puffin*	Opened Strand, 18/7/61	(French, 1963)
		Transferred to Duchess, 18/9/61	
		Duke of York's, 17/12/62–16/3/63	
98.	*The Chalk Garden*	Haymarket, 11/4/56–9/11/57	(French, 1953)
99.	*Nude with Violin*	Globe, 7/11/56–1/2/58	(French, 1956)
100.	*Watch it Sailor*	Opened Aldwych, 24/2/60	(French, 1961)
		Apollo, 14/11/60–5/8/61	
101.	*The Gazebo*	Savoy, 29/3/60–27/5/61	(ETG, 1959)
102.	*Signpost to Murder*	Cambridge, 9/2/62–9/2/63	(French, 1963)
103.	*Bell, Book ,and Candle*	Phoenix, 5/10/54–3/12/55	(French, 1952)
104.	*The Private Ear* and *The Public Eye*	Globe, 10/5/62–31/8/63	(French, 1962)
105.	*Chase Me Comrade*	Whitehall, 15/7/64–21/5/66	(ETG, 1966)
106.	*Five Finger Exercise*	Comedy, 16/7/58–2/1/60	(French, 1958)
107.	*The Waltz of the Toreadors*	Criterion, 27/3/56–30/11/57	(French, 1953)
108.	*Romanoff and Juliet*	Piccadilly, 17/5/56–13/4/57	(ETG, 1957)
			(Heinemann, 1967)
(71.)	*The Affair* (TV List)	Strand, 21/9/61–18/8/62	(French, 1962)
109.	*Who's Afraid of Virginia Woolf*	Opened Piccadilly, 6/2/64	(Penguin,
		Transferred to Globe, 20/7/64	1962)
		Garrick, 25/1/65–19/6/65	
110.	*The Masters*	Opened at Savoy, 29/5/63	(French, 1964)
		Piccadilly, 28/9/63–11/1/64	
111.	*The Tunnel of Love*	Opened Her Majesty's, 3/12/57	(French, 1957)
		Apollo, 8/12/58–14/2/59	
112.	*Hostile Witness*	Haymarket, 4/11/64–27/11/65	(Evans, 1965)

Name Index

Subject Index